# WOMEN WORKERS AND THE SWEATED TRADES

# Women Workers and the Sweated Trades

The Origins of Minimum Wage Legislation

JENNY MORRIS

Gower

Published by
Gower Publishing Company Limited
Gower House
Croft Road
Aldershot
Hants GU11 3HR
England

Gower Publishing Company
Old Post Road
Brookfield
Vermont 05036
USA


British Library Cataloguing in Publication Data

Morris, Jenny
    Women workers and the sweated trades:    the
    origins of minimum wage legislation.
    1. Wages —— Women —— Great Britain ——
    History
    I. Title
    331.4'21'0941          HD6061.2G7

Library of Congress Cataloging-in-Publication Data

Morris, Jenny, 1950—
    Women workers and the sweated trades.

    Bibliography: p.
    1. Sweating system--Great Britain--History.
2. Women--Employment--Great Britain--History.
3. Labor policy--Great Britain--History. 4. Wages--
Minimum wage--Law and legislation--Great Britain.
5. Wages--Women--Law and legislation--Great Britain.
I. Title.
HD2339.G7M67   1986        331.4'23        86-9850

ISBN 0 566 05188 5

Printed and Bound in Great Britain by
Paradigm Print, Gateshead, Tyne and Wear

# Contents

# Introduction

The Trade Boards Act of 1909 has been somewhat neglected by historians of social policy. Even those historians who have given some space in their work to the Act have not chosen to examine its origins in any great detail; for this reason there are few references to secondary sources in this thesis, most of the evidence being based on primary sources and original research. Yet the Trade Boards Act was an important piece of legislation. The implementation of a minimum wage, even though limited to a few industries, was a fundamental step in the development of state intervention in the economy. By stipulating that employers in certain trades must not pay their workers below a certain level of wage, the state intended to act as a definite check on the power of employers, and of the forces of supply and demand, to determine workers' wages. Furthermore, as we shall see, politicians were aware that the imposition of a minimum wage might have a fundamental effect on a particular trade, the product and the workers, and those who supported the legislation were willing to see a trade disappear rather than allow the payment of excessively low wages and poor working conditions. Why was this? Why was the Trade Boards Act passed in 1909?

In attempting to answer this question, my research has been guided by the principle that the making of social policy should not be considered in isolation from the reality of the social conditions to which it is addressed. Moreover, the problem as perceived by those pressing for a particular development of social policy should not be taken as necessarily an accurate reflection of that reality. The treatment of the evidence which was available to contemporaries on a "social problem" such as sweated labour tells us much about the aims, ideas and assumptions within which social policy is formulated. However, it is also necessary to attempt a more detailed analysis of the "social problem" and this will highlight, not only the relationship of social policy to the reality to which it is addressed, and the importance of ideology in the development of social policy, but also provide an important setting for any examination of the workings of social policy once legislation is enacted.

There is another very important reason for a detailed analysis of sweated labour and that is to question the way in which historians have traditionally viewed the existence of the sweated trades. Most studies which involve any consideration of sweated labour assume that the phenomenon was a residual characteristic of an earlier stage in the development of industrial production. This assumption particularly applies to the system of outworking and the existence of homeworkers, in that it is commonly believed that it is only earlier and more backward types of industrial production which rely on outworking and homeworkers. These two phenomena are assumed to disappear in the sections of the trades which are based on modern factory production and sweated labour generally is not associated with the modernisation of industrial production but with those sections of trades which remain undercapitalised and technologically backward. One purpose of this thesis will be to examine this question and to try and assess to what extent sweated labour at the turn of the century could be called a residual phenomenon.

The first three chapters of this thesis therefore examine the evidence on sweated labour at the end of the nineteenth century and, having established a definition of sweated labour, attempt an analysis of its causes. Chapter 1 commences by setting the contemporary investigations in the context of the wider concern about poverty. We then go on to identify the characteristics of the sweated trades which were revealed by the investigations into sweating between 1888 and 1908. This discussion does two things - it reveals the evidence available to the social reformers of the time and provides the background to the development of a particular type of concern about poverty; and secondly, the evidence provides the historian with a number of clues as to where a more detailed analysis of sweated labour should be concentrated. This more detailed analysis follows in Chapters 2 and 3 and is designed to shed light on the whole question of sweated labour by investigating, first the development of one notoriously sweated trade - the tailoring trade - and second, the position of women in the labour market, as women appear, from the evidence discussed in Chapter 1, to be a particularly important group of sweated workers.

Chapters 1 to 3 therefore deal with the nature of the sweated trades and sweated labour and thus provide a vital background to subsequent chapters which examine how the Trade Boards Act came to be passed.

J.R. Hay[1] sums up the conclusions reached from the work of those historians who have paid any attention to the Trade Boards Act, when he says:

"The Trade Boards Act of 1909 ... was the result of pressure
from women's organisations; individual politicians, including
Ramsay MacDonald and Sir Charles Dilke, quoting American and
Australian practices respectively; and a public campaign
mounted by the Daily Mail"[2]

One purpose of this thesis will be to re-examine, in more depth, the
influence of the groups and individuals referred to by historians such
as R. Davidson[3] and also to assess the importance or otherwise of what
J.A.M. Caldwell calls the erosion of the principles of laissez faire[4].
"The trade unions played little part", says Hay[5], summarising research
already published.   Chapter 4 re-examines this and seeks to answer the
question, why didn't the trade unions play an important part in an issue
which was highly significant for trade unionists?   Chapter 5 looks at
the women's organisations to which other historians have referred and
attempts an assessment of their motivations and the extent of their
influence.

Recent research has focussed on the attitudes of employers to social
policy[6].   In Chapter 6 of this thesis we examine in detail the response
of employers' organisations to the development of arbitration and
conciliation procedures and to minimum wage legislation.   We will also
use original research material to show the particular involvement of one
important employer in the campaign for Wages Boards.

In Chapter 7 we discuss the state's response to the mounting pressure
during the 1890s and early 1900s for action on the sweated trades and
assess the reasons for the limitations of this response.   With Chapter
8 we move on to detail the setting up of the campaign for Wages Boards,
the motivations behind this campaign and the events leading up to the
passing of the Trade Boards Act in 1909.   Chapter 9 brings together
the evidence presented and attempts to answer the question posed by the
title of the thesis, while finally, in Chapter 10, we look, very briefly,
at how successful the legislation was in fulfilling the aims of its
initiators.

References - Introduction

1.   "The Origins of the Liberal Welfare Reforms" 1906-1914 (1975).

2.   Ibid., p.53.   He would be more accurate if he referred to the
     Daily News rather than the Daily Mail.

3.   R. Davidson, "Sir Hubert Llewellyn Smith and Labour Policy, 1886-
     1916", Cambridge PhD, (1971).

4.   Caldwell, "Social Policy and Public Administration 1909-1911",
     London PhD (1956).

5.   Hay, (1975), p.53.

6.   See K. Burgess, "The Challenge of Labour" (1980) and the articles
     by J.R. Hay and J. Brown in P. Thane (ed.), "The Origins of British
     Social Policy" (1978).

# 1 The sweated trades

In this Chapter we begin the examination of the phenomenon to which the Trade Boards Act was addressed - the problem of sweated labour.  As we shall see, the terms "sweating" and "sweated labour" were applied to those trades or sections of trades characterised by low wages, long hours of work and insanitary conditions.

There are three aims of the chapter.  Firstly, we seek to provide a background to the first major illustration of concern about excessively low wages and poor working conditions, namely the 1888-1890 House of Lords Select Committee on Sweating.  Secondly, we then extract from the evidence to the House of Lords Select Committee and from the subsequent investigations over the next twenty years, what were considered to be the major characteristics of sweating.  Finally, we introduce a brief discussion on the possible causes of sweated labour.  The Chapter thus sets the stage for the more detailed analysis of the tailoring trade which follows in Chapter 2 and the analysis of the position of women workers in Chapter 3.

## II

According to Duncan Bythell[1], the House of Lords Select Committee on Sweating[2] "lifted the lid off something highly unpleasant"[3].  To a certain extent, however, the lid was already off by the time the Select Committee was appointed in 1888.  Evidence of low wages, long hours and insanitary conditions was publicised by a number of writers in the three decades before 1888[4].  A lot of this evidence was about London and its trades. The decline of the traditional London industries of silk-weaving and ship-building and the increase of casual work and unemployment were subjects much written about by philanthropists, journalists and social reformers.  The depression of the mid-1880s saw an increase in their concern.  Nationally, there had been a decline in average real wages between 1874 and 1887 and wages in the  sweated  trades were squeezed more than most[5].

Charles Booth[6] and others made enquiries into the conditions of life in the East End of London in the late 1880s and were horrified by what they found, not only because of the human suffering involved but also because

of what they considered to be, the possibility of a revolutionary
situation arising out of these conditions[7].   As Stedman-Jones has
pointed out, almost all commentators on social conditions in the 1880s -
from the Charity Organisation Society (COS) to the Social Democratic
Federation (SDF) - divided the working class into two distinct camps -
the "true working class" and the "casual residuum"[8].   The "true working
classes" were represented by the skilled male worker who usually
belonged to a trade union;  the "casual residuum" was the unskilled or
semi-skilled casual worker who suffered often chronic poverty, was
unorganised and frequently out of work.   Many of the workers who
conformed to this latter description were in fact women workers but
social commentators tended to concentrate on the men, who were often
said to be "brutalised" and dangerous.   The fear (or, in the case of
the SDF, the hope) was that the "casual residuum" would be led by the
"true working classes" into bringing about severe social upheaval and
these fears seemed justified by the events of 8, 9 and 10 February 1886,
when large violent demonstrations of East End unemployed attacked the
respectable and prosperous West End[9].

As the very word indicates, those who identified the "residuum" made
certain assumptions about the phenomenon's causal factors.   It was the
shortcomings of the casual workers which were identified as the problem
rather than the economic system in which they found themselves.   As
Stedman-Jones puts it:

> "The chronic poverty of the casual residuum was due not to the
> problems of casual employment but to their 'feeble and tainted
> constitutions', the product of generations of decaying slum
> life.   The prevalence of casual employment was determined
> primarily not by a demand for irregular work, but by the ready
> availability of a supply of degenerate labour which was lazy,
> shiftless and incapable of regular work".[10]

During the depression of 1884-1887, both parliamentary and private
investigations[11] showed that the chronic poor were not the dwindling
number of London's population previously thought.   Studies of  sweating
in the late nineteenth century were part of this "discovery" of a
persistent poverty, yet the image of the  sweated  worker was somewhat
different from that of the casual labourer.   From the literature
written during this period, the term "sweated labour" conjures up the
picture of an over-worked seamstress whereas the term "casual labourer"
presents the picture of an idle, demoralised (usually male) member of
the "residuum".   Studies of  sweating  opened up a new perspective on
poverty - the poverty of people who worked desperately hard for very low
wages.

It was the publication of a number of sensationalist articles and pamphlets such as those by Arnold White[12] in the late 1880s which heralded the need for a more objective look at the problem of sweating.    In his book, published in 1886, White voiced the theory of urban degeneration in an extreme form.    Over-crowding, early marriage and immigration were to blame for the chronic poverty of London's East End, said White, and his sentiments were shared by a whole spectrum of middle class opinion, albeit in a diluted form, when he wrote:

> "If it be monstrous that the weak should be destroyed by the
> strong, how much more repugnant it is to instinct and to
> reason that the strong and capable should be overwhelmed by
> the feeble, ailing and unfit."[13]

In 1885, a more respectable and prestigious gathering of politicians, economists, capitalists, and trade unionists had met to consider the problem of poverty and its threat to society, but had come to remarkably few conclusions[14].    The motivation behind this Conference, chaired by Sir Charles Dilke, MP, is well expressed in a statement which the anonymous backer made to the Pall Mall Gazette.    "Wealth, luxury and extravagance among the few", he said, "accompanied by poverty, misery and want among the many is a great danger to the commonwealth"[15].    The national newspapers generally agreed with these sentiments and applauded the prospect of the Conference, the _Times_ arguing that there was a need for reform because "The old relation of capital and industry ... has not succeeded in giving satisfaction to one of the two parties [i.e. labour] to the transaction"[16].

It almost looked as if inroads were rapidly being made into the principles of "laissez-faire" with one of the speakers at the Conference quoting Adam Smith in justification for state intervention[17].    But there was only one form of state intervention really considered - land reform, which assumed that structural un/under-employment in the London trades could be solved by encouraging workers to leave the city and set up as small-scale farmers.    Frederic Harrison, the last speaker at the Conference, commenced with the brave words, "... the evils of our industrial system are the direct product of the industrial system itself"[18], but baulked at the possibility of state intervention. Instead, he concluded, "industry must be moralised - infused with a spirit of social duty from top to bottom ..."[19].

cf Dicey's
dating

Arnold White's sensationalist journalism and the general interest in the problems of low wages exhibited by such events as the Industrial

7

Remuneration Conference prompted the Board of Trade to instruct its
Labour correspondent, John Burnett, to prepare a report on the sweating
system in the East End of London[20]. Public interest in the problems
of sweated labour was heightened by investigations carried out by The
Lancet, the journal of the British Medical Association. The findings
of their investigations into the London tailoring trade, published in
1887, attracted a lot of attention and criticism. The report[21] had high-
lighted not only appalling sanitary conditions but also low wages and
long hours. The Lancet replied to accusations that their report had
been exaggerated by giving the example of a Manchester woman who was
charged with attempted suicide - her reason being that during the whole
of the previous week she had worked as a costume finisher from 8.30 am -
7 pm and only earned 2/2d[22].

In early 1888, East London MPs pressed the Government to take some action
on sweating[23]. In the House of Lords, Lord Dunraven successfully
proposed that a Select Committee of the House of Lords be set up to
investigate further the problems of the East End clothing trade[24].
During the next few months, an outbreak of smallpox in the part of Leeds
where the domestic and workshop tailoring trade was concentrated, prompted
first The Lancet and then the Board of Trade, to carry out investigations
into the Leeds clothing trade[25]. Their findings brought about the
extension of the House of Lords Select Committee, under the chairmanship
of Lord Dunraven, to cover sweating in all trades throughout the country[26].

In all, the Select Committee considered evidence on twenty-seven
different trades which exhibited some or all of the following
characteristics[27]:
> "1. a rate of wages inadequate to the necessities of the worker
>    or disproportionate to the work done;
>
> 2. excessive hours of labour;
>
> 3. an insanitary state of the houses in which the work is
>    carried on."[27a]

Table 1 gives the list of the trades concerned and the numbers of workers
employed. In most of these trades there was a core of workers (usually
skilled) whose wages were adequate and it is therefore impossible to
accurately assess the number of "sweated" workers. In total, these
trades accounted for 1,754,369 workers in 1891, 24% of the industrial
workforce[28].

actually

TABLE 1.1 Trades considered by the House of Lords Select Committee on Sweating: Numbers occupied in these trades according to the 1891 Census Returns (PP 1893, CVI, Cd. 7058)

| Trade | Employees | | Working on own account[2] | | Total | |
|---|---|---|---|---|---|---|
| | M | F | M | F | M | F |
| Boot and Shoe | 138,185 | 41.644 | 38,190 | 1,300 | 176,375 | 42,944 |
| Cabinet and Upholstery | 57,591 | 10,023 | 8,796 | 1,748 | 66,387 | 11,771 |
| Docks[1] | 54,996 | | | | 54,996 | |
| Furmaking | 4,616 | 3,868 | 265 | 157 | 4,881 | 4,025 |
| Shirtmaking | 1,594 | 32,614 | 105 | 13,678 | 1,699 | 46,292 |
| Tailoring | 83,117 | 77,472 | 13,659 | 5,628 | 96,776 | 83,100 |
| Basketmaking | 6,367 | 1,736 | 1,996 | 424 | 8,363 | 2,160 |
| Chainmaking | 4,071 | 1,728 | 76 | 116 | 4,147 | 1,844 |
| Dressmaking | 2,943 | 223,357 | 306 | 136,634 | 3,249 | 349,991 |
| Gun Trade | 7,928 | 180 | 410 | 8 | 8,338 | 188 |
| India Rubber and leather/waterproof | 5,757 | 3,935 | 121 | 11 | 5,878 | 3,946 |
| Nail-making | 4,331 | 4,418 | 301 | 116 | 4,632 | 4,534 |
| Nut and Bolt making | 6,278 | 3,119 | 75 | 8 | 6,353 | 3,127 |
| Umbrella making | 3,745 | 3,844 | 898 | 318 | 4,643 | 4,162 |
| Cutlery | 15,418 | 2,110 | 914 | 19 | 16,332 | 2,129 |
| Bookbinding | 13,401 | 10,038 | 55 | 74 | 13,456 | 10,112 |
| Paper Box | 1,655 | 16,039 | 118 | 246 | 1,773 | 16,285 |
| Artificial Flower | 430 | 3,828 | 138 | 270 | 568 | 4,098 |
| Lace making | 11,277 | 17,567 | 335 | 1,963 | 11,612 | 19,530 |
| Fancy Goods | 1,598 | 5,125 | 238 | 1,357 | 1,836 | 6,482 |
| Straw Hat | 2,364 | 9,585 | 258 | 3,531 | 2,622 | 13,116 |
| Trimmings | 923 | 6,498 | 57 | 546 | 980 | 7,044 |
| TOTALS | 979,275 | 479,652 | 107,164 | 168,278 | 1,086,439 | 647,930 |

37% of
1754369

Notes: 1. This figure is for dock labourers.

2. This figure relates to those who classified themselves as neither employers nor employees and is the most accurate estimate of the number of homeworkers in each trade. It must be pointed out, however, that these workers were not necessarily working in their own home; some worked in hired rooms or "sittings", or in small workshops shared with similar workers.

During the following twenty years an increasing amount of evidence
became available about these sweated trades.   The Royal Commission on
Labour, appointed in 1891, heard evidence of low wages, excessive hours
and poor working conditions - although they also heard evidence of, and
concluded that, the condition of manual (male) workers in general had
improved greatly over the previous forty years[29].   The Annual Reports
of the Factory Inspectorate produced valuable information on the sweated
trades, particularly after the appointment of women Factory Inspectors
in 1893[30].   The Royal Commission on Housing also heard evidence on homeworking and the conditions under which it was carried out.   After the
turn of the century, there was increasing concern about the effect of
low wages and poor working conditions, particularly following the 1904
Report on Physical Deterioration[31].   Later chapters will analyse the
motivations behind this concern.


III

We now move on to consider the characteristics of the sweated trades which
were revealed by the investigations carried out between 1888 and 1908.
This discussion has two functions - firstly, to illustrate the type of
evidence available to contemporary social reformers and which forms the
background to the development of concern and the policy proposals put
forward by the various groups of people considered in Chapters 4 to 7;
secondly, to provide pointers for the more detailed analysis of sweated
labour which is necessary in order to relate the reality of the social
problem to the ideas and assumptions held by social reformers.

The characteristics of the sweated trades revealed by contemporary investigations fall into five categories.   The first two are probably the
most important - namely the nature of the labour force in the sweated
trades, and the organisation of production of the three remaining
characteristics.   Of the three remaining characteristics, two relate to
the organisation (or lack of it) amongst employers and employees, and
the final point which emerged from the investigations was the unregulated
nature of the trades concerned.

1.   The Labour Force in the Sweated Trades
Much of the evidence about the sweated trades is of the type of labour
which was employed.   The earlier investigations tended to concentrate
more on foreign immigrant labour while the later investigations were
particularly concerned with homeworkers.   Almost all the evidence,
however, points to the preponderance of women amongst those designated
10

as sweated workers and also reveals that sweating was apparent amongst
factory workers as well as those engaged in non-factory production


(a)  Women Workers
Apart from evidence relating to the docks and the building trade, the
evidence to the House of Lords Select Committee, and indeed all subsequent investigations on sweating, focussed on women workers.    In
fact, if we ignore for the moment these two trades, the majority of
sweated workers in the trades considered by the Select Committee were
women:  646,880 women workers compared to 440,900 men.    Over half of
these women were to be found in the dressmaking trade, however, and it
is still the case that from the national statistics the majority of the
sweated trades were dominated by male workers.    However, these national
statistics are misleading, for within each trade, in the areas and in
the type of work where very low wages were common, there was a higher
proportion of women workers.

The analysis of the tailoring trade in Chapter 2 illustrates how women
were employed in the lowest paid types of work, and Chapter 3 demonstrates
a similar sexual division of labour in other areas of employment for
women.    Furthermore, within a number of the sweated trades examined by
the House of Lords Select Committee, there was a higher proportion of
women in the geographical areas where sweating was more common.    This
is illustrated by two examples:

(i)  In the tailoring trade, the major areas of sweating were identified
as East London, Leeds, Manchester and Essex.    Table 1.2 shows that in all
these areas more women were employed than men in the tailoring trade.
On the other hand, the House of Lords Select Committee commented that
the Newcastle and Sheffield tailoring trades did not suffer so much
from low wages, long hours and insanitary conditions[32] - it was said
that the "sweating system" had not even been introduced into Newcastle[33].
It will be seen from Table 1.2 that women made up a very small proportion
of the workforce in the tailoring trade in Newcastle and only half of
the workforce in Sheffield.

(ii)  In the nail-making trade, although women made up 48% of the workforce nationally, in the Staffordshire nailmaking trade, where examples
of very low wages and appalling working conditions were common[34], women
formed the major part of the workforce (69%) as Table 2.2 again illustrates.

11

Table 1.2    **Male and Female** workers in two sweated trades in 1891

|  |  | Male | Female | Women as % of workforce |
|---|---|---|---|---|
| (a) | Tailoring |  |  |  |
|  | E. London | 9,030 | 12,836 | 59% |
|  | Leeds | 4,774 | 10,916 | 70% |
|  | Manchester | 3,611 | 3,736 | 51% |
|  | Essex | 1,709 | 3,463 | 67% |
|  | Newcastle | 1,171 | 267 | 19% |
|  | Sheffield | 990 | 485 | 33% |
| (b) | Nailmaking |  |  |  |
|  | England and Wales | 5,127 | 4,816 | 48% |
|  | Staffordshire | 783 | 1,943 | 69% |

Figures taken from the 1891 Census PP 1893 CVI Cd 7058.

Contemporary investigations recognised this link between sweating and women workers.   The Royal Commission on Labour asked for special reports on women workers and concluded that women's wages were generally low[36].   The Commissioners found that the average wage for women and girls in 1891 was 11/3½d (12/8d for women;  7/- for girls) compared with the average of 12/- in the sweated trades found by the House of Lords Select Committee on Sweating.   The Royal Commission concluded that "in the majority of cases, women's wages are low"[37].   Furthermore, as contemporary investigations found, the majority of homeworkers - the lowest paid group of workers - were women, many of them tied to the home through the need to look after children or elderly/sick relatives. Investigators of the problem of very low wages in the late nineteenth and early twentieth centuries paid much attention to women workers and since low wages appear to be a particular phenomenon of the female labour force, a separate chapter is devoted to a detailed analysis of women workers during this period.   It is sufficient here to emphasise that what was perceived as the problem of the  sweated  trades between 1888 and 1908 was very much seen to be also a problem relating especially to women workers.   It is also the case that a woman was far more likely to be earning a below-subsistence wage than a man, but this is something which we will discuss in Chapter 3.

## (b) "Foreign Immigration"

Foreign immigrants were held by many to be the cause of the forcing down of wages and the perpetration of insanitary conditions. In 1881, there were already sizeable Jewish communities in London, Leeds and Manchester. Between 1882 and 1914 their numbers were added to by another 200,000 Jews - most of them refugees from Russia and Poland. These immigrants tended to settle where the Jewish community was already established, in particular in East London where, by 1900, it was calculated that nearly one person in every three in Whitechapel and one in every four in the parish of St. George's was Jewish[38]. Many of these immigrants found, or created, work in the tailoring trade, utilising the craftsmanship which many of them already had and taking advantage of the ease of entry into the trade[39].

When the House of Lords Select Committee was first set up, it was foreign immigration that was primarily blamed for low wages and insanitary working conditions[40]. Lord Dunraven continued to be of the opinion that controls on foreign immigration were necessary but the final report of the House of Lords Select Committee recognised that sweating existed where there were no immigrants[41]. The Royal Commission on Alien Immigration reported in 1903 that the cities affected by immigration were confined to London, Birmingham, Cardiff, Leeds, Liverpool, Manchester, Reading, Sheffield and part of the mining districts of Scotland[42]. On the other hand, as an important private investigation on sweating published in 1908 pointed out[43], sweated industries were found throughout the country.

There is little conclusive evidence that foreign immigrants displaced English workers or that they pulled wages down. Nevertheless, this association of sweating with Jewish immigrants contributed to the pressure which brought about immigration controls incorporated in the Aliens Act of 1902. But by the time the Select Committee on Homework reported in 1908 it, and the campaign against sweating at that time, paid little attention to the question of Jewish immigrants; it was evident to most people that this was not an important factor in the problem of low wages.

## (c) Homeworkers

The typical sweated worker has often been assumed by historians[44] to be the homeworker. Although a closer study of the contemporary investigations

13

reveals that the characteristics of sweating were also found amongst
workshop and factory workers, there is no doubt that very low and
starvation wages were more common amongst homeworkers than any other
class of worker.    The Select Committee on Homework in 1908 stated that

> "We have had evidence to convince us (indeed, it is almost
> common knowledge) that the earnings of a large number of
> people - mainly women who work in their own homes - are so
> small as alone to be insufficient to sustain life in the most
> meagre manner, even when they toil hard for extremely long
> hours"[45].

The Select Committee found that these homeworkers fell into three groups[46]:

(a)    Single women;  widows or deserted separated wives;  women
       whose husbands were permanently unemployed or unable to work.
       These were regular homeworkers and some were engaged on skilled
       work.

(b)    Wives who obtained work when their husbands are out of work.
       These were casual workers and were usually unskilled.

(c)    "Wives and daughters of men in regular employment, who wish to
       increase the family income.   They usually elect pleasant work,
       and do not ordinarily work very long hours".


With reference to the third category of homeworker, the Select Committee
under-estimated the extent to which even men in regular employment
often did not earn a wage adequate to support a wife and children.   The
wife of such a man would not, therefore, be taking in homework merely
for "luxuries" but to provide a vital part of the family income.   This
question of whether the average male worker's wage constituted a "family
wage" will be discussed in Chapter 3.


(d)   Factory Workers

Both the House of Lords Select Committee on Sweating and the House of
Commons Select Committee on Homework twenty years later concluded that
very low wages were not confined to homeworkers but were also found
amongst factory workers[47].    Chapter 2 will examine the evidence of low
wages in tailoring factories and Chapter 3 indicates the low wages
earned by women workers generally and by some men workers in both
factory and non-factory production.   The characteristics of sweating
are often thought to be symptoms of residual forms of production, a
system left over from earlier stages of capitalist development of
industry.    The evidence which came to light between 1890 and 1908 and
which is discussed in Chapters 2 and 3, was that this was not the case
at all but that low wages, long hours and poor working conditions were

found in some of the most modern industries and were by no means confined
to backstreet workshop or domestic production.


2.   Lack of Trade Union Organisation

Low-paid and unskilled workers were very unlikely to be organised and a
causal connection was often drawn between a lack of unionisation and
the existence of sweating.   George Shipton, Secretary of the London
Trades Council, told the House of Lords Select Committee, "The weaker
the union, the more subject are the trades to the sweating system"[48].

Workers in the sweated trades did attempt to organise but more often than
not it would appear that the forces ranged against them proved to be too
powerful.   In the Leeds tailoring trade, for example, when the Leeds
Jewish tailors went on strike for a 58-hour week, the work was sent by
the Leeds employers to East London workers[49].   There were  a few
isolated cases where unskilled workers were successful in getting
organised.   One such case is that of women workers in the rope making
trade in Leeds who managed to get an increase in wages but only after
an 11-week strike, and this was not something that many workers could
afford to do[50].

The Select Committee on Homework drew attention to the lack of organisation amongst homeworkers which resulted in their having

> "to bear more than their share of the consequences of un-
> certainty and irregularity in the trades in which they are
> engaged;  and they are powerless to resist the tendency to
> reduce rates which is caused by the keen competition by the
> employers to undersell each other"[51].

Generally, investigations into the sweated trades echoed the opinion of
the Royal Commission on Labour - that unskilled workers were very
vulnerable in that a plentiful supply of unskilled labour put them in
an extremely weak position in any bargaining for better conditions of
work.   The Royal Commission also drew attention to what were said to
be particular problems in organising women workers "... unmarried women
frequently consider their employment as one which will be terminated by
marriage and not as a life affair"[52].   This particular question, that
of the unionisation of women workers, will be considered in more detail
in Chapter 4.

## 3. Lack of Employer Organisation

The investigators of the sweated trades commented on the fierce competition amongst employers which meant that

> "the cutting of prices in contract work follows as a natural consequence, the less reputable employers underbidding their competitors and seeking to recoup themselves by reducing the remuneration of the workers"[53].

Some employers informed the House of Lords Select Committee and the Royal Commission on Labour that they would be willing to pay higher wages were it not for competition from other employers - or from foreign competitors - forcing their prices down[54]. The Royal Commission on Labour received evidence of attempts in the tailoring industry to impose uniform rates which, however, failed under pressure of competition[55], and the Commissioners concluded that so long as, in such trades, small employers and contractors remained unrecognised and in bitter competition for small profits from the work put out by wholesalers, the problem of excessively low wages would continue[56].

## 4. The Organisation of Production

Contemporary investigations revealed two major features of the organisation of production of the sweated trades. The first was the common incidence of sub-contracting and a dividing up of production into different stages and more detailed work tasks, a phenomenon which appeared to be found in both the factory and non-factory sections of many trades. The second was the fluctuations in the demand for the product and therefore the level of employment in the sweated trades.

The dilution of labour skills which accompanied the development of a more detailed division of labour is only briefly referred to in the following paragraphs; the subject merits a closer examination and this will be done at the end of this chapter and throughout Chapters 2, in the context of the tailoring trade, and Chapter 3 when we discuss women workers.

### (a) Sub-contracting and the dividing up of the production process

A system of sub-contracting appears to have been very common in the trades examined by the House of Lords. This was particularly the case in the clothing trades. John Burnett's evidence to the Select Committee, based on his investigations into the East London and Leeds clothing trade set out in detail the many stages of contracting out that each piece of

16

work went through.  He emphasised that the expansion of the clothing trade had brought about the expansion of the role of middleman/contractor who himself often contracted the work out further.  The Lancet's investigations found that the contract system was accompanied by a dilution of labour skills which in itself led to a vulnerable workforce. The production process had been fragmented to the extent that the worker was "so unskilled and therefore so helpless that [he/she] cannot but accept the very lowest of remuneration"[57].  The contracting out system in the clothing trade will be examined in more detail in Chapter 2.

The contracting out system was not, however, confined to the clothing trades.  The House of Lords Select Committee heard evidence of other trades where the organisation of manufacture was also based on contracting work out.  For example, the Secretary of the Sheffield Federated Trades Council gave evidence on the Sheffield cutlery trade and detailed the system of sub-contracting.  Those known as "manufacturers", i.e. those who sold the finished product to the wholesaler placed orders with a number of outworkers/sub-contractors, who either hired rooms in factories (i.e. buildings equipped with steampower) or worked in small workshops.  In both cases, the outworker worked alongside his few employees who in some instances were members of his own family.  Some of the work was given out further to domestic workshops and to homeworkers[58].

The Select Committee also heard evidence on the sub-contracting method in lace-making, a phenomenon still evident in 1907 when the Daily Express published a description of lace-making in Sheinton.  In that densely crowded part of East Nottingham, the employer/"manufacturer" gave the work out to a middlewoman, known locally as a "Lace Duchess", who then gave it out to outworkers, many of whom were homeworkers.  The work was divided up into four parts - dipping, drawing, scalping and jennying - and the Daily Express' main concern was with the employment of children to do the drawing, i.e. the pulling out of threads.

> "The following case [they reported] is typical of many
> families.  The youngest child, a girl of seven is called from
> her bed at 6 o'clock.  She starts work, pulling, pulling,
> pulling till nearly 9.  Then she has a meal of bread and jam,
> and after that goes to school ... and after school in the evening
> the same weary round goes on.  She reaches her bed again at 11".[59]

Sub-contracting and sub-contractors were often blamed for the phenomena of low wages and insanitary working conditions.  Some witnesses to the

House of Lords Select Committee went so far as to say that sweating
was in fact an abuse of the sub-contracting system and that where there
was no sub-contracting there would be no sweating[60].    The Select
Committee concluded, however, that the sub-contract was in fact a consequence rather than the cause of sweating[61], as, twenty years later,
did the House of Commons Select Committee on Homework.    By adopting
a definition of sweating which was based on the phenomenon of low wages,
the Select Committee rejected a definition based on excessive profits
being made by sub-contractors by "grinding the face of the poor".
This was a recognition of the fact that sub-contractors were in fact
usually not making large profits and were indeed often as badly off as
their employees[62].

Charles Booth, in his evidence to the Royal Commission on Labour,
attempted to dispel some of the common misunderstandings about sub-
contracting[63].    The process was far from being a sign of a "backward"
industry, nor were the "middlemen" or "middlewomen" so often accused
of being the "sweater" of the poor, more than scapegoats.    The evidence
was that sub-contracting was part of the development of a more sophisticated
organisation of production which was taking place in many industries at
this time.    The processes of retailing and distribution were becoming
more complicated, the wholesaler was becoming a more significant feature
and, as the production process in many industries was being divided into
many different stages, firms were more likely to specialise in one
particular stage of production.

(b)   Seasonal Fluctuations

The term "sweating" infers overwork as well as low wages and insanitary
conditions.    Most of the trades examined by the House of Lords were
subject to seasonal fluctuations, where a period of little or no work
was followed by a period of rushed orders in the clothing trades and
frantic bottling, pickling and preserving in the perishable foods trades.
The building trade was also subject to seasonal fluctuation and dockers'
work varied almost from day to day.

Even in the regulated trades, the Factory Inspectorate seems to have
been powerless in most cases to prevent excessive hours[64], not only
because of the successful evasion by employers but because in many
cases excessive hours in fact were still perfectly legal.    During the
months of June to September, there was no limitation on the hours of

workers engaged in the process of cleaning and preparing fruit.
Similarly, the "gutting, salting and packing of fish immediately on
arrival in the fishing boats" was altogether outside the regulation by
the Factory Acts, whether for hours or sanitation, and even children's
work was unregulated until the Factory Act of 1901.   The hours worked
by women in the Grimsby fish-curing trade during the busy season were
usually sixteen hours a day[65].

The other side to these periods of overwork was periods of idleness when
many workers were laid off and contractors found orders very difficult
to obtain.   Some workers were then lucky enough to obtain work in other
seasonal trades but for many such alternatives were not available.
Married men then fell back upon the earnings of a wife or daughter - if
their own trade was not going through a slack season - and women who
were on their own often had to resort to the Poor Law or charity.

The seasonal fluctuations in many of the trades to be found in inner
city areas contributed to the vulnerability and poverty of the workforce,
and at the same time the availability of such a workforce attracted to
such areas industries whose employers could not or would not stabilise
demand for their product[66].

5.   Unregulated Trades

The investigations of the late-nineteenth century into sweated labour
also drew attention to the unregulated nature of the trades concerned.
The docks, building trades, and domestic workshops were not covered by
the Factory Acts and some of those trades that were, for example, jam-
making, fish-curing, were exempt from many of the regulations because
of the perishable nature of their raw materials.

Even where the Factory and Workshop Acts did cover the workers concerned,
their requirements were often not complied with.   The Lancet's inquiry
into the East End tailoring trade found that the Factory Inspector's
visits were useless, for

>  "on the appearance of any stranger the women are often
>  distributed about the private parts of the house - in the
>  bedrooms, kitchens and so forth"[67].

John Burnett also concluded from his investigation into the East London
sweating system that the conditions of the Public Health Acts and the
Factory and Workshop Acts were often disregarded.   He deplored the fact

that the system of inspection was inadequate and estimated that not more than a third of the "sweating shops" in the East End were known to the Factory Inspectors[68].

Beatrice Potter even went as far as to say that the sweating system referred to "all labour employed in manufacture which has escaped the regulation of the Factory Acts and the trade unions"[69].

IV

Having surveyed the main characteristics of the sweated trades as revealed in contemporary investigations we can now begin to ask what were the reasons for the existence of sweating.

Of the possible reasons for the existence of sweated labour there are two factors which are predominant. The first is the existence of surplus labour and all the implications this has for wages, conditions of work and the vulnerability of the workforce; the second is the evidence of the dilution of labour skills which was going on in a number of industries in the last part of the nineteenth century and the implications that this had for the type of labour employed, levels of unemployment and of wages.

1.    The most comprehensive study to date of the East London labour market, an area on which many investigators of sweating concentrated, illustrates the significance of a surplus labour supply.    G. Stedman-Jones[70], concentrating on male workers, finds that the supply of male unskilled labour in East London during the second half of the nineteenth century bore no necessary relation to the actual demand for such labour. The sources of recruitment to the male unskilled labour market were:

(a)    declining industries (silk-weaving, ship-building, building and railway construction) which threw men out of work;

(b)    a regular influx of seasonably unemployed and of retired soldiers;

(c)    boys and young men entering the labour market with no industrial skill or training.

"The result" [states Stedman-Jones] "was the existence of a large stratum of under-employed workers.    This situation provided the pre-conditions for a large casual labour market and for the growth of trades which depended for their existence upon the cheap labour of the casual's family".[71]

The existence of an underemployed male labour force created a greater
need for women to work and thus further expanded the pool of surplus
labour.   This situation, according to Stedman-Jones, made the existence
of sweated trades in London almost inevitable in that there was a
captive labour force, extremely vulnerable to any attempts to reduce
wages.

A surplus labour force was also evident in other parts of the country
where sweated trades were found.   In Leeds, for example, the rapidly-
expanding tailoring trade drew on the female workforce thrown out of
employment by the decline of the linen industry;   in Glasgow, the lack
of secure, well-paid skilled work for men, drove their wives and
daughters to seek work wherever they could find it and made the town
one of the blackest spots for sweating[72].   In Leeds, Glasgow and also
Manchester and London, the problems created by a ready supply of cheap
female labour were added to by the competition for work from the Jewish
communities in these cities.   These communities expanded during the
late-nineteenth century owing to the influx of refugees and although
they created work by setting up new businesses and particularly by
creating new markets in the ladies' outerwear trade, they were also a
substantial addition to the supply of labour.

It was not just inner city areas that suffered a surplus of labour:
in towns such as Colchester surrounded by rural areas where the main
employment for men was low-paid agricultural work, the need for their
wives and daughters to work attracted the new light clothing factories
to the area.

2.   Many industries were being transformed at the end of the nineteenth
century by a breaking down of the production process into detailed work
tasks.   This development followed from the introduction of new machinery
and from the accompanying more sophisticated division of labour.   The
various investigations of the time noted the relationship between this
dilution of skills and very low wages - just two examples are the watch
trade in Coventry, where handwork previously done for 18/- pw and upwards
was now done by machine for 12/- pw[73];  and in the Sheffield cutlery
trade, the increased use of machinery and a greater sub-division of
labour was blamed for starvation wages[74].   Other commentators, such
as The Lancet, identified a fundamental link between sweating and the
dilution of skills[75].

The more unskilled the work was, the more likely there was to be a glut of labour, a surplus of people desperately chasing work; furthermore, those skilled workers thrown out of work by the dilution of skills added to the supply of labour. These factors all contributed to a downward pull on wages.

In industries undergoing technological change, the investment in new machinery both prompted and made possible the employment of cheaper labour. In the workshop trades of East London employers were also faced with the need to reduce costs, but in this case because of provincial factory competition and high rents and rates in London. This latter factor also discouraged capital investment particularly as there was a ready supply of cheap labour. Labour-intensive production with costs squeezed to a minimum was therefore the reaction of these workshop employers[76]. In both cases, however, - i.e. in both factory and non-factory production - the results were very low wages and a tendency to employ the cheapest source of labour - women and girls.

## V

Bythell[77], in dealing mostly with the earlier part of the nineteenth century, uses a definition of "sweating" based on the outwork system, by which he means the giving out of work to be done, primarily under workshop or domestic conditions. Together with other historians, Bythell assumes the phenomenon of sweated labour to be an indication of the backwardness of a particular trade and that with the "modernisation" of industry - the development of factory production - sweating (i.e. the payment of excessively low wages, long hours of work and insanitary working conditions) becomes a thing of the past. However, those concerned with the problem of poverty in the late-nineteenth century recognised that wages so low as to be a social problem were to be found throughout the country, in factory as well as in workshop and domestic production. Furthermore, a preliminary analysis of the causes of sweating indicates that the most important factors were those associated with the development of industrial production and of industrial society, namely the dilution of labour skills brought about by a more sophisticated division of labour and the existence of a surplus labour force brought about by a mismatch between the demand for and supply of the industrial labour force. The evidence also points to the importance of a con-sideration of women workers in any analysis of the problem of sweating. A detailed analysis of the position of women in the industrial labour

force at the end of the nineteenth century will be carried out in
Chapter 3.   Before doing this, we will first test the contention that,
contrary to common assumption, sweating (as defined by contemporary
investigators) was to be found in factory as well as non-factory
production, by a detailed analysis of the development of the tailoring
trade.

References - Chapter 1

1. Duncan Bythell: "The Sweated Trades: Outwork in Nineteenth-Century Britain" (1978).

2. House of Lords Select Committee on the Sweating System:
   First Report, PP1888, XX Cd.361
   Second Report, PP1888, XXI Cd.448
   Third Report, PP1889, XII Cd.165
   Fourth Report, PP1889 XIV Pt. I Cd.331
   Fifth Report, PP1890, XVII Cd.169.

3. D. Bythell, (1978), p.232.

4. The most well-known is Henry Mayhew's book, "London Labour and the London Poor" (1861) but G. Stedman-Jones gives a number of other sources in his Bibliography "E" in "Outcast London" (1971, Oxford).

5. G.H. Wood: Real Wages and the Standard of Comfort Since 1850, in Journal of the Royal Statistical Society (1909) No.72, pp.91-103. A.L. Bowley: Wages in the United Kingdom in the Nineteenth Century (1900). Even though real wages did not fall below the 1871 level, this relative decline was obviously of significance.

6. Charles Booth: The Inhabitants of Tower Hamlets, their Conditions and Occupations, in Journal of the Royal Statistical Society (1887) Vol L, pp.326-91. Charles Booth: Conditions and Occupations of the People of East London and Hackney, in JRSS, Vol LI (1888), pp.276-339.

7. G. Stedman-Jones: (Oxford, 1971), Chapter 16.

8. Ibid, p.288.

9. Ibid, pp.291-4.

10. Ibid, p.287.

11. For example, Royal Commission on the Housing of the Working Classes, PP1884-5 XXX, Cd.4402. Andrew Mearns "The Bitter Cry of Outcast London" (1883) C. Booth, (1887), (1888).

12. A White": The Nomad Poor of London", in Contemporary Review, Vol. XLVII, May 1885. A. White: "Colonisation and Emigration", in Contemporary Review, Vol. XLIX, March 1886.

13. A. White: "Problems of a Great City" (1886), p.30.

14. Industrial Remuneration Conference, 1885.

15. Pall Mall Gazette, September 8, 1884.

16. The Times, 11 October 1884.

17. Industrial Remuneration Conference, 1885.

18. Ibid.

19. Ibid.

20. Report to the Board of Trade on the Sweating System in the East End of London, PP.1887 LXXIX (Cd.331).

21. The Lancet, 10 December 1887.

22. The Lancet, 30 June 1888.

23. Parliamentary Debates, House of Commons, 14 February 1888; 12 May, 15 May, 1888.

24. Parliamentary Debates, House of Lords, 28 February 1888.

25. Report to the Board of Trade on the Sweating System in Leeds, PP.1888 LXXXVI (Cd.5513).

26. See Note 2 for full list of the Select Committee's Reports.

27. This figure is calculated using the 1891 Census returns for the trades investigated by the House of Lords. It does not include what the Select Committee called the "match trade", "the gunlock filing trade", "the military harness and accoutrements trade" or the "iron trade" as the 1891 Census does not list appropriate occupations which cover these trades.

27a. Fifth and Final Report of the House of Lords Select Committee on the Sweating System, PP.1890, XVII (Cd.169), p.xlii

28. This percentage is calculated using the 1891 Census Returns total for the industrial workforce.

29. Fifth and Final Report of the Royal Commission on Labour, PP.1894, XXXV (Cd.7421).

30. See Chapter 7, p.175 .

31. Report of Interdepartmental Committee on Physical Deterioration, PP.1904, XXXII (Cd.2175).

32. Fourth Report of the House of Lords Select Committee on Sweating, QQ.26584-26671; QQ28431-35; PP.1889, XIV Pt.I (Cd.331).

33. Ibid, QQ.26584-16600..

34. Third Report of the House of Lords Select Committee on Sweating, PP.1889, XII (Cd.165) Q.19564. See also Report as to the condition of nailmakers and small chainmakers in South Staffordshire and East Worcestershire by the Labour Correspondent of the Board of Trade, pp.1888 XCI (Cd.385).

36. The Royal Commission on Labour included three reports on women workers.
(1) Reports of the Lady Assistant Commissioners on the Employment of Women PP 1893-4, XXXVII PtI (Cd.6894). These lady Assistant Commissioners were appointed especially to carry out this work, the first time that women were thus employed.
(2) Report by Clara Collet on the Statistics of Employment of Women and Girls, PP.1894 LXXXI (Cd.7564).
(3) Fifth and Final Report of the RC on Labour, Appendix III Employment of Women. PP.1894 XXXV (Cd.7421).

37. Fifth and Final Report, App. III, p.477.

38. S. Aris, "The Jews in Business" (1970), p.37.

39. See Chapter 2, p.42 .

40. Parliamentary Debates, House of Lords, 28 Feb. 1888, 1604.

41. Fifth Report, p.xlii.

42. Report of Royal Commission on Alien Immigration, PP.1903, IX
    (Cd.1741) Vol.I, p.1.

43. E. Cadbury and G. Shann, "Sweating" (1908), p.iv.

44. Notably by Duncan Bythell (1978).

45. Report of Select Committee on Homework, PP.1908, VIII (Cd. 240).

46. Ibid, p.iv.

47. Ibid, p.iii.

48. House of Lords Select Committee on Sweating, 4th Report and Mins.
    of Evidence. PP.1889, XIV Pt.I (Cd.331) Q32142.

49. Ibid, 1st Report and Minutes of Evidence, PP.1888 XX (Cd.361) Q3616.

50. Webb   Trade Union Collection Section A, Volume 47.

51. PP.1908 VIII (Cd.246) p.vi.

52. RC. on Labour Fifth and Final Report, App.III.

53. Select Committee on Homework, 1908, VIII, Cd.246, p.vi.

54. See G. Askwith,"Industrial Problems and Disputes",(1920), p.205.

55. Digest of Evidence, Vol.II.  PP1892  XXXVI Cd.6795 - III, p.30.

56. RC on Labour, Fifth and Final Report, PP1894 XXXV Cd.7421.

57. The Lancet, 12 May 1888, p.933.

58. House of Lords Select Committee on Sweating, 3rd Report and Mins.
    of Evidence, PP1889 XII (Cd.165) QQ24700-24910.

59. Daily Express, 22 June 1907.

60. Fifth and Final Report, 1890 XVII Cd.169, pxlii.

61. Ibid, p.xliii.

62. House of Commons Select Committee on Homework, Report, PP1908, VIII,
    (Cd.246) p.iii.

63. RC on Labour, Minutes of Evidence before Commission sitting as a
    whole.  PP1893-4, XXXIV Pt.I (Cd.7063) Q.5415.

64. Anderson, (1922) p.29.

65. Ibid, p.30.

66. G. Stedman-Jones (1971).

67. The Lancet, 10 December 1887, p.1176.

68. Report to the Board of Trade on the Sweating System in the East End
    of London, 1887, p.7.

69. House of Lords Select Committee. 1st Report and Mins. of Evidence.
    PP1888 XX (Cd.361).

70. G. Stedman-Jones (1971).

71. Ibid, p.97.

72. M.H. Irwin, "The Problem of Homework" (Glasgow, 4th ed. 1907).
    "Homework Amongst Women - (1) Shirtmaking, shirt finishing and
    kindred trades. (2) Miscellaneous Trades - Report of an Inquiry
    concluded for the Glasgow Council for Women's Trades (Glasgow,
    nd, 1898?).

73. Royal Commission on Labour, APP.III, p.480, PP1894, XXV (Cd.7421).

74. House of Lords Select Committee. 3rd Report and Mins. of Evidence
    QQ24708-24877.

75. The Lancet, 12 May 1888, p.933.

76. G. Stedman-Jones (1971), p.23.

77. D. Bythell, (1978).

# 2 The tailoring trade

We have seen that the major concern of the House of Lords Select
Committee was the payment of very low wages and that it was the
tailoring trade which first attracted attention to the problem of
sweating. We have also mentioned that the assumption is commonly made
(and was made by some contemporary investigators) that the payment of
below-subsistence wages was a residual phenomenon, something that would
disappear with the modernisation of industry. Below-subsistence wages
were especially assumed to be associated with what were considered to
be backward sections of the clothing trade, in particular with workshop
production in the tailoring trade where the employment of immigrant
labour was common. This chapter sets out to challenge this assumption
by examining the evidence on wages in the different branches of the
tailoring trade. To date no detailed analysis has been undertaken of
the tailoring trade at the turn of the century and it is the purpose of
this chapter to analyse the statistics on wages and other primary sources
on the structure of the tailoring trade in the late nineteenth and early
twentieth centuries. Using this material, we will then attempt an
explanation of the reasons for the widespread payment of very low and
below-subsistence wages in the tailoring trade.

II

## Tailoring as a Sweated Trade

The House of Lords Select Committee on Sweating and subsequent investigations concentrated on the phenomenon of very low wages when discussing
the sweated trades. The particular concern of contemporary investigators
was that relating to wages which were so low as to be "inadequate to the
necessities of the worker"[1]. Two other characteristics were also a
matter of concern - long hours of work and insanitary working conditions
- but the main focus was on below-subsistence wages; this is also the
characteristic of sweating the incidence of which is easiest to measure.
Before examining the structure and development of the tailoring trade,
we will first attempt an assessment of the incidence of sweating in the
trade by examining how many and what type of workers earned an income
which was considered at the time to be inadequate for the necessities
of life.

Information on wages in the tailoring trade falls into two categories -
one is the official collection of data through the Enquiry into Hours
and Earnings[2]; the other is the individual examples of wages and rates
received by factory and workshop workers and homeworkers, this information
being available in official reports such as the Select Committee's
report on Homework and also in contemporary studies and journalistic
accounts of the tailoring trade. The accuracy of these figures - even
of the Earnings and Hours Enquiry - is limited but the information is
useful in that it demonstrates the cause of concern to social reformers
and politicians.

We must first set some standard of subsistence wage. Cadbury and Shann
in their book published in 1908, set subsistence wages at 25/- per week
for men and 14/- to 16/- per week for women[3]. This subsistence wage
of 25/- for men is higher than that set by B.S. Rowntree of 21/8d[4].
Cadbury and Shann state that their reasons for doing this are because
Rowntree's figure covers only the barest necessities and does not allow
any amount at all for travelling, recreation, sickness expenses or even
funeral expenses. York - the town that Rowntree was studying - was a
small provincial town in 1900 and the cost of living there was appreciably
lower than in towns such as Leeds and certainly lower than the cost of
living in London. Charles Booth, who used roughly the same standard
as Rowntree, admitted in a letter to Rowntree that

"It is very possible that few of those classed by you or me
as poor would pass muster as sufficiently nourished, clothed
and housed according to this standard"[5].

It therefore seems reasonable to adopt the standard set by Cadbury and
Shann, especially since we will deal with wages in the two cities which
were the main centres of the tailoring trade, namely Leeds and London.

Cadbury and Shann set 14/- to 16/- as the subsistence wage for women
on the following basis[6]:

"Assuming that the average family is of five persons, a woman
worker should be able to pay one fifth of the rent, which for
the minimum of decent accommodation would work out at 1/- to
1/6d as a house with three or four rooms cannot be obtained
for less than 5/- to 7/6d per week. Food, with share of fire,
lighting etc. would cost at least 8/- per week, and 4/- would
be needed for clothes, boots, etc. Then there is recreation,
holidays and medical attendance."

This measurement of a subsistence wage for women - while more accurate
than many - does of course assume that a woman's wage is supplementary
to a man's wage (her husband's or her father's). This assumption is,

however, to a large extent unjustified; many women not only had to
support themselves but also had to support dependents. Furthermore,
the assumption that a man's wage was necessarily sufficient to support
a family can also be questioned and this is discussed in detail in
Chapter 3.

Cadbury and Shann's subsistence wage for women is based on the assumption
that it was only necessary for her to contribute the money necessary
for her own needs. Yet many married women, whose husbands earned low
wages and/or were in irregular work, needed to work in order to provide
food, clothing and housing for their children. As we shall see in
Chapter 3, for a significant proportion of the workforce, a man's wage
was not sufficient to support a family.

Bearing the above considerations in mind, it does not seem unreasonable
to take the upper limit mentioned by Cadbury and Shann - namely 16/- -
as a measurement of a subsistence wage for women.

Another point which must be borne in mind, is the irregularity of work
in all branches of the tailoring trade. In the London bespoke trade,
directly affected by seasonal demand, the busiest times of the year were
between March and August, October and December, but in between workers
were often locked out for many weeks[7]. The ready-made trade also
suffered from fluctuations. Beatrice Potter estimated that "indoor"
workers for large contractors and the most skilled tailors throughout
the trade averaged 4½ days in work per week throughout the year[8]. Mr.
Isaacs, Secretary of the Jewish Master Tailors' Federation, was more
pessimistic; he estimated that his members, who were skilled tailors
taking contract work from wholesalers or retailers, averaged 3¼ days to
the week, that is, about 28 full weeks in the year[9].

These two examples refer to the top end of the trade where wages were
higher. At the cheaper end of the London tailoring trade there were
more violent fluctuations in work available. Potter estimated that
2½ days and under was the average employment throughout the year for
those workers at this end of the tailoring trade.

The workers in the factories of the Leeds ready-made trade experienced
greater regularity of work. Amongst some sub-contractors, however,
the volume of work to be done fluctuated as in London, according to
season, to export orders and to government orders. The eight sub-

contractors who Beatrice Potter and John Burnett met in 1888 experienced
irregularity of work from 3½ to 5 days a week[10].   The workers for
these sub-contractors stated that their average working week was 3 days[11].
Any assessment figures provided by the Earnings and Hours Enquiry,
therefore, must be qualified by this irregularity of work.

Perhaps the nearest we can get to an assessment of the average variation
in the working week is by looking at the variation in the weekly wages
bills of firms who made returns to the Earnings and Hours Enquiry.   This
assessment will, however, be an optimistic one for the firms with the
most irregular hours - those whose existence was more precarious - were
unlikely to have made such returns.

According to the returns made to the Earnings and Hours Enquiry in
respect of the average weekly wages bills (for indoor workers) throughout
the year, the following variations were shown by the London and Leeds
tailoring trade[12]:

           London bespoke tailoring      - 42.9% variation
           London ready-made tailoring   - 30.1% variation
           Leeds ready-made tailoring    - 19.1% variation

It therefore seems reasonable to assume that some idea can be obtained
of wage levels if we calculate what workers in the London and Leeds
tailoring trade would have been earning if they worked for 4 days and
5 days a week respectively (the particularly high variation shown by
the bespoke London trade would have been partially offset in the case
of individual workers because these skilled tailors often found work
in the ready-made trade during the slack season, thereby putting the
not so skilled worker out of work).

It will be seen from the figures in Tables 2.1 and 2.2 that, taking account
of the fluctuations in the trade, the average wage for both men and women
in the London bespoke and ready-made sections of the trade was below the
subsistence level set by Cadbury.   The average wage for women in the
Leeds ready-made trade was also below subsistence.   The average man's
wage in the Leeds ready-made trade (Table 2.3) was 1/5d above subsistence but even then, it can be seen that this was only because of the
relatively high wages of the foremen, cutters and piece-work pressers
who pulled the average wage up;   all other types of male worker earned
below the subsistence wage thought necessary to support a family.
Chapter  3 discusses the evidence that a significant number (although
a minority) of women workers were sole breadwinners for their families.

Table 2.1[1] London Bespoke Tailoring: Wages of workers if they averaged 4 days a week

| | | Average | Lower Quartile | Median | Upper Quartile |
|---|---|---|---|---|---|
| MEN: | Foremen - Time | 35/7 | 28/- | 33/3 | 46/6 |
| | Cutters - Time | 57/5 | 33/3 | 53/3 | 73/3 |
| | Journeymen - Time | 26/6 | 20/- | 26/6 | 34/3 |
| | Tailors - Piece | 28/- | 24/- | 28/- | 32/- |
| | Machinists - Time | 22/5 | 19/- | 21/6 | 26/6 |
| | - Piece | 23/- | 20/- | 23/3 | 26/6 |
| | Other Men - Time | 20/4 | | | |
| | - Piece | 23/5 | | | |
| | ALL MEN | 28/5 | | | |
| | | | | | |
| WOMEN: | Machinists - Time | 11/1 | 8/- | 10/3 | 13/3 |
| | - Piece | 9/- | 7/3 | 8/6 | 10/- |
| | Other Women - Time | 11/7 | | | |
| | - Piece | 9/- | | | |
| | ALL WOMEN | 10/7 | | | |

1. All figures in this and the following two tables are calculated from the REHE Vol.II.

Table 2.2 London Ready-made Tailoring: Wages of workers if they averaged 4 days per week

| | | Average | Lower Quartile | Median | Upper Quartile |
|---|---|---|---|---|---|
| MEN: | Foremen - Time | 36/8 | 29/3 | 33/3 | 42/- |
| | Cutter (hand) - Time | 23/7 | 20/- | 23/6 | 28/- |
| | - Piece | 26/3 | 23/6 | 27/3 | 29/6 |
| | Cutters (machine) - Time | 22/2 | 20/- | 24/- | 26/6 |
| | Basters - Piece | 17/8 | 14/- | 16/3 | 19/3 |
| | Machinists - Piece | 19/8 | 14/2 | 18/3 | 21/- |
| | Pressers - Piece | 23/2 | 20/- | 23/3 | 27/- |
| | Warehousemen and Packers - Time | 20/7 | 16/6 | 20/- | 23/3 |
| | Other Men - Time | 22/7 | | | |
| | - Piece | 24/6 | | | |
| | ALL MEN | 24/1 | | | |

Table 2.2 (continued)

|  |  | Average | Lower Quartile | Median | Upper Quartile |
|---|---|---|---|---|---|
| WOMEN: | Forewoman | 41/1 | 11/6 | 14/- | 15/3 |
|  | Basters | 8/1 | 5/- | 6/6 | 12/2 |
|  | Machine Sewers (hand or foot)   - Time | 8/2 | 7/3 | 7/9 | 9/9 |
|  |                  - Piece | 8/9 | 7/3 | 8/9 | 10/2 |
|  | Machine Sewers - Piece | 8/2 | 6/6 | 7/9 | 9/9 |
|  | Hand Sewers & Finishers | 6/3 | 5/- | 6/3 | 7/3 |
|  | Pressers | 7/6 | 5/9 | 7/3 | 9/2 |
|  | Other Women   - Time | 8/1 |  |  |  |
|  |                  - Piece | 8/- |  |  |  |
|  | ALL WOMEN | 7/9 |  |  |  |

Table 2.3   Leeds Ready Made Tailoring:   Wages of workers if they averaged 5 days per week

|  |  | Average | Lower Quartile | Median | Upper Quartile |
|---|---|---|---|---|---|
| MEN: | Foremen - Time | 39/3 | 29/9 | 33/2 | 41/5 |
|  | Cutters (hand) - Time | 25/5 | 23/2 | 26/6 | 27/8 |
|  | Cutters (machine) - Time | 27/- | 24/9 | 26/6 | 29/- |
|  | Basters - Time | 23/- | 20/4 | 24/- | 24/9 |
|  | Fitters - Time | 22/10 | 21/6 | 23/2 | 24/9 |
|  | Pressers - Time | 21/9 | 18/7 | 19/- | 23/7 |
|  |          - Piece | 27/4 | 23/2 | 26/6 | 31/11 |
|  | Warehousemen & Packers | 24/9 | 19/11 | 22/9 | 27/4 |
|  | Enginemen & Stokers | 25/6 | 18/2 | 24/9 | 29/- |
|  | Other Men   - Time | 22/6 |  |  |  |
|  |              - Piece | 23/9 |  |  |  |
|  | ALL MEN | 26/5 |  |  |  |
| WOMEN: | Forewomen   - Time | 18/1 | 16/8 | 18/3 | 20/9 |
|  | Basters      - Piece | 11/3 | 9/11 | 10/9 | 12/10 |
|  | Machines    - Time | 12/10 | 10/9 | 12/5 | 14/11 |
|  | (Power)      - Piece | 11/9 | 9/6 | 11/7 | 14/1 |
|  | Hand Sewers & Finishers | 9/7 | 7/5 | 9/6 | 11/7 |
|  | Pressers | 13/4 | 10/9 | 12/5 | 13/4 |
|  | Other Women - Time | 11/3 |  |  |  |
|  |                - Piece | 9/11 |  |  |  |
|  | ALL WOMEN | 11/3 |  |  |  |

In this context, it is relevant to point out that none of the average
wages for women in the different sections of the tailoring trade were
high enough to meet the subsistence wage set by Cadbury and Shann as
necessary for a man to support his family.

The above tables do not cover homeworkers, and there is no way of
accurately assessing an average wage for homeworkers.   However, the
following examples may be given from evidence to the Select Committee
on Homework in 1908.   Mr. Holmes, a Police Court Missionary, gave
evidence of a mother and daughter making women's costumes at home.   The
skirt and coat were

> "made throughout with seven seams round the bottom, five seams
> up the side, a band put on and the placket worked round for
> 1s. 1d. finding their own machine and thread"[13]

The mother and daughter working together for two days from 9 am to
12.30 am could make seven costumes so if they worked, say, an average
of four days per week throughout the year their average weekly wage
would be 7/6½d each.   The costumes sold in the shops for about 29/-
to 39/-.

This particular witness had connections with the Homeworkers' Aid
Association which had about 1,000 members who were mainly "engaged in
this work simply and solely for the purpose of getting their own
living"[14].   He maintained that the homeworkers with whom he had contact
were working for their own living and not supplementing the wage of a
husband or father.   On the other hand, E.G. Howarth found that of
600 homeworkers in West Ham, 53% were supplementing the casual or
irregular earnings of other members of the family[15].   In both cases,
however, it is obvious that the earnings of homeworkers would not be
mere 'pin money' but were essential to the individual's or the family's
survival.   Miss Vines, a Factory Inspector, had visited a family of
three adults and two children who were entirely dependent on the earnings
of the mother who worked at home on "trouser finishing".   "Finishing"
meant putting the pockets and linings in, sewing on eleven buttons,
making five buttonholes, soaping and pressing the seams and felling the
legs of the trousers.   She could do one pair at 2½d in two hours and
one pair at 3½d in three hours.

> "She had to find her own trimmings, thread, cotton, grimp and
> also soap and heat for irons, and lost from about half an hour
> to an hour daily in fetching and returning the work"[16].

Some witnesses to the Select Committee did not wish homework to be

abolished and quoted wages which would have been adequate to live on.
Others no doubt deliberately cited the worst instances of low rates
received and it is difficult to assess how many homeworkers were paid
wages below subsistence level.  Other evidence, however, backs up the
general picture of very low wages indeed being earned.  Cadbury and
Shann, for example, compiled a table of hours of work and earnings of
homeworkers from their own investigations and from the Daily News
Exhibition on the Sweated Trades held in 1906[17].  The following are
the items relating to the tailoring trade[18]:

Table 2.4

|  | Average Working Day (Hours) | Average Earnings Per Week |
|---|---|---|
| MEN'S CLOTHING: |  |  |
| Trousers | 16 | 5/- |
| Waistcoats | 14 - 15 | 9/- to 10/- |
| WOMEN'S  CLOTHING: |  |  |
| Skirts | 14 | 6/9 |
| Holland skirts | 14 | 6/- |
| Melton cloth skirts | 10 | 5/- to 6/- |
| Voile skirts | 10 - 13 | 10/- to 18/4 |
| Bolero and Chesterfield costumes | 14 | 21/- (between 2) |

Generally the wages and conditions of homeworkers were of a lower standard than those of the majority of "indoor" workers.  There is much
evidence of the long hours worked and the need for assistance from other
members of the family in order to get a sufficient amount of work done.

There is also evidence that some homeworkers were paid such low wages
that they had to resort to poor relief to supplement their earnings.
According to Margaret Irwin's study of homeworkers in Glasgow,

   "The returns of the inspectors of the poor show that many outworkers, who are in receipt of wages too small to support them,
   though working full-time, are helped from the rates.  Moreover,
   although to an extent which it is impossible to ascertain,
   many of the outworkers on low wages are assisted by the
   churches and by charities."[19]

The Handbook of the Sweated Industries Exhibition gives another example; a trouser-maker - "a widow with four children, the eldest of whom is 9 years and the youngest 3 years. She is in receipt of parochial relief"[20]. Although the subsidising of homeworkers by poor relief was not in fact as common as many observers believed[21], such a practice did exist to some extent and was of much concern.

From the foregoing evidence is would appear that below-subsistence wages were a feature of the more advanced sections of the tailoring trade as well as what is usually considered to be the residual sector of home-working and domestic workshops. The payment of below-subsistence wages to women was especially prevalent. In order to shed further light on the phenomenon of low wages, we will now examine the structure and development of the tailoring trade in London and Leeds at the turn of the century. In doing this, we will be looking for indications of why very low wages were common in both workshop and factory production.

### III

We must first make clear what is meant by "tailoring". A tailor is either employed in the making of men's and boys' suits and coats or in the mantle and costume trade, that is, women's and girls' costumes, coats, and skirts. Before the development of wage labour in the trade, tailoring was a handicraft occupation carried out by men working on their own, making up cloth which they or their customer had bought and often travelling from house to house or village to village. However, as early as 1721, when 15,000 journeymen tailors in London formed a trade union and struck for better conditions of employment, it was obvious that the nature of the trade was changing for these tailors were waged workers, striking for higher day-wages and shorter hours of work against capitalist employers[22]. The late seventeenth century and early eighteenth century had in fact seen the emergence of master tailors and tailor/shopkeepers who bought cloth and employed workers under them to make up garments for sale, and the beginnings of an expanding market which marked this development also marked the emergence of seasonal fluctuations in the demand for clothing and an expansion in the retail and wholesale distribution of the product. One pattern was now used to cut out many garments instead of a pattern being drawn up to suit the measurements of a particular customer. Wholesale ware-houses entered into this "ready-made" section of the trade but so too did retailers who either employed tailors on their premises or gave

work out already cut to be made up.   The journeymen tailors were,
however, still skilled workers and the garments were mostly made
throughout by one worker.   Their union was a strong craft union,
insisting on proper apprenticeships and negotiating regional "logs"
(rates of payment).

Handicraft tailors had always tended to give over certain parts of the
finishing processes to members of their family, for example, buttons
and button-holing were fairly simple tasks and could be done while the tailor
was engaged on another part of the garment.   With the expansion of wage
labour in the trade, at the beginning of the nineteenth century, master
tailors started to employ women to do these types of tasks in their
workshops.   It is of fundamental importance that these women bore a
subordinate relation to the male workers - they were brought in to fill
a position that neither journeymen nor apprentices had filled and as
such no one - least of all the journeymen - sought to apply the union
wage to them.   Where women were employed in the tailoring trade,
therefore, it was either as waged workers brought in at low wages by
the master tailor or sub-contractor or it was as unpaid assistants to
their husband or father.   In this context, a sexual division of labour
developed whereby certain tasks in the making of a garment were
separated out and given to women in such a way that the main part of
the work on a garment was done by the tailor while women did things
like felling the lining, turning cuffs, sewing buttonholes, etc.   It
is also important to emphasise that women went to work in the tailoring
trade before the introduction of machinery;  tailoring is an example of
a trade which had previously been male-dominated until the development
of a division of labour (brought about by its transition to a capitalist
basis of production) pulled in women to perform tasks subordinate to the
work tasks - central to the production process - performed by men.

As the market for ready-made clothing expanded, an intensification of
competition brought about the development of a sub-contracting system
of production which was well established in the larger urban centres
by the mid-nineteenth century.   Many journeymen now became sub-
contractors of work to be done for master tailors and tailor/shopkeepers
outside the latters' establishments.   The work was executed either in
a workshop or a "sitting" hired by the tailor/journeyman, or in his own
home.   The narrow margin of profit on which the sub-contractors
operated meant that, where the work was done in workshops there was an
impetus to a more sophisticated division of labour and where the work

37

was done in the tailor's own home, the assistance given to him by his
wife and family became even more important than before.  The sub-
contracting system beame the dominant form of organisation of production
of outerwear clothing in most of the large towns, particularly in Leeds,
Manchester, Glasgow and the East End of London;  for example, by 1850,
it is estimated that two-thirds of the tailors in Glasgow were working
for sub-contractors[23].

In 1851, a viable sewing machine was marketed and was quickly introduced not only into the workshops but also into the homes of individual
outworkers.  The majority of sewing machines produced in the second
half of the nineteenth century were hand or treadle operated and were
inexpensive;  in 1865, a Singer's "New Family" machine could be bought
for £4 4s and could be paid for by hire purchase, a system developed
by Isaac Singer especially for the sale of his sewing machine to homeworkers[24].  In the twenty years from 1865, four million of this
particular model alone were sold and at one time, Singers' employed
thirty collectors in the East End of London "who visit the customers
every week and spend the remainder of their time touting for custom"[25].

Power-driven machines were used in the trade by the larger employers,
such as John Barran of Leeds, the first Leeds tailor to move into what
the 1878 Factory Act defined as factory production, but - as we shall
see - the decision to introduce power-driven machinery and the development of large units of production by no means inevitably followed the
invention of the sewing machine.

The other essential piece of machinery for the tailor in the second
half of the nineteenth century was the band-knife, an adaption of the
band-saw used for cutting furniture veneers, which made possible the
cutting out of more than one garment at a time, and this was also
inexpensive enough for the small workshop employer to buy.  The band-
knife was not a bulky piece of equipment and had been rapidly introduced
into tailoring workshops from 1858.  This had made possible the cutting
of several garments at once and was followed by the subdivision of the
tasks of making the garment into many different operations.  A coat,
for instance, was divided up into five or six operations, unskilled
machinists being employed on most of them -

> "Gradually, this division of labour was extended and with
> each substitution of less skilled labour for more skilled,
> costs were reduced still further."[26]

The buttonhole machine, which was patented in 1884 and 1889 and could sew six buttonholes a minute, was more expensive but could be hired. A series of "goose" irons were installed in some workshops and factories which were fitted with a small flame inside fed from a common gas supply, the heat being varied on each iron by a foot pedal.

With this mechanisation of production, ready-made clothing in the tailoring trade underwent further considerable expansion in the second half of the nineteenth century. The new ready-made clothes had at first met a demand from small tradesmen, office workers, etc. and their families but towards the end of the nineteenth century there was an acceleration in demand from the skilled and semi-skilled manual workers and their families. This was accompanied by a reduction in prices and the development of a sophisticated division of labour in the workshops.

The splitting up of the production process required the division of the workforce in each workshop into teams and in some workshops - particularly the ones in Leeds - these teams were very large and the division of labour extremely sophisticated.

> "In some cases, where each operative concentrates on some small part of the garment, ceaselessly repeating the same process in a mechanical manner, there is nothing to distinguish the workshop from the factory, except the technical distinction that it contains no power-driven machinery."[27]

The new tailoring industry developed most rapidly in Leeds where the declining linen industry provided workshop and factory space and a pool of female labour in an area where engineering firms were alert to the possibilities of new mechanical developments. Leeds also prospered because of the large number of Jewish immigrants, most of whom had been craft tailors and were quick to take advantage of the new developments. In fact the new division of labour in the tailoring workshops was first associated with Jewish sub-contractors who accepted work from the retail tailor at a fixed price per garment. Other areas where there was a steady expansion in the production of ready-made clothes were Colchester, Norwish, Bristol and the East End of London.

Mechanisation and the development of the division of labour in workshop production together with the transition to factory production meant that the tailoring industry in the last quarter of the nineteenth century experienced an increase in the number of women and girls employed (see Table 2.6 for the Leeds figures).

This increase in female labour was due not only to the dilution of labour skills in the workshops and factories but also to the increase in contract work in the form of homework.

> "The simpler operations such as button sewing and plain machining ... were within the compass of the elderly, the sick, and the young mother tied to her home by growing children".[29]

The initial increase in female labour in the tailoring trade took place within the context of some introduction of machinery but very little introduction of power-driven machinery.   Much work was still done by hand although subdivided into many separate stages.   In all branches of the clothing trade there was little incentive to apply power to machinery and bring the workers all under one roof - i.e. into the factory - while contract workers still managed to meet the demand for ready-made clothing and to bear the brunt of seasonal and cyclical fluctuations.   It was the transition from craft production where the tailor made the garment almost  throughout  to a form of production where the production process was separated out into a complicated division of labour which was initially responsible for the increase in female labour in the clothing trade.


IV


## The London Tailoring Trade

The London tailoring trade was divided into two sections - the production of ladies outerwear and the production of men's and boy's outerwear.   Our analysis will concentrate on the men's tailoring trade as this is more appropriate to a comparison with the Leeds (men's and boy's outerwear) tailoring trade, but a brief consideration of the mantle and costume trade is of interest.


## 1.    The Mantle and Costume Trade

Certain parts of London at the beginning of the twentieth century - particularly Whitechapel - were the centre of the mantle and costume trade.   Before the 1880s there was no ready-made trade in ladies' outer- wear in London.    There was a made-to measure trade in the West End but women's ready-made suits and coats were imported, mainly from Germany.

The new trade in ready-made ladies' coats and suits was created by the
Jewish refugees fleeing from Russia and Poland after 1882 who settled
mainly in Leeds, Manchester and London.  By 1900, imports of ladies'
coats and suits had virtually ceased.  Morris Cohen, a wholesale
mantle and costume maker in Bishopsgate and a witness to the Select
Committee on Homework in 1908, described how he started his business
in the 1880s, the first, he believed, of its kind in Britain.  Before
then, he said,

> "if a lady wanted a particular costume made or a jacket, she
> would of course, go to a tailor's shop or have one made;  but
> the bulk of the goods for the City warehouses and to supply
> shop-keepers used to be imported."

But now, he estimated, there were 20,000 people in the ready-made ladies
costume and mantle trade in Britain[30].

One important factor in the mantle and costume trade was the amount of
control which the ladies' tailor retained over the production process.
Ladies' tailoring was, and is, particularly prone to seasonal fluctuations
and changes in fashion;  the product was highly differentiated and ready-
made production (that is, the cutting of many garments from one pattern)
was limited to short runs.  Sub-division of work did take place in the
mantle and costume workshops but not to the extent that it did in the
men's outerwear trade.  The differentiated nature of the product
prevented this, and although his earnings were often low, the male
worker's status in the mantle and costume trade did not degenerate to
that of the "hands" in the other parts of the trade.

The product of the mantle and costume trade was sold in the shops concentrated around Regent Street and Oxford Circus, the work being given
out by wholesalers to tailors who either rented workshops (or "sittings"
in a workshop) or who set up workshops in their own homes.  The firm
paid the tailor a piece-rate and often gave out the work already cut,
but however detailed the division of labour, the tailor usually
maintained the job of "putting the garment together".  Machinists in
the mantle and costume trade were mainly men and were considered to be
skilled workers;  women were employed sometimes as plain machinists but
more often as hand workers on the finishing processes.  Girls were
first employed as "improvers" which often meant just "trotting" - i.e.
running errands - and then progressed to working on various parts of
the finishing processes, e.g. buttonholes, felling, braiding, etc.

Women were also employed on skirts, sometimes making the skirt throughout (a skilled job) but they were almost never employed on coats other than on the subsidiary tasks. Skirts were often given out to women "skirt hands" who worked either in their own homes or in the workshop or home of a middleman or middlewoman. There was no regular apprenticeship system for girls; boys ("greeners"), on the other hand, were apprenticed to the tailor and were taught the different processes involved in making a coat whereas girls were usually only taught one subsidiary task, such as how to make sleeve linings and sew them in.

## 2.  Men's Tailoring

Both Jewish and Gentile workers were found in the production of men's outerwear in London. In the bespoke men's trade, traditionally dominated by men and with the minimum amount of subdivision, an increasing amount of work was put out to, mainly Jewish, sub-contractors in whose workshops a detailed division of labour was common, one result being an increase in the number of women and girls employed. Even within the bespoke trade, certain operations were often given out yet again by the sub-contractor, for example, buttonhole-making or the addition of various trimmings. Furthermore, the trousers and waistcoats ordered in a West End shop were frequently given out already cut and basted to women homeworkers in the East End. The West End of London had always been the centre of high class bespoke tailoring and this continued to be the case (although German immigrants provided a less expensive made-to-measure service in some of the boroughs just outside the West End, for example, in Islington and St. Pancras). It was from this class of tailoring that the Amalgamated Society of Tailors drew its membership, that is, from journeymen tailors and their apprentices. The dependence even of bespoke tailoring on the sub-contracting system is demonstrated as early as 1867 when the strike of 2,000 journeymen tailors was supported by outworkers employed by the firms concerned, including about 300 women who were allowed to attend business meetings of the union for the first time and were paid strike pay equal to the men[32]. The strike was against such leading firms in London as Henry Poole's of Saville Row and Robert Lewis's of St. James' and most of the work that was given out was completed in workshops rather than in the homes of tailors[33].

The cheaper end of the market for men's outerwear was characterised by a very detailed division of labour. Unlike the mantle and costume trade, the production of ready-made men's outerwear - jackets, coats and

trousers - was very easily broken down into stages in such a way that
the tailor's skill was no longer required and he tended to lose control
over the production process.  Not only was there a sophisticated
division of labour within the workshop but there was a multiple "giving
out" of work.  An example of the way in which the trade developed is
found in the history of the firm, Moss Bros[34], who started trading in
second-hand men's clothing and buying up "mis-fits" in 1860.  In the
1880s Moses Moses started to buy up the remnants that cloth merchants
were left with at the end of the season and to make up suits, cut out
by his son, George Moses, and put together by the tailors who were
experiencing a "slack time" as the West End season was over.  These
tailors, who received work from both shops and wholesalers, themselves
often gave out parts of the work to be done outside their own workshop
or home.  Sometimes, most of the work was done by one tailor who gave
the subsidiary tasks to be done by a woman; e.g. an account is given in
the 1890s of a West End tailor

> "employed at a shop where all the work is put out, each tailor
> having to find his own workroom - [he] told me that he pays a
> woman 12/- for doing work which at the same quality and for the
> same quantity he would have to pay a man at least 18/-".[35]

These women and girls would either be employed in the tailor's workroom
(sometimes they were the wives and daughters of the tailors) or they
took the work into their own home, such as, for example, where it was
reported in 1913 that journeymen tailors in the West End farmed work out
to homeworkers, contending that it was their business only to make the
elaborate part of the garment[36].  Other tailors took large amounts of
work either direct from shops or from wholesalers and employed several
people under them.

In these workshops the workers were divided into teams corresponding
with the division of the garment into several stages of production.  The
work was divided as follows:  the tailor basted the garment, then it was
passed to the machinist (often a woman) to machine the main seams, then
the tailor fixed the shoulder seams and the collar; a woman would be
employed to fell the linings and to stitch the buttonholes.  In the
larger workshops, the work was further divided according to parts of the
garment, for example, one machinist would do nothing else but stitch
sleeves or make pockets.  The tailor-employee retained his status as
long as he was only assisted by, say, a couple of tailoresses, a machinist
and a couple of apprentices but as soon as the work was divided amongst
a larger team - particularly when the pressing and the main tailoring
parts of the work were separated - the majority of tailors became little

43

more than "hands".  An example of a larger team was a foreman-tailor,
two tailors, two machinists, two finishers, one presser and one girl
apprentice.  If the tailor did not have a large enough workshop the
garment would be given out to be pressed by an individual worker or
workshop specialising in pressing.  Often, even if the jacket or coat
was completed within one workshop, the trousers would be given out,
ready cut out and basted, for machining by, usually, a woman machinist.
Waistcoats were, by this time, firmly established as "women's work".
In 1834, the Grand Lodge of Operative Tailors had fought the Lodge of
Female Tailors over the entry of women into waistcoat-making[37] but by
the end of the nineteenth century, waistcoat-making was almost completely
in the hands of the cheapest labour offered on the market - that is,
female labour - and was often done by homeworkers.

The distribution of cheap to medium quality men's suits and coats underwent rapid development at the end of the nineteenth century.  In the
1880s and 1890s large shops were established in the West End which -
like Moss Bros. - integrated both manufacturing and selling functions by
contracting work out to tailors - most of whom lived in the City or the
East End.  Furthermore, by the end of the nineteenth century there was
a booming export trade in cheap men's outerwear, especially to South
Africa and to Australia.  The Select Committee on Sweating had been
told that the export of clothing had doubled in the previous twenty
years[38].

In this ready-made section of the London Tailoring trade - where a
prospering tailor would employ a number of machinists - power-driven
sewing machines were most likely to be introduced.  These changed
workshops into factories overnight, for often new premises were neither
sought nor available.  For example, Mr. Thomas, the District Factory
Inspector for North London, reported in 1905 that the introduction of a
small electric motor was common in some of the small workshops and
resulted in many small factories being added to the register where only
a few people were employed on each premises[39].  The possibility of
dividing up the work into many different stages many of which could now
be completed by machinery was obviously one incentive to mass production;
another was the development of standardised cutting in men's tailoring
(with the introduction of new cutting techniques such as the "West End
system")[40].

It was in one expanding section of the trade - namely the production of army, navy, police and railway uniforms where large production runs were needed - that factory production in the London tailoring trade was most advanced.  Men did all the cutting out and also worked on the better class of work (for example, the officers' uniforms were usually made almost throughout by tailors) but - apart from the supervisory and warehouse tasks - women were employed at every other stage of the production process.  Each stage was divided up into corresponding departments - machining, finishing, buttonholing and pressing - and within these divisions there was further sub-division according to the type of garment being made;  for example, a woman or girl might be employed specifically as a "tunic hand" or a "trouser hand".

It must be emphasised, however, that the high rents and the increasing rates which prevailed not only in central London but also in the East End, were a strong discouragement to the larger premises which were required where more than a very few power-driven machines were installed. Moreover, the seasonal nature of the demand for clothing was also a con- straint on investment, particularly as London trade generally was especially prone to seasonal fluctuations owing to its commercial life being dominated by the Parliamentary and "society" season which not only directly affected the retail bespoke section of the tailoring trade but indirectly affected all sections, for the 'quiet season' that almost all London trades experienced meant that working-class demand for clothing also diminished.  Fluctuations in demand for the product of the larger production unit were also fairly common therefore, and to a large extent the smaller factories, the workshops and the homeworkers acted as a buffer against these fluctuations (not always successfully) by taking on the extra work in the busy season.  Even in the most advanced sections of the London tailoring trade, homework was used as a buffer between the factory and seasonal fluctuations.  The rush of work at certain times meant that women and girls were often sent home with work at night. Ada Nield Chiew[41] experienced this when working on a government order in a large factory and, although this giving out of work to "indoor workers" was banned under the Factory and Workshops Acts, the employers resorted to it as necessary overtime which was less visible to the Factor Inspector's eye than working illegal hours in the factory.

The work available to tailors and tailoresses varied throughout the week as well as throughout the year.  Shops and wholesalers, in desperate competition with each other, offered early delivery dates which set workers - who were in turn in competition with one another - impossible deadlines. The Sunday Chronicle in 1913 ran an article headed "The Tragic Song of the Saturday Certain", which included an account of a presser who said that in the busy season he frequently started work on Tuesday morning at 5 am and worked from then until 11 pm on Friday without any break except for five hours sleep each night. Another presser said he had worked as long as thirty-six hours at a stretch[42].

The overwhelming impression that one gets from looking at the London tailoring trade at the turn of the century is that of what the Select Committee on Homework called "the anarchy of competition". Various factors would seem to have encouraged the predominance of small units of production which frantically competed with each other in undercutting prices. These factors are:

1. Ease of entry into the production of ready-made clothing: workshops and domestic workshops could be set up or homework could be undertaken fairly easily as the essential tool - the sewing machine - was relatively cheap and as we have seen, could be bought on hire purchase. Machines were also lent to tailors by employers and by organisations such as the COS and the Jewish Board of Guardians. There was often only a thin dividing line between being a worker and becoming an employer. A tailor could take work from a wholesaler and employ his family and neighbours on the various parts of the production process, and little or no capital would have been required. In the East End, there was a proliferation of what were ironically called "garden workshops", that is, an extension into the backyard of the home.

2. At the same time, the high rents in London and the scarce opportunities to build factories discouraged the physical expansion of small workshops or factories even when they prospered. Successful employers tended to move out of London into Essex, and these provincial factories heightened competition amongst the small London employers.

3. The seasonal nature of the London tailoring trade was a severe curtailment to its prosperity and further discouraged employers from capital investment in space and machinery which would be under-used for perhaps four or five months of the year. A wholesaler was thus better advised to contract his work out in the busy season.

4.   The weakness of unionism and of employers' organisation at the turn
of the century in the London tailoring trade was no doubt a result of
the economic vulnerability of the industry.   This lack of organisation
meant that there was little constraint on the anarchy of competition
amongst both employers and workers.   Workshops and small factories
sprang up overnight in the busy season only to disappear in the chaos
of price-cutting in the slack season and the lack of effective organisation amongst the workforce or amongst the employers and sub-contractors
meant that there was little hope of stabilising the trade and therefore
sparse encouragement to large-scale investment.

Against this background, the clearest correlation with low wages in
both factory and workshop production is the employment of women and
girls.   The breaking down of the production process - first made by
the workshop or individual tailor and later by the introduction of power-
driven machinery - brought about the employment of women and girls on
detailed parts of the garment.   The result was that the skill content
of the work deteriorated and the workers' control over the work situation
was diminished.   Women were brought in by the skilled tailor to assist
them;   they were brought in as unskilled unapprenticed labour and it was
not in the interests of the tailors' unions to allow them into their
organisation.   The following table (Table 2.5) indicates that at the
beginning of the twentieth century, there was a clearly-defined sexual
division of labour in both branches of the London tailoring trade.
This sexual division of labour was associated with the clear-cut wage
differentials between men and women employed in the trade demonstrated
in Tables 2.1 and 2.2.

Where the tailor retained control of the work process, as in the bespoke
men's and ladies' tailoring trades, wages for these men remained
relatively high.   The production of a garment was not broken down into
semi- and unskilled tasks and the employment of women and girls was
limited.   This was the more traditional part of the tailoring trade.
By contrast, when the bespoke trade developed into wholesale bespoke
and ready-made - a process associated with the advancement of
industrialisation - skilled workers lost a great deal of control, semi-
and unskilled work increased, together with the employment of women and
girls and the payment of very low wages was more common.   Below
subsistence wages could not be said, in this case, to be a feature of
an under-developed trade.   However, it is often assumed that there
were particular factors operating in London which, in creating a

Table 2.5   The Sexual Division of Labour in the London Tailoring Trades

(a)   Men and women returned as engaged in the bespoke tailoring trade
       in London in 1906 shown according to what percentage of total
       men and total women were returned as foremen, cutter, machinist, etc.

|  | Type of Worker | Percentage so returned |
|---|---|---|
| Men: | Foremen | 1.9 |
|  | Cutters | 8.3 |
|  | Journeymen Tailors | 51.6 |
|  | Machinists | 16.3 |
| Boys: | Apprentices | 48.1 |
| Women: | Machinists (the remainder were hand workers) | 14.0 |
| Girls: | Machinists (the remainder were hand workers) | 87.6 |

(b)   Men and women returned as engaged in the ready-made tailoring
       trade in London in 1906 shown according to what percentage of
       total men and total women were returned as foremen, cutter,
       machinist, etc.

|  | Type of Worker | Percentage so returned |
|---|---|---|
| Men: | Foremen | 12.0 |
|  | Cutters    (hand) | 28.8 |
|  |            (machine) | 6.2 |
|  | Basters | 8.8 |
|  | Machinists | 10.0 |
|  | Pressers | 13.8 |
|  | Warehousemen and Packers | 11.1 |
| Women: | Forewomen | 1.9 |
|  | Basters | 5.0 |
|  | Machinists    (hand) | 16.0 |
|  |               (power) | 30.0 |
|  | Hand Sewers and Finishers | 26.0 |
|  | Pressers | 5.6 |
| Girls | Machinists | 53.2 |
|  | Hand Sewers and Finishers | 4.5 |

(The number of boys returned are not given according to type
 of worker)

Figures taken from the REHE 1906 Vol.II Clothing Trades, referring to
people who worked full-time, pp.xvii, xviii etc.

proliferation of small businesses in the tailoring trade and discouraging
the installation of power-driven machinery and the expansion of a business,
were responsible for the London tailoring trade being a sweated trade.
The high rents and rates in London were obviously a discouragement to the
expansion of factory production, but is it the case that such an expansion
would have diminished the incidence of sweated labour?   We have already
seen that the payment of below-subsistence wages was common in factory
as well as workshop and domestic production.   We will now go on to
examine in more detail the tailoring trade in its most advanced form at
the turn of the century, namely the tailoring trade in Leeds.


V

## The Leeds Tailoring Trade

In the second half of the nineteenth century, Leeds developed as an
important centre of the wholesale trade in ready-made men's and boy's
outerwear.   In the 1850s, John Barran was the first wholesale tailor
in Leeds to introduce power-driven machines together with the first
bandknife and goose irons.   Barran had been a cloth dealer but now he
went into the business of cutting cloth and bringing in machinists,
finishers and pressers to make it up.   He also relied heavily on
Jewish sub-contractors to do the work for which his premises had not
the capacity[43].   The expansion of the trade encouraged a sub-division
of labour.   Previously although some of the finishing processes had
been undertaken by subsidiary workers, the garment had been 'put together'
by the tailor.   Now the making up of coats and jackets was divided up
into, at first, five or six different operations, and then even more
sub-division took place, unskilled and semi-skilled workers being
introduced to replace the skilled tailor.   When John Burnett carried
out his investigation into the Leeds tailoring trade, he found for
instance, that some women were employed solely to sew on buttons[44].   The
sub-divisional system in Leeds was generally agreed to be more advanced
than that in London[45], and this system was developed at its most
sophisticated level in the Jewish outworkers' (i.e. contractors) workshops, most of whom were new immigrants, while the small English tailors
in Leeds tried desperately to preserve their skill and status.   In the
Jewish workshops the workers were split up into teams, each person
specialising on one part of the production process.   The workshops were
larger than those of the London outworkers, indeed some of them should
strictly be called factories for small gas engines were installed to
drive the machines.   Yet it was in some of these more modern workshops/

factories that contemporary investigators found sweating to take place.
John Burnett reported that "The largest sweating master in the Leeds
trade has 40 machines, and the average of machines to each master is
somewhere between 20 and 30"[46].   The largest workshops in London, on
the other hand, had about 8 to 10 machines.

As the dilution of skilled labour progressed, so the numbers of women
and girls employed increased as the following table indicates[47].

Table 2.6   Census Returns of those Employed in the Leeds Tailoring
            Trade

|        | Men   | Women  |
|--------|-------|--------|
| 1861*  | 951   | 20     |
| 1871*  | 1,523 | 483    |
| 1881   | 2,148 | 2,740  |
| 1891   | 4,773 | 10,916 |
| 1901   | 5,792 | 14,021 |

* The figures for 1861 and 1871 refer to men and
  women of and above twenty years of age.

1881, 1891 and 1901 figures refer to all workers.
The returns made for each year included dealers.

This influx of women and girls into the Leeds tailoring trade, accompanied
as it was by a division of labour and a dilution of labour skills was
also associated with the payment of low wages revealed by Table 2.3.

The changing representation from the clothing trade on the Leeds Trades
Council[48] reflects the development of the tailoring trade from production
dominated by skilled tailors to that dominated by machinists, pressers
and other semi-skilled workers.   Furthermore, it illustrates the influx
of Jews and of women into the trade.   In the 1850s tailors formed the
largest membership represented on the Trades Council and the delegates
were English, who referred to themselves as master tailors.   In 1855,
the first tailors' machinists appeared on the Trades Council and these
were Jewish men, the forerunners of the fluctuating but steadily growing
Union of Jewish Tailors, Tailors' Machinists and Tailors' Pressers.   By
1891, the master tailors had lost their dominance of the Trades Council[49],
and the Council was helping the Wholesale Clothiers' Operatives Union to
increase its membership.   In 1889, the tailoresses (that is, machinists)
working at Messrs Arthur and Co., wholesale clothiers, came out on
strike for the abolition of the 1d charge for steam power.   Two male

delegates to the Leeds Trades Council, together with two middle-class
feminists Isabella Ford and Clementina Black, helped the striking women
to form the Leeds Tailoresses Union, and their delegates, Lily Thackray
and Maud Storey, were the first women to be elected onto the Trades
Council[50].

Throughout the second half of the nineteenth century Leeds employers
engaged in the making of men's and juveniles' outerwear went from
strength to strength. The 1870s and 1880s saw an expansion of both
size of firm and number of tailoring firms. In February 1879,
John Barran moved into new premises in Park Square. It was a four-
storey building and was divided up according to the sub-division of the
production process. The reporter from the Leeds Mercury gave a detailed
account of what went on inside this new clothing factory and it is worth
quoting extensively from this article[51] for an indication is given of
the way that the clothing industry was developing.

In the basement were situated the three gas engines, two of which drove
the cutting machines, the hoist and the sewing machines while the third
was held in reserve. Also in the basement was the cutting room. The
bales of cloth were brought down to the cutters-out who chalked out the
pattern on the top of a bale 100 or 200 thicknesses thick and then
carried it across the room to be cut by the band-knife machine.

> "Then comes the process of separating all the parts, and
> packing each suit in a compact bundle, together with the
> linings, trimmings, buttons, etc. which are needed to make
> it complete. To the bundle a ticket is affixed, on which
> are marked all the particulars as to the style in which the
> suit is to be made up that are needed for the guidance of the
> work people through whose hands it has still to pass"[52].

The bundles were then either passed to the machinists on the floor of
the building or to outworkers, and during the busy season more and more
work would have gone to outworkers as the three hundred machines on the
top floor could not be added to whereas there were always many outworkers
crying out for work.

The Leeds Mercury's reporter who visited the machine room, commented:

> "... one's attention is called to the admirably ingenious
> arrangement, invented and patented by Mr. John Barran, Junior,
> by which each sempstress has the needle of the machine she
> tends completely under her control. A simple movement of the
> foot enables her to regulate with perfect accuracy the speed
> of the machine, and thus prevents the confusion which would
> inevitably arise if all the machines were being driven at a

uniform rate, regardless of the character of the work they are
doing."[53]

After the seams had been machined the "bundle" then passed down to the
second floor where the finishing processes were carried out, that is,

"... buttons are fastened on;  button-holes are made;
certain parts of the garment strengthened by hand sewing;
the basting taken out, and, in short, the clothes finished".[54]

The final process was the ironing of the suits.   The <u>Leeds Mercury</u>
reported

"the irons, which are of the ordinary 'goose' shape, are kept
constantly hot by means of one hundred gas jets burning inside
them, and the ironer, by the simple application of her foot to
a pedal beneath the table can bring enormous pressure, at any
moment she pleases, to bear upon the iron she is using."[55]

Barran's main output was juvenile suits and five or six hundred different
styles were manufactured.

Although, as we shall see, Barran and firms like his were not exempt from
the accusation of  sweating  (i.e. paying subsistence or below-subsistence
wages and providing unhealthy working conditions), they did attempt to
build up a disciplined and efficient workforce.   With such heavy investment in machinery a reliable workforce was essential and, in fact,
employers would sometimes refuse to allow their workers to leave the
premises at dinner time "because they could not trust them to return"[56].
Barran, like many other large factory-owners, provided a dining-room
for his workers[57].   He also paid three weeks sick leave automatically[58],
but some of the other practices introduced in pursuit of a reliable
workforce were the source of much bitterness, particularly the fines
imposed.

In 1888, Barran opened yet another new factory in Leeds and the large
capital investment seems to have increased his concern for a disciplined
workforce.   New rules and fines were introduced, not only to discourage
shoddy work but also to ensure good time-keeping.   These rules were
written in the front of the books in which an individual's work was
entered and the workers had to sign a declaration that they would be
bound by them.   They were fined for lateness - 1d for arriving between
8.05 am and 8.15 am, 2d for between 8.15 and 8.30 am and after 8.30 the
doors were locked until after dinner[59].

Barran's successful expansion into the wholesale ready-made trade in
men's and juvenile's tailoring signalled the entry of other firms, some

of whom like Barran's had previously been dealers in cloth, all of them
benefitting from the ready supply of skilled female labour created by
the decline of the linen industry[60] and by the movement of the woollen
industry from the centre of Leeds to its outskirts[61].   In 1887, the
Yorkshire Post reported that following Barran's success,

> "one after another, in rapid succession, new firms have
> successfully embarked on the business and at this moment
> Leeds stands unrivalled as a metropolis for the production
> of attire for men and boys"[62].

It was estimated that more than a dozen wholesale clothiers had been
opened in the previous ten years.


Most of the large factories were concentrated around the Park Square area
in the centre of Leeds.   Messrs Buckley, took over the whole of one side
of Greek Street and a large part of Bedford Street and then, like many
other wholesale clothiers, took over a mill which was no longer in
business, where they employed over 600 clothing operatives[63].   Barran's
continued to expand and in 1888 built another factory (a five-storey
building this time) on a site formerly known as Park Lane Mills where
they employed 1,200 people.   In 1879 their three gas engines in the
Park Square factory had been 8 hp, now their engines ran at 80 hp.
Some of the new buildings were built in a very grand style, for example,
that of Arthur & Co. in Park Square, built "in the Italian style and
towering to the extent of six storeys" which employed 1,000 people, 300
of them machinists[65].   The reporter also mentions that Arthur & Co
were using the new Reese buttonhole machine, an American invention, which
turned out at least 700 buttonholes a day and was "minded" by a girl.


Leeds manufacturers were reported to be paying increasing attention to
the colonial ready-made trade and in this direction they entered into
competition with the London trade, a development which probably took
some responsibility for the driving down of wage rates at the cheaper
end of the London trade.   It was Hepworth's venture into the retail
business, however, which was probably the biggest step forward for the
Leeds tailoring industry.   In 1884, Norris Hepworth, son of Joseph
Hepworth, the wholesale manufacturer, set up retail shops to sell the
firm's own product, and by 1891 was so successful that he had seventy
or eighty such shops[66].   The increased trade was reported to have
meant that in spite of enlarged premises, Hepworth had had to give more
work out, not only to workshops but also to homeworkers[67].   In 1891,
the firm opened what was claimed to be the largest factory in the world

(100,000 square feet) - and Norris Hepworth was elected to the Leeds County Council. Later on, of course, Montague Burton greatly contributed to the expansion of the Leeds tailoring trade by his development of the wholesale made-to-measure trade, but this was not until the turn of the century.

By the late 1880s, Hepworth had five factories - in Leeds, Manchester, and London - and contemplated concentrating all production in Leeds[68]. It was also reported that ready-made clothing firms had moved to Leeds from Glasgow, London, Newcastle, Abingdon, Leicester and Bristol[69]. Evidence to the House of Lords Select Committee on Sweating demonstrated the tendency for large clothing firms to move production to Leeds. Small Jewish employers and Jewish workers were also reported to be moving from, for example, Glasgow and Birmingham, to Leeds[70]. An example of a firm of wholesalers which moved to Leeds from Glasgow was J & W Campbell who opened a factory in Leeds in 1882 employing 300 people and by 1889 were about to move onto a new site where it was planned to employ 2,000 people[71]. Campbell's were one of at least four large factories which were established by Glasgow firms who moved to Leeds, despite the availability of cheaper female labour in Glasgow. Clara Collet, an investigator for the Board of Trade explains this preference for the more expensive Leeds female labour in terms of Leeds supplying "a better class of labour, which is really less costly than that of Glasgow"[72]. The Leeds linen and woollen industry had traditionally provided skilled work for women and girls so skilled female labour was available but Collet also posits a relationship between the type of jobs available for men and the quality of female labour.

> "The great diversity [in Leeds] of skilled men's labour ensures the existence of a class of girls whose work is more likely to be efficient than that of the daughters of un-skilled labourers" [who were predominant in Glasgow][73].

There was little opportunity for skilled work for men in Glasgow and the female workers there were more likely to be the wives and daughters of unskilled and semi-skilled workers, whereas amongst Collet's sample of female workers in Leeds the majority were daughters or wives of skilled workmen[74].

Although women's wages were higher in Leeds than in London, they were still below subsistence level. This is in spite of the fact that towards the end of the nineteenth century the claim was often made that the Leeds tailoring trade was so much more advanced in terms of factory development than the London trade that very low wages and insanitary conditions were not the problem in Leeds as they were in East London. The following table indicates this more advanced nature of the Leeds trade.

Table 2.7     Numbers employed in Factory and Workshop Production in the Clothing Trades[1]:  1904

|  | Persons Employed in: | | % of Total employed in Factories |
|  | Factory Production | Workshop Production | |
|---|---|---|---|
| North London | 13,419 | 32,337 | 29.2 |
| South London | 6,017 | 21,707 | 21.7 |
| West London | 6,932 | 11,785 | 37.5 |
| Special West London Area | 2,323 | 26,526 | 8.0 |
| East London | 12,957 | 28,702 | 31.0 |
| Total in London | 41,648 | 121,057 | 25.6 |
| Leeds | 24,316 | 12,692 | 65.7 |
| United Kingdom | 307,157 | 359,118 | 46.2 |

1. Sources:  Report of the Chief Inspector of Factories and Workshops 1904 (Supplement) Tables 2 and 3, PP1907 X (Cd.3323).

NB These figures include, of course, the dressmaking trade.  The Special West London district covered the high class bespoke ladies tailoring and dressmaking which accounts for the extremely low proportion of factories in the area.


Factory production was much more common in the Leeds tailoring trade than in London.  Yet the Leeds employers were also subject to the accusation of sweating.

In 1888 The Lancet published an article which claimed that insanitary conditions and the payment of below-subsistence wages existed in Leeds to a far greater extent than was claimed by the large wholesalers.  The journal's concern - and that of the people of Leeds - had been aroused by the outbreak of smallpox in an area where tailoring workshops and homeworkers were common.  The Lancet's investigators visited a neighbour-hood in Leeds which was known for frequent outbreaks of typhus fever and they found work being carried on in unsatisfactory conditions.

"Immediately opposite the door of the common lodging-house, from whence nine small-pox patients were removed, separated from this door only by the width of a narrow street, is the entrance to an old abandoned mill, where there are no less than five sweaters' workshops.  Here, altogether, from 300-400 people for the most part women, are engaged in tailoring".[75]

They also found homeworkers in this district, for example, an Englishwoman who worked for a "very large firm of wholesale clothiers" making boys' vests and short trousers[76].

The sanitary conditions amongst both homeworkers and Jewish workshops were sometimes very bad. The Lancet reported that although the workshops in Leeds tended to be bigger than those in East London, they were often just as insanitary[77]. In the "Jewish Quarter" of the town The Lancet's investigators entered a house where there were three different workshops, employing altogether about 160 people and exuding "a most appalling stench" owing to the lack of sanitary facilities. In the uproar which followed the publication of The Lancet's report, the Leeds Mercury took up the investigation. They agreed with the findings of The Lancet that, while the workshops were large and the middlemen few the amount of contracting out was enormous and much work was done by homeworkers. Very low wages were common. One of the homeworkers visited earned between 5/- and 17/- per week, but "she has to pay out of this sum for her thread and trimmings, rent, gas, iron - in fact, every incidental expense"[78]. Much was made of the inadequate sanitary facilities.

> "The sanitary accommodation is altogether inadequate, and in some cases, the most revolting consequences ensue. In one street, where a great number of tailors live, we found only two closets for seven houses. The houses on this side of the street have no back yards or back windows; and it is therefore no easy matter to supply proper sanitary accommodation ... As a result, the whole passage leading to these two closets is one mass of filth. People come here and empty utensils outside the closets, being fearful to approach such foul places. The flagstones are covered with soil, the liquid is seen oozing from under the stones, where it contaminates the subsoil, and passing out into the street, stains the pavement of the causeway till it reaches the gutters. The stench is so great that in a cottage on one side of the passage in question we found the inhabitants could not open their windows. Yet the little room thus deprived of ventilation contained, when we looked in, no less than nine persons huddled together, one of them was a tailor, and there was a child suffering from whooping-cough."[79]

The Yorkshire Press, on the other hand, joined with most of the large Leeds wholesalers in condemning The Lancet's report[80] and the Leeds Medical Officer of Health, the Sanitary Inspectors and the Sanitary Committee maintained that "a most rigid inquiry will show the statements made in the London medical journal to have been greatly exaggerated"[81]. Nevertheless, the Medical Officer of Health was sacked and the Sanitary Inspectors instructed to increase their inspection of workshops.

But accusations of sweating, particularly those relating to the payment of very low wages, were not confined to workshop employers.    John Barran was frequently accused of sweating his workers[82] and the conditions at his factory prompted many tailoresses employed there to attempt to organise into a trade union.    A tailoress reported in 1889 that during the previous six years, the prices paid to workers for each garment had been pulled down.    This, she said, was a direct result of new machines being introduced, for "... as the manager believed that they would run quicker than the old ones and do the work in less time, the prices were reduced"[83].    Low wages were also reported to be paid in the finishing department of another large Leeds factory where a girl received 4½d for finishing an Eton jacket and vest.

> "For this amount she has to fell the neck of the vest, to put
> the buttons on the coat and waistcoat, then to take the coat and
> vest to the button-hole machinists and pay 3d for the button-
> holes on the coat and vest and ½d for the button-holes on the
> jacket, so that only one penny is left for payment for the rest
> of the work".[84]

Table 2.3 (page 34) illustrates the extent of the payment of below-subsistence wages in the Leeds ready-made tailoring trade.    Although the level of wages for women was higher in Leeds than in the London bespoke or ready-made trades, the average woman's wage was still below subsistence - only forewomen earned a wage adequate for subsistence needs.    The average man's wage in the Leeds trade was 1/5d above subsistence level but within six of the eleven different types of work for men in the trade, the average wage was below subsistence.

"Pocket money" wages for girls were universal in the Leeds tailoring trade - as elsewhere in the country.    At Barran's, for example, a girl named Mary Ellen Ashton was taken on at fifteen years of age for 6/- per week. This was increased by 1/- three months later and then by 1/- per year so that by 1893 she was earning 11/- at the age of nineteen[85].

The above two examples of girls being paid below-subsistence wages touch on two fundamental features of the tailoring trade:  the competition between indoor and outdoor workers, and the employment of young girls at very low wages.    The first girl was competing with homeworkers for the finishing work, for coats and waistcoats were frequently sent out to be finished by homeworkers who accepted the work for lower rates than that paid to "indoor" workers[86].    Although the number of homeworkers was said to be smaller in Leeds than in East London, they were still estimated to make up between one fifth and one eighth of the total workforce engaged in the trade[87].    Wages amongst finishers employed directly by the whole-saler were therefore very vulnerable to being forced down by competition.

Both cases demonstrate the way in which girls, who generally lived with their parents, could be paid a below-subsistence wage on the grounds that they themselves did not have to meet the full cost of their sub-sistence.   This question is taken up in more depth in Chapter 3.

People such as Charles Booth maintained that the development of factory production in the clothing industry "with its better sanitary condition and greater regularity of earnings"[88] was diminishing the incidence of sweating in towns such as Leeds.    This conception of the nature of factory production, I would contend, is a mistaken one.    Bad sanitary conditions may have been less common in factory production but long hours and low wages were encouraged by the system of contracting work out, a system on which the ready-made trade evolved in response to the fluctuations in demand for the products of the clothing trades.    The Leeds ready-made trade - just as the London trade - was "essentially a seasonal trade"[89].    This seasonal nature of the trade, together with the ease of entry into tailoring, made its employees especially vulner-able to the inevitable outcome of intense competition - the forcing down of wages.    Contracting work out was as inherent a part of the Leeds tailoring trade as it was of the East London trade.    Large wholesalers were more common in Leeds and more work was done on their own premises, but much work was contracted out, not only to workshops and homeworkers but also to smaller factories.

The Secretary of the Jewish Tailors' Trade Society described to the House of Lords Select Committee what happened to the "bundles" of work which were given out from Barran's to a contractor.    This contractor took the bundles into his own large workshop and then gave them to a fitter-up:

> "from the fitter-up he hands them to the machiner;  from the machiner in some particular branches, it goes to the under-presser;  some other parts of the garment go to the tailor, what they call a tailor, that is, a baster out, and a baster under him;  then there is the lining maker that pieces linings before they are put into a garment, to be stitched together and made up ready to be sent to the presser.    Then the presser presses the garments off ... and they have to go through the finishers, feller hands, and button-hole hands, and then they come to, what they term, a brusher off, the garments then being all ready for going to the warehouse."[90]

Sometimes all these processes would have been carried on in the same
workshop but sometimes the work would be "given out" yet again to a
smaller workshop, a domestic workshop or a homeworker.    Within the
men's tailoring trade, the customary practice was for coats to be given
out to the Jewish workshops, men's vests (waistcoats) to the English
workshops, and trousers were made up on the wholesalers' premises[91].
All of these processes, however, especially during the busy season,
could be found to be executed by homeworkers and in domestic workshops.
The large amount of work given out by wholesalers is reflected in the
way in which their premises were commonly called warehouses.

Clothing manufacturers in other towns were aware that work could be done
cheaply in Leeds.    For example, a Sheffield master tailor, who claimed
that sweating was common in Leeds, told the House of Lords Select
Committee that they had made-to-measure suits made up in Leeds rather
than Sheffield because it was cheaper to do so[92].

Like the London trade, therefore, the Leeds tailoring trade was divided
up into three levels of production, all intimately linked by contracting
and sub-contracting.    The wholesale businesses in Leeds were run by
English businessmen (who sometimes went into retailing as well) - many
of whom had been dealers in cloth or clothing.    Although some of the
wholesalers had attempted to carry out all production under their roof
it was common practice that much of the work was contracted out.    The
next level was therefore the workshops and smaller factories who took
the contracts and the final level was the homeworkers who took work
from both wholesaler and contractor.

The fundamental characteristic of sweating - the payment of below-
subsistence wages - was to be found in Leeds as well as in the London
tailoring trade.    And again, having discussed the development and
changing structure of the tailoring trade, it is clear that the major
section of the workforce which received below-subsistence wages were
the women and girls in both factory and workshop production (see Table
2.3).    It is also clear that, as in the London trade, there was a very
definite sexual division of labour which accompanied the large wage
differentials between male and female workers (Table 2.8).

Table 2.8   The Sexual Division of Labour in the Leeds Ready-made
            Tailoring Trade.

            Men and women returned as engaged in the ready-made
            tailoring trade in Leeds in 1906 shown according to what
            percentage of total men and total women were returned as
            foremen, cutter, machinist, etc.[1]

|  |  | Percentage so returned |
|---|---|---|
| Men: | Foremen | 11.7 |
|  | Cutters   (hand) | 26.4 |
|  |           (machine) | 4.8 |
|  | Basters | 4.7 |
|  | Fitters | 8.6 |
|  | Pressers | 12.2 |
|  | Warehousemen and packers | 15.0 |
|  | Enginemen and stokers | 2.8 |
| Boys: | Apprentices | 11.3 |
| Women: | Forewomen | 0.6 |
|  | Basters | 1.2 |
|  | Machinists   (power) | 58.7 |
|  | Hand sewers and finishers | 30.0 |
|  | Pressers | 4.7 |
| Girls: | Basters | 1.6 |
|  | Machinists   (power) | 58.1 |
|  | Hand sewers and finishers | 24.4 |
|  | Pressers | 2.4 |

1.    Taken from REHE (1906) Vol.II


                              VI

From the general discussion of the sweated trades in Chapter 1 and from
the more detailed analysis of the tailoring trade in this chapter, it is
evident that the problem of sweated labour was by no means a problem
confined to workshop or domestic production:  it is also clear that outworking (i.e. the sub-contracting out of work) was as much the basis of
the more "advanced" Leeds trade as it was of the supposedly backward
London trade.    The main characteristics of sweating - the payment of
very low wages - was found in factory as well as workshop production.
It is also evident that below-subsistence wages were particularly a
phenomenon found amongst women workers.    Chapter 3 sets out to examine

the more general position of women workers at the turn of the century
before we move on to an analysis of how women's work and sweated labour
were perceived and what was the political response to the problem.

References - Chapter 2

1.  House of Lords Select Committee on Sweating, Fifth Report 1890
    XVII (Cd.169) p.xlii.

2.  UK Board of Trade:  Report of an Enquiry into Earnings and Hours
    of Labour of the Workpeople of the United Kingdom, Vol.II Clothing
    Trades, PP1909, LXXX, Cd.4844 (hereafter referred to as REHE).

3.  E. Cadbury and G. Shann, "Sweating" (1908).

4.  B.S. Rowntree, "Poverty:  a Study of Town Life" (1901), p.110.

5.  Ibid., p.300.

6.  Cadbury and Shann, 1908, pp.14-15.

7.  C. Booth, "Life and Labour of the People of London" (1902), Vol.4, p.53.

8.  Ibid., p.54.

9.  Report of the Committee appointed to consider and advise with regard
    to the application of the National Insurance Act to Outworkers,
    Vol.I, PP1912-13 XLII (Cd.6178).

10. Report to the Board of Trade on the Sweating System in Leeds,
    PP1888, LXXXVI, (Cd.5513), p.5.

11. Ibid., p.6.

12. REHE, Vol.II.

13. Select Committee on Homework, PP1908, VIII (Cd.246), p.14.

14. Ibid., p.14.

15. E. Howarth and M. Wilson, "West Ham - A Study in Social and
    Industrial Problems" (1907).

16. Select Committee on Homework, Minutes of Evidence, PP1908, VIII,
    (Cd.246), Q.1133.

17. R. Mudie-Smith (ed.):  Sweated Industries:  Being a Handbook of
    the Daily News Exhibition.  (1906).

18. Cadbury and Shann (1908), pp.25-34.

19. Margaret H. Irwin (1897).

20. R. Mudie-Smith (1906), p.93

21. Royal Commission on the Poor Laws and Relief of Distress:  Appendix
    to Vol.XVII - C. Williams and T. Jones:  Report on the Effect of
    Outdoor Relief on Wages and the Conditions of Employment, PP1909,
    XLIII, Cd.4690.

22. This section on the history of the tailoring trade draws on the
    following sources:
    - F.W. Galton, "The Tailoring Trade" (1923).
    - J. Thomas, "History of the Leeds Clothing Trade", Yorkshire

Bulletin of Economic and Social Research, Occasional Paper No.1, 1955.
- Clara E. Collet, "Women's Work in Leeds" in Economic Journal Vol.I, No.I, 1891.
- Charles Booth (1902) Vol.7.
- S.P. Dobbs, "The Clothing Workers of Great Britain (1926).
- B. Drake, "The West End Tailoring Trade" in "Seasonal Trades" edited by S. Webb and A. Freeman (1912).
- R.R. Gilbert, "Sewing Machines" (1970).
- E.B. Giles, "History of the Art of Cutting in England" (1887)
- W.H. Hulme, "The English Tailor, A Short History of the Tailoring Trade" (nd 1920s. Typescript manuscript deposited in Leeds Reference Library)
- Report to the Board of Trade on the Sweating System in the East End of London PP1887 LXXXIX, (Cd.331).
-    - ditto - in Leeds PP1888 LXXXVI (Cd.5513).

Evidence contained in the House of Lords Select Committee on Sweating 1888-1890.
        - ditto - in House of Commons Select Committee on Homework, 1907-8.
        - ditto - Royal Commission on Labour

- "Austin Reed Ltd:  Fine and Fifty" (History of the firm published on their Golden Jubilee) (1950)
- M. Steward and L. Hunter, "The Needle is Threaded - a History of the Clothing Industry" (1964)
- W.S. Tute, "The Grey Top Hat, the Story of Moss Bros. of Covent Garden" (1961)
- Board of Trade, Handbooks on the London Trades - Clothing (1915)
- S. Aris, "The Jews in Business" (1970)
- Apprenticeship and Skilled Employment Association, "Trades for London Girls" (1907)
- L. Davidoff, "The Employment of Married Women in England 1850-1950" (Unpublished MA Thesis, London 1956).
- I. Pinchbeck, "Women Workrs and the Industrial Revolution, 1750-1850" (Reprinted 1969)
- W.F. Neff, "Victorian Working Women" (1960)
- Alice Clark, "The Working Life of Women in the Seventeenth Century" (reprinted 1968)
- "Lloyd, Atree and Smith Ltd:  One Hundred Years" (History of a firm of Manufacturers of Menswear) (1957)
- National Union of Tailors and Garment Workers, "Ever Since the Fig Leaves Came into Fashion, the Tale of the Tailors' Union" (1947)
- Leeds Clothing Firms, business records and newspaper cuttings deposited in Leeds (Chapeltown) Archives Dept.


23.  M. Irwin, (1897).


24.  J. Thomas:  A History of the Leeds Clothing Industry (Yorkshire Bulletin of Economic and Social Research, Occasional Paper No.1) 1955, p.34.

25.  C. Booth, (1902), Vol.4, p.45.

26.  J. Thomas, (1955), p.10.

27.  S.P. Dobbs:  The Clothing Workers of Great Britain" (1926), p.15.

28.  See REHE, Vol.II.

29.  Stewart and Hunter:  The Needle is Threaded (1964), p.116.

30.  Report of the Select Committee on Homework, PP1908 VIII (Cd.246)
     QQ1473-1475.

32.  Stewart and Hunter (1964), pp.91-92.

33.  See B. Drake (1912).

34.  W.S. Tute (1961).

35.  Webb Trade Union Collection, Section A, Vol.47, Item 31.

36.  Daily Citizen, 5.12.1913.

37.  See   F. Galton (1923);  Stewart & Hunter (1964).

38.  House of Lords Select Committee on Sweating, 1889, XIV (Cd.331)
     Q.32055, 32060.

39.  Report of the Chief Inspector for Factories and Workshops 1905, p.5.

40.  E.B. Giles:  A History of the Art of Cutting (1887).

41.  Ada Nield Chew, "Victims of Our Industrial System - I Tailoresses"
     in Young Oxford  Vol.II No.18, March 1901.

42.  Sunday Chronicle, 30.3.1913.

43.  Joan Thomas (1955).

44.  House of Lords Select Committee on Sweating, 2nd Report and Mins.
     of Evidence, PP1888, XXI (Cd. 448) Q.17351.

45.  See Charles Booth's evidence to the House of Lords Select Committee
     and also John Burnett's Report to the Board of Trade PP1888 LXXXCI
     (Cd.5513).

46.  Report to the Board of Trade on the Sweating System in Leeds
     PP1888, LXXXVI (Cd.5513) p.4.

47.  This increase in the proportion of women and girls employed in the
     trade was not uniform throughout the workforce.   Jewish tailors
     were reluctant to employ Jewish women and girls in their workshops
     and where they had to employ women they mainly employed gentiles.
     This strength of social custom is reflected in the figures given
     below which show that amongst the non-Jewish workers in the Leeds
     tailoring workshops, women and girls outnumbered the men by some-
     thing like two to one, whereas amongst Jewish workers, the reverse
     is the case.

Break-down of the male and female workforce in tailoring
workshops in Leeds:  1894

| ORDINARY WORKSHOPS: | | | | DOMESTIC WORKSHOPS | | | |
|---|---|---|---|---|---|---|---|
| Jewish workers | | Others | | Jewish workers | | Others | |
| Male | Female | Male | Female | Male | Female | Male | Female |
| 960 | 455 | 289 | 740 | 57 | 34 | 2 | 16 |

Source:  Report of the Chief Medical Officer of Health for Leeds,
1894, p.144.

It is also of interest to note Joan Thomas' statement that there is some evidence that in Leeds the Jewish women and girls were employed on more skilled work than the English women working in the same shop.

48. Leeds Trades Council: Annual Reports for the years 1850-1900.

49. There were now a larger number of delegates from the engineering trades.

50. Leeds Trades Council: Annual Report for the year 1889.

51. Leeds Mercury, 15 February 1879.

52. Ibid.

53. Ibid.

54. Ibid.

55. Ibid.

56. Royal Commission on Labour Summaries of Evidence, Vol.II PP1894 XXXV (Cd.7421) p.30. Evidence of John Allen, President of the Master Tailors Association.

57. Leeds Mercury, 15 February 1879.

58. Leeds Archives Department, Barran Coll. Item 29.

59. Leeds Mercury, 18 October 1889.

60. Thomas (1955); Collet (1891).

61. Yorkshire Post, 23 February 1887.

62. Ibid.

63. Ibid.

64. Leeds Mercury, 22 September 1888.

65. Leeds Mercury, 10 June 1889.

66. Leeds Mercury, 14 January 1891.

67. Ibid.

68. Leeds Mercury, 22 September 1888.

69. Leeds Mercury, 25 August 1888.

70. Report of Chief Inspector of Factories and Workshops for the year ending 31 October 1891. PP1892 XX (Cd.6720) pp.16-17.

71. Leeds Mercury, 11 June 1889.

72. C. Collet (1891).

73. Ibid.

74. Ibid.

75. Report of Special Sanitary Commission on the Sweating System in

Leeds, Part I.   The Lancet, 9 June 1888, p.1147.

76. Report ... Part II.   The Lancet, 16 June 1888, p.1209.

77. Report ... Part I.   The Lancet, 9 June 1888, p.1147.

78. Leeds Mercury, 16 June 1888.

79  Leeds Mercury, 16 June 1888.

80. Yorkshire Press, 12 June 1888.

81. Ibid.

82. Yorkshire Daily Observer, 4 May 1905.

83. Leeds Daily News, 18 October 1889.

84. Ibid.

85. Barran Collection, Wage Book 1884-1893.

86. Yorkshire Post, 23 February 1887.

87. Yorkshire Post, 23 February 1887 and 12 June 1888.

88. House of Lords Select Committee on Sweating, 1st Report and Mins. of Evidence, PP1888 XX (Cd.361) Q307.

89. Report of Chief Inspector of Factories and Workshops PP1892 XX (Cd.6720) p.17.

90. House of Lords Select Committee on Sweating, 1st Report and Mins. of Evidence PP1888 XX (Cd.361) Q.3029.

91. House of Lords Select Committee on Sweating, 4th Report and Mins of Evidence, PP1889 XIV Pt.I (Cd.331), Q.30262-5.

92. Ibid, Q.28974-82.

# 3 Women's work and wages

I

As we have seen, the problem of sweated labour was to a large extent a problem of cheap female labour. When we come to consider the campaign for a minimum wage it will become obvious that those arguing for a minimum wage were primarily concerned about the low wages and unsatisfactory working conditions suffered by a significant number of women and the social consequences of this. In order to shed light on the reality which prompted their concern, the first part of this chapter attempts an analysis of the industrial female labour force at the turn of the century with particular reference to the question of sweated labour. In the second half of the chapter, the issue is raised as to why women earned such low wages.

The first question to be answered is how widespread was sweating amongst women workers. The House of Lords Select Committee on Sweating received evidence on twenty-seven trades where sweating was evident and posited that sweated labour exhibited one or all of the following three characteristics:

> "i. a rate of wages inadequate to the necessities of the
>     worker or disproportionate to the work done;
>
> ii. excessive hours of labour;
>
> iii. the insanitary state of the houses in which work is
>      carried on."[1]

The House of Lords Select Committee did not confine itself to the most exploited section of sweated labour - the homeworkers - but was also concerned with the incidence of sweating in workshops and factories and of course with the phenomenon of casual dock labour. Low wages was the complaint most frequently voiced by witnesses to the Select Committee and, in their conclusions, the Lords gave greatest weight to this particular characteristic of sweating. We have argued that (with the exception of the docks) women dominated the low paid sections of the trades considered by the House of Lords (Chapter 1, p.12 ). We will now address the question of how widespread low wages were amongst women workers generally.

1.  Wages

The most important source of information on wages at the beginning of
this century is the Board of Trade's Earnings and Hours Enquiry (the
Wages Census) carried out in 1906 and 1907.  The accuracy of the Wages
Census results is limited;  for example, not all employers in the trades
covered made returns to this enquiry and those that did would have
tended to be the larger, more responsible employers.  The average wage
rates returned therefore may well be over-estimates of the reality.
Adelaide Anderson, the Principal Lady Factory Inspector for many years,
commented, that although the Wages Census shows an average wage for women
over eighteen in non-textile industries of 12/11d per week, the Reports
of the women Factory Inspectors show that for a large number of women
their wages did not rise above 7/- to 8/- per week[2].  However, the
inquiry is the most comprehensive source of information on wages available, and will therefore be used to examine the level of women's wages
whilst keeping these reservations in mind.

Three industries in 1901 accounted for almost 75% of all women workers -
textiles (16%), the clothing trades (17%) and domestic service (including
laundry workers, charing etc. - 40%).  Domestic service was not covered
by the Enquiry and, although undoubtedly characterised by long hours and
low wages, was never considered as a "sweated trade".  Another industry
which accounted for a significant number (7.2%) of women workers was the
food and allied trades.  This category covered a number of different
processes - from jam-making to fish curing.  It will be seen from Table
3.1 that no other industry accounted for much more than 2% of women
workers, although in some of these industries women made up a significant
proportion of the workforce - for example, paper and printing trades
(32.6%);  skins, leathers, etc. (24%);  chemicals (20.8%);  brick and
cement (18.9%).

In Chapter 2 we discussed a subsistence wage for women, assessed by
Edward Cadbury and George Shann[3] to be 14/- to 16/- per week and accepted
this as a reasonable assessment of a "living wage" for women.  Tables
3.2 to 3.6 indicate in six of the seven trades mentioned above, the
percentage of women earning 15/- and under 16/- per week and those
earning 10/- and under 15/-.  Separate figures are also given for those
earning less than 10/-.  The figures relate to women over eighteen and
two sets of figures are given:  one for those women who worked a full
week during the week the returns were made, the second for all women,

Table 3.1    Returns of Women and Girls Occupied According to the
             1901 Census

| Occupation | Females returned as percentage of category | Female workers as percentage of total female workforce |
|---|---|---|
| General or local government | 13.4 | 0.6 |
| Professional occupations and their subordinate services | 48.8 | 7.1 |
| Domestic offices or services | | |
|    (1) Domestic services | 84.5 | 31.9 |
|    (2) Other | 85.7 | 8.6 |
| Commercial occupations | 10.2 | 1.4 |
| Conveyance of men, goods and messages | 1.5 | 0.5 |
| Agriculture | 5.4 | 1.4 |
| Metals, machines, etc. | 5.4 | 1.5 |
| Precious metals, etc. | 12.5 | 0.5 |
| Wood, furniture, etc. | 9.6 | 0.6 |
| Brick, cement, etc. | 18.9 | 0.8 |
| Chemicals | 20.8 | 0.6 |
| Skins, leathers, etc. | 24.0 | 0.6 |
| Paper, printing etc. | 32.6 | 2.2 |
| Textiles (including hosiery) | 57.4 | 15.9 |
| Dress | 62.8 | 16.8 |
| Food, tobacco, etc. | 27.9 | 7.2 |

Table 3.2    Women's Wages in the Textile Trades, 1906.

| Trade | Percentage of Women Earning | | | | | |
|---|---|---|---|---|---|---|
| | Under 10/- | | 10/- and under 15/- | | 15/- and under 16/- | |
| | A* | B* | A | B | A | B |
| Woollen and worsted | 10.7 | 16.3 | 55.6 | 53.4 | 7.5 | 6.8 |
| Linen | 41.7 | 45.2 | 49.1 | 46.2 | 3.4 | 3.2 |
| Jute | 6.2 | 10.8 | 66.4 | 63.8 | 10.4 | 5.6 |
| Silk | 38.9 | 46.3 | 47.8 | 42.6 | 4.4 | 3.6 |
| Hosiery | 14.5 | 17.4 | 44.4 | 43.9 | 8.4 | 8.0 |
| Lace | 18.1 | 20.8 | 49.3 | 48.3 | 8.4 | 8.0 |
| Cotton | 3.0 | 5.6 | 20.9 | 21.5 | 6.5 | 6.4 |
| Carpet | 15.3 | 23.8 | 49.8 | 46.2 | 8.2 | 7.3 |
| Hemp | 47.1 | 54.4 | 39.6 | 35.1 | 4.0 | 3.1 |
| Fustian and cord cutting | 47.1 | 61.2 | 41.7 | 30.6 | 2.3 | 1.7 |
| Bleaching, printing, dyeing and finishing of textiles | 27.0 | 31.2 | 51.6 | 48.3 | 5.0 | 5.1 |

* A = Those who worked full-time

  B = All women including those who worked more or less than full-time.

70

Table 3.3   Women's Wages in the Clothing Trades

| | Under 10/- | | 10/- and under 15/- | | 15/- and under 16/- | |
|---|---|---|---|---|---|---|
| | a | b | a | b | a | b |
| Dress, millinery etc. | | | | | | |
| (i) Workshop | 28.0 | 29.1 | 36.2 | 36.1 | 6.6 | 6.5 |
| (ii) Factory | 12.6 | 17.2 | 39.5 | 38.1 | 8.1 | 7.8 |
| Shirt, blouse etc. | 22.2 | 26.6 | 46.0 | 43.7 | 7.3 | 6.9 |
| Tailoring | | | | | | |
| (i) Bespoke | 15.4 | 22.5 | 42.4 | 40.8 | 9.3 | 8.4 |
| (ii) Ready-made | 24.0 | 29.1 | 46.6 | 43.5 | 7.0 | 6.4 |

Table 3.4   Women's Wages in Paper and Printing

| | Under 10/- | 10/- and under 15/- | 15/- and under 16/- |
|---|---|---|---|
| Percentage of those who worked full-time | 26.5 | 52.2 | 5.8 |
| Percentage of those who worked more or less than full-time | 30.5 | 49.0 | 5.4 |

Table 3.5   Women's Wages in the Food, Drink and Tobacco Trades

| | Under 10/- | 10/- and under 15/- | 15/- and under 16/- |
|---|---|---|---|
| Percentage of those who worked full-time | 37.8 | 44.2 | 5.1 |
| Percentage of those who worked more or less than full-time | 41.0 | 40.6 | 4.7 |

Table 3.6   Women's Wages in the Pottery, Brick, Glass and Chemical Trades

| | Under 10/- | 10/- and under 15/- | 15/- and under 16/- |
|---|---|---|---|
| Percentage of those who worked full-time | 31.0 | 49.7 | 7.0 |
| Percentage of those who worked more or less than full-time | 36.0 | 46.5 | 6.3 |

i.e. including those who worked either overtime, part-time or short-time, so as to give some allowance for variations in wages. These figures are not as accurate a picture as that arrived as in Chapter 2 when we discussed wages in the tailoring trade, because there is no allowance made for fluctuations in employment throughout the year; but if anything the average rates given will be an over-estimate of women's wages.

It will be seen from the Tables that a significant number of adult women in each trade earned at or below a subsistence wage. In the cotton industry, one of the highest paying industries for women workers, 27.1% of all women working in the industry earned 14/- or under per week and another 13.1% earned 15/- or 16/- per week. In the woollen and worsted industry, where it was possible for women weavers to earn high wages it was, however, also the case that 70% of adult women earned 14/- or under per week and another 12% earned 15/- or 16/- per week. In some of the textile industries, significant numbers of adult women earned under 10/- per week: 45.2% in the linen industry, 20.8% in lace; 23.8% in carpet; 54.4% in hemp and 61.2% in fustian and cord cutting.

The figures for the clothing trades (Table 3.3) also reveal the extent to which women workers earned below subsistence wages - 29.1% of all women workers in the ready-made tailoring trade earned below 10/- per week and a total of 72.6% under 15/-. In the paper and printing trade (Table 3.4), 30.5% of women earned under 10/- and a total of 79.5% under 15/- per week; in the food and allied trades (Table 3.5) 41% earned under 10/- and a total of 81.6% under 15/- per week, while in the pottery, brick, glass and chemical trades (Table 3.6), 36% received less than 10/- per week and a total of 82.5% under 15/-.

The payment of below-subsistence wages to adult women workers was, therefore, very widespread indeed.

The bare statistics on average wages, however, do not give the complete picture - many women were piece workers. The Particulars Clause of the Factory Acts was intended to rationalise the piece rate system and to enable workers to know what rates they were being paid. The legislation, however, was not effectively implemented, and Adelaide Anderson commented that "piece workers (suffered) an intolerable uncertainty as to what their rates really were"[4]. Violations of the Truck Acts with respect to fines and deductions were also particularly found in industries with

a high proportion of women workers.   The Factory Inspectors found that
out of a wage of 7/- or 8/-

> "came deductions for disciplinary fines, charges for cotton,
> needles, etc. use of power, standing room, cleaning of the
> factory, damage, or purchase of damaged articles, hospitals,
> supply of hot water for tea"[5].

One investigation of women's work found examples of a charge of 2d in
every shilling earned for power;   a charge of 2d a week for hot water
(charged whether hot water was used or not);   and that it was common for
women to be fined the price of an hour's work for arriving five minutes
late[6].   The Report of the Factory Inspectors in 1898 showed that
because of fines and deductions "a rate of 6/6 would emerge as 5/5, of
7/6 as 6/5, of 12/- as 9/9"[6a].   The Annual Report of 1897 reported on
young women workers soldering tins containing perishable goods, engaged
on a fixed weekly wage but rarely receiving that full wage as 1d was
deducted for every ten trays (twenty-four tins on each) short of the
total required daily, which was 190 trays containing 4,560 tins.   The
woman Factory Inspector examined the books of eleven workers during five
weeks and none reached the total required.   Again, in a biscuit factory
labellers were employed putting labels on four sides and the top of a
tin, paid at the rate of 1d for twelve tins;   for any one label damaged
1d was deducted, so that twelve tins would then have been labelled for
nothing[7].

Truck in its traditional form of payment in "unprofitable wares" rather
than "lawful money", survived amongst outworkers in rural areas, e.g.
in Cornwall and Somerset, over wide areas in Ireland and in Scotland[8].
For example, Cornish women knitted yachtsmen's guernseys and were paid
in drapery goods from the employer's shop "at whatever price and of
whatever quality the employer chooses to supply"; "a poor cripple woman
was found in great distress with a man's coat on her hands when she
sorely needed money for her rent"[9].

The Truck Act of 1887 gave the Factory Inspectorate the power to enforce
the 1831 Truck Act, and the 1896 Truck Act made fines and deductions
from wages illegal unless set out in a definite agreement or contract.
However, a series of unsuccessful prosecutions brought by the women
Factory Inspectors and two subsequent High Court decisions resulted in
a situation where any outworker, who was not under an explicit contract
to execute the work, was outside the protection of the Truck Acts[10].

## 2. Hours of Work

The second characteristic of sweated labour to which the House of Lords
Select Committee pointed was the incidence of excessive hours of work.
This is a more difficult phenomenon to assess.  A large number of women
workers at the beginning of this century were covered by the Factory
Acts' regulations on hours of work, although workers in non-factory
production were only brought under the Acts' protection at the end of
the nineteenth century, shop workers and laundry workers in the early
1900s and domestic servants remained without protection.  Employers
making returns to the Board of Trade, therefore, were unlikely to admit
to breaking the law.  There is evidence, however, that very long hours
were often worked by women and the case can also be made that long hours
were more common amongst women workers than amongst men, although it is
difficult to know how common.  Contemporary investigators drew attention
to excessively long hours worked by women and girls, J.A. Hobson (the
economist) being just one among many who argued that female workers
suffered unduly[11].

The legal maximum working week for women workers was 55½ hours in textile
factories and 60 hours in non-textile factories, with the conditions that
they could not be employed for longer than 4½ and 5 hours, respectively,
without a meal-break of at least half an hour.  Men's hours of work
were not regulated by legislation, with the exception of the miners
after 1908.  It might be assumed therefore that women workers at the
turn of the century generally worked fewer hours than men.  However,
there is evidence which questions this assumption - the inability of the
Factory Inspectorate to adequately implement the Act because of ineffective sanctions and shortage of staff;  the ways in which employers
legally and illegally exceeded the hours of work laid down for women
workers;  and the way in which trade union organisation amongst male
workers was effective in reducing men's hours of work.  The Factory
Inspectorate - charged with implementing the legislation on hours of
work - was understaffed and the penalties when employers were brought to
court do not seem to have been prohibitive.  For example, in 1905, the
Factory Inspector for East London reported

> "After receiving and investigating several complaints about
> the hours worked in a large laundry, I succeeded at last in
> collecting enough evidence to justify a prosecution.  The
> proceedings were treated as a joke;  the magistrate complimented
> my witnesses on their complexions, which he said had not
> suffered from overwork, and convicted in costs only".[12]

When fines were levied they apparently did not serve as an effective
deterrent.   This was a general complaint amongst Factory Inspectors,
who deplored the small fines which were meted out to convicted
employers[13].    In 1902, the average penalty in each case where conviction
resulted was 16/10d[14].    An example of an employer who was not even
deterred by larger fines is found in the case of the firm in the
theatrical costume industry, an industry which produced a large number
of complaints about excessive hours, illegal homework, Sunday employment
and so on.   The Factory Inspectorate reported in 1911 that one employer
had been prosecuted twelve times in ten years.   In 1911 he was found on
three occasions to be seriously contravening the law,

> "a typical instance of long hours being Friday 8 a.m. to
> 12 midnight, followed by 7 a.m. - 9 p.m. on Saturday with
> some Sunday employment following".

He was fined £20 but the Factory Inspector commented that this was not
sufficient deterrent[15].

The Factory Inspectors found cases of excessive hours being worked which
were in fact within the letter of the law.   Employers were found who
arranged the working day in such a way that long hours were worked which
were yet not illegal.   In non-textile factories and workshops, a common
practice was to work two five-hour spells with a break at mid-day of one
hour and on Saturday an unbroken spell of five hours.   This meant an
eleven-hour working day, including the meal-break, on weekdays, and
Anderson commented that

> "the heavy burden of labour on this basis was a perennial
> source of complaint from women and girls for which there was
> no remedy in the Factory Acts".[16]

Factory Inspectors received many complaints about excessive hours in
seasonal trades in particular, which, on investigation, were found to be
inside the law.   An example is the fancy stationery factory where

> "fifty girls over eighteen years of age had been working
> weekly from 8 a.m. to 10 p.m. on three days, from 8 a.m. to
> 8 p.m. on two days and from 8 a.m. to 4 p.m. on Saturdays
> and this carried on for six to eight weeks during the trade's
> busy season".[17]

Indeed, seasonal trades were allowed quite a lot of flexibility in that
very long hours were permissible during the busy seasons.   An example
is the exemption of the jam-making and fruit preserving trade from the
normal restrictions on hours during the fruit season which enabled
employers to create very long working days for even young girls of
thirteen and fourteen, who were found in one jam-making factory to be

employed from 6 in the morning until 11 o'clock at night[18]. Fish curing
is another trade which was exempt during the "busy" season which enabled
the legal employment of women from "8 in the morning until 10.30 or 11
at night for several nights in the week and for many weeks on end"[19].
Women engaged in the "gutting, salting and packing of fish immediately on
arrival in the fishing boats" at Lowestoft and at Grimsby took strike
action in 1910 and 1911 against the long hours of work[20].

The Factory Inspectorate also found cases where women employees were
sent home with work to be done.   For example, in 1908, the Factory
Inspectors reported of a woman employed in the silk industry who, having
worked from 6.30 am to 5.45 pm in the mill, brought home ties to tassel
which occupied her from 8 to 10 pm[21].   Anderson commented on the widespread practice of sending work home when the women finished work in the
factory.   "Portable articles of manufacture could easily be, and often
were, sent home with the worker at the close of the legal day".   She
felt that the practice "was really rooted in starvation wages"[22].   The
Factory Inspector in Birmingham found in 1913

> "Workers in the warehouses of a pen factory had been regularly
> taking home cards to thread with elastic for the reception of
> pens, compasses, india rubber, etc.   The workers, who mostly
> lived some way from the factory, arrive at their homes about
> 7.15 pm and in nearly every case worked steadily for three
> nights in the week for three hours or more.   Many of the girls
> with large quantities of cards to do received help from their
> relations;   even where this was given, their leisure was en-
> croached on to the extent of 1½ to 2 hours, and where it was
> lacking entirely, work sometimes went on till midnight, or
> spread to four or five evenings in the week."[23]

Edward Cadbury and George Shann, in their study of sweating, also report
of women who worked in a factory during the day and carded buttons or
hooks and eyes before and after going to the factory - "One such woman's
working day was from 3 or 4 in the morning to 11 or 12 at night"[24].

The practice of sending work home with employees after the official end
of the working day was particularly common in the clothing trade, a trade
which was a major source of employment for women.   The practice was
even carried on in the factories making uniforms for the army, navy and
police force, although such firms were thereby breaking their contract
with the government.   One worker in such a factory wrote in 1901,

> "I have myself, repeatedly, for weeks at a time, taken four
> hours' work home with me every night, besides Saturday after-
> noons, and have done it, and this after a close, hard day's
> work in the factory ...   The foreman of the department in which

I worked even went through the farce of standing at the door sometimes, with the professed object of preventing work being taken out and we have passed him with our arms full of it"[25].

A well-researched investigation in 1903 reported that, although legislation had been "to a great extent" effective in abolishing night work for women in the printing trade, cases were found where printers' folding was "being done, legally, by women in separate premises at night"[26].

The Factory Inspectorate found that employers used even more dubious ways of evading the Factory Acts. In 1900, a woman Factory Inspector, Miss Vines, reported that the Factory Act was being evaded by West London laundries by the employment of workers on two different types of work, e.g.

> "... women are sometimes employed as washers at the beginning of the week and as ironers at the end. The 60 hours limit may thus easily be exceeded without detection"[27].

In the food trade factories, women and girls were often employed on several different processes within the same factory. Thus women were found employed on making jam at the end of the day - a working day extended supposedly because of the seasonality of the fruit - when earlier in the day they had been employed on making pickles or mustard, etc.[28] It was common for jam-making factories to also be engaged in the confectionery, pickle-making, ginger preserving, potted meat and mince meat-making and candied peel-making trades. The busy seasons of these trades did not coincide and this confusing situation enabled employers to employ women and girls for long hours, sometimes "until a late hour at night"[29], either in such a way that they were within the law or so that it would be very difficult to detect whether the regulations were being flouted.

In the factory food trade (an expanding area of women's employment) the way in which workers and factory could be directed to different food processes at different times of the year meant that women and girls did not just suffer long hours of work during, say, the fruit season. Once the fruit season had finished, the fish curing season began and as the Factory Inspectors' Reports commented, "The tired and worn facts of the women show only too plainly how much they suffer" from the long hours engaged in fish curing, when they had been employed "in the fruit trade under similar conditions during the months of June, July, August and September"[30].

All the evidence gathered by the 1888 House of Lords Select Committee
on Sweating and the House of Commons Select Committee on Homework
twenty years later points to homeworkers working excessive hours.  The
majority of homeworkers were women and although there were some whose
earnings were not essential to their survival, most of those homeworkers
whose conditions were reported on appear to have been in a situation
where their wages were essential for themselves and their dependents
and where pitifully low wage rates necessitated long hours of work.
The Factory Inspectors Report of 1904 reported that it seemed to be the
nature of homework that homeworkers

> "suffered either from grinding overwork or from absolute lack
> of work.   There was no normal period of employment.   Either
> abnormally long hours were worked, or else no work was to be
> obtained."[30a]

Employers recognised the advantages of the "flexibility" of homeworking -
one example being a Stockport clothier who explicitly praised the advantages of homeworking because it meant that the women worked long hours
when necessary and he was free from all responsibility[31].

There is plenty of evidence therefore that women **workers** tended to work
very long hours.   The Factory Inspectorate found that particularly
in the unorganised trades, the legal maximum hours were "frequently
and widely exceeded"[32].   Even in the textile industry where trade union
organisation was stronger than any other women's trade, the practice of
"time-cribbing" was common.   This was the practice whereby legal
maximum hours were exceeded in small instalments - work was carried over
into the meal breaks and encroachments were made at the beginning and end
of the working day.   Even where women and girls in the textile trades
were nominally members of a trade union they were often inactive members
and were unlikely to be able to defend their working day.   On the other
hand, although male workers were not covered by legislation on hours of
work, (until the 1908 Act which brought in the eight-hour day for miners)
trade unions were fairly successful in bringing about a shorter working
week for men in the organised industries.

An inquiry carried out in 1903 found that "in men's industries influenced
by trade unions, the hours are very rarely so many as 60"[33].   The 1918
Reconstruction Committee, in looking at the period before the war,
confirmed that male workers in general worked fewer hours than the legal
maximum laid down for women.   A.M. Anderson felt that trade union

organisation had done more to bring down the hours that men worked than protective legislation had to bring down the hours that women worked.

> "In spite of protective laws [she found] a working day and week in which the standard hours worked by women frequently exceeded those for which men in certain great trades had by means of trade unions secured recognition from employers"[35].

The 1903 investigation into women's employment also supported the idea that trade unionisation had done more to bring down hours than had protective legislation[36], and the 1918 reconstruction Committee reported of industry before the war:

> "In very few cases are the recognised hours for men as long as those permitted by the Factory and Workshop Acts to be worked by girls of 14 in non-textile trades (i.e. 60 hours). In the great majority of districts they are shorter than those permitted for girls in the textile trades (i.e. $55\frac{1}{2}$)"[37]

Furthermore, the formal regulation by employers and employees of a standard working week for men was usually accompanied by the agreement of a minimum standard wage or piece rate and an agreement on overtime rates. This was not the case with women. The Reconstruction Committee found in the few instances where women were paid extra for extra hours worked, "it has always been regarded as a gratuity and not as a payment to which the woman has a legal claim"[38].

It is of course the case that men in unorganised industries (and the majority of men were not in trade unions) suffered long hours and poor working conditions. It is significant, however, that politicians and social reformers were rarely concerned with the working conditions of men; they concentrated instead on the working conditions of women. The relevance of the evidence presented above is twofold - firstly, that excessive hours of work occurred in industries which were thought to be "modern" and not just in the supposedly backward workshop and homework trades; and secondly, that where men workers were organised (and a higher proportion of the male workforce was involved than the female workforce) it appears that they were more successful in shortening their working week than protective legislation was on behalf of women.

## Conditions of Work

The third characteristic to which the House of Lords Select Committee on Sweating referred was that of "insanitary conditions in the houses in which the work is done". In this case, they were referring mainly

to homeworkers.  As all the investigations showed, women made up the
majority of homeworkers and therefore this characteristic of insanitary
conditions was more likely to affect them than male workers.  However,
unsatisfactory environmental conditions were also found in factory and
workshop production.  The poor working conditions - lack of ventilation,
overcrowding and inadequate sanitation - and the high level of accidents
found in many factories and workshops had as great an impact on the
health and lives of factory and workshop workers as did insanitary
conditions on the lives of homeworkers.  We will therefore examine the
extent to which women workers (apart from homeworkers) especially
suffered from poor working conditions.

Men as well as  women suffered fom working conditions detrimental to
health but women in particular had little control over their working
conditions;  they were primarily employed when the production process
was split up into more detailed tasks (as for instance in the tailoring
trade) or when machinery was introduced and workers were required as
machine minders of one kind or another (as in the textile industry).
They were therefore devoid of the knowledge and training which enabled
craft and skilled workers to exert influence over the pace and
conditions of production.   This lack of influence by women over their
working conditions was commented on by the Ministry of Reconstruction
in their report on women's employment published in 1919 which looked
back on women's working conditions before the war and remarked on how
the introduction of machinery had brought about "lower grade work and
diminished self-respect for women workers"[38a].

Both men and women workers suffered from sometimes appalling working
conditions as a result of "the tyranny of machinery" so ably described
by a number of historians[39] but whereas men attempted through their trade
unions to improve their working conditions, women had to rely on the
actions of the Factory Inspectorate whose reports reveal their inability
to make much of an impact.   The Factory Inspectorate also commented on
the failure of the trade unions to look after the interests of women
workers[40].

The working conditions in the textile industry in the earlier part of
the nineteenth century are well documented, but unhealthy and unhygienic
working conditions were still found in textile factories and mills at
the beginning of the twentieth century.   High temperatures were a
constant complaint for example.   In 1910, a woman Factory Inspector

found, when investigating thirty cotton mills in Preston, Darwen, Manchester and Hyde, that during December when there was an outside temperature of 40°F, nine mule-spinning rooms had temperatures of 90 - 100°F and one over 100°F[41]. On the other hand, excessively cold temperatures were found in the sorting rooms of some mills.

Lack of ventilation, combined with the problem of fibre dust created severe health problems. The 1892 Factory Inspector's Report had commented that a carder's average length of life in the flax mills was 16.8 years of work. "If a girl gets a card at 18, her life is often terminated at 30"[42]. The 1906 Report drew attention to the problem of excessive dust in silk waste carding and spinning. The medical adviser found, in samples given to him by the Factory Inspector, debris of silk-worms, containing, "an enormous number of hook-like structures, probably portions of the thoracic and abdominal segments of the pupa case". Anderson comments that

> "this gave support to the apparently strange opinion of the workers expressed to Miss Squire [the Factory Inspector] that they were coughing up not silk but silkworms"[43].

In 1902, attention was drawn to the health hazards of mercerised cotton yarn which gave rise to "shivering and sickness with cough and oppression in the chest"[44].

There are many more examples to be found in the Factory Inspector's Reports of the bronchial problems caused by dust and inadequate ventilation in the textile industry; they also drew attention to the accidents caused by improperly guarded and dangerous machinery. The 1906 Annual Report commented on the hosiery industry:

> "How closely the machines are packed in some factories is exemplified by the case of a girl of 15 sitting down by her machine and in drawing her handkerchief from her pocket her thumb was caught and lacerated by an adjacent machine. 'The machines are too close together to allow of sitting down in this way with safety', remarks the Certifying Surgeon. In another case a girl of 14, in taking out the needle of her machine, threw her hand back, and it was caught by the revolving guide of another machine causing rather severe injury. In another factory, a little girl of 13, a mule piecer, was crushed between the mule and a fixed portion of the machine".[45]

B.L. Hutchins, in her study of women industrial workers published in 1915, also reported on the health problems resulting from working conditions in the textile industry.∗

> "Where steaming is used, colds and rheumatism are very prevalent. It is noticed by the weavers that the sickness rate is lower in times of bad trade and indeed slack seasons

81

are regarded as times for much-needed recuperation".[46]
She also commented on the detrimental effect of the speeding up of
machinery on workers' health - "Weavers are now said to be doing as much
work in a day as in a day and a half 12 or 13 years ago"[47] - and
throughout all factory industries she found that while the hours of
work had been very little reduced since 1874, the strain of work had
been considerably increased[48].


The women Factory Inspectors found unsatisfactory working conditions in
almost all the industries in which women were employed.   Miss Paterson,
the Factory Inspector for West London, commented on the dressmaking
industry

> "... nowhere have I seen so much overcrowding, so many dirty
> ceilings and walls - and such disregard for the comfort of
> workers as is shown by the absence of fires or stoves.  I may
> add that nowhere have I seen workers so much and so obviously
> afraid of their employers"[49].

Damaged eyesight was a common hazard of workers in the dressmaking trade
and lack of ventilation and dust was also a problem in the clothing trade
generally, as for example, in the Manchester "making-up" warehouses
where young women were employed who suffered from chest and throat complaints as a result of the excessive dust given off by the material with
which they worked[50].


The 1907 Factory Inspector's Report described some of the accidents caused
by machinery in the clothing trade which had been reported to them.

> "One girl ... in picking up a piece of paper, squeezed her
> head through the guard rods of the low shafting (of a sewing
> machine) and had the right side of her scalp torn off and her
> hand lacerated.   Another girl of 13 in wringing rags for
> pressing had her hand drawn in between the rollers and severely
> injured.   In another case, a girl was employed in dusting her
> collar polishing machine.   The board had been removed with the
> guard attached and the child had the bone of her elbow-joint
> severely fractured".[51]

The inadequate guards and safety mechanisms on sewing machines resulted
in many accidents involving lacerated fingers.


Complaints to the Factory Inspectorate of poor ventilation, badly drained
and unhygienic workplaces appear to have been increasing at the turn of
the century as were complaints about inadequate sanitation and extreme
temperatures[52].   The reports of the Sanitary Inspectors, who were
responsible for the implementation of certain sections of the Factory and
Public Health Acts relating to conditions in factories and workshops,
also contain evidence of poor working conditions.   Many local

82

authorities appointed Sanitary Inspectors especially to deal with the inspection of factories, workshops and outworkers' premises, following increasing pressure put on them by the Local Government Board and the Home Office to fulfil their obligations under the 1901 Factory and Workshop Act. Their reports reveal not only the large numbers of defects relating to ventilation, over-crowding and sanitary conditions, but also the difficulty of implementing the legislation when the sanctions available to both the Factory and Sanitary Inspectorates were so inadequate. One example of a large employer getting away with failing to fulfil his obligations on working conditions was that of Peter Robinsons Ltd. who were successfully prosecuted by the Westminster Sanitary Inspectorate for failing to ensure a reasonable temperature in their Oxford Street workrooms which employed 350 people (mostly women) making ladies clothing, but who won the appeal. Even if the appeal had been lost, the fine of 20s was hardly prohibitive[53].

Complaints about poor working conditions and those about accidents in the workplace, were made of all industries in which women were employed. The health hazards of dust were found in all branches of the textile and clothing industries, even in the lace-making industry[54]. In other industries also, women's health was found to suffer as a result of poor working conditions - in the Sheffield electro-plate industry, phthisis and anaemia were common[55]; thick clouds of dust were found in asbestos carding rooms causing "a considerable amount of phthisical, bronchial and gastric trouble"[56]; the health hazards of working with lead were well documented[57]; in the new steam laundries, there was a common incidence of leg ulcers, phthisis, rheumatism and bronchitis as a result of constant exposure to steam, standing on wet floors, great heat and long hours of exhausting work[58].

The House of Lords Select Committee, when referring to working conditions, had in mind the situation of homeworkers. They expressed their concern that insanitary conditions were not only a health hazard to the buyer of the goods but also very damaging to the health of the worker, and in particular, to women workers. However, as discussed above, the evidence suggests that working conditions were also to be found in factories and workshops which were detrimental to the health of women workers.

From the evidence cited above we must conclude that the most important characteristic of sweating, namely below-subsistence wages, was a very common experience amongst women workers and that long hours and unhealthy working conditions were also common. This poses the wider question of why women earned such low wages. Why was the average wage for women in 1906 only 42% of the average wage for men?[59]

Before we look at explanations offered for this, it will be useful to focus on some general characteristics of women's employment which are pertinent to any attempt to answer this question. There are five points to be made: the decline of women's participation in productive activity and their confinement to certain industries; the existence of a sexual division of labour in industry and the wage differentials associated with this; the relationship between a dilution of labour skills and the employment of women and girls; the higher proportion of younger women in the female labour force compared with the proportion of younger men in the male workforce, and lastly, the extent to which women were less likely to be the sole breadwinner for a family.

1. It would appear that women's participation in production declined with industrialisation compared to pre-industrial production and their opportunities were limited to particular industries. This is the hypothesis which Richards puts forward, drawing from the earlier work of Pinchbeck and Collet[60]. Briefly, the argument is as follows: what evidence there is for the pre-industrial period suggests that women's participation in production (particularly in agriculture) approached the maximum. This would seem reasonable given the high dependency/low productivity rate characteristic of pre-industrial societies and the fact that the household was the unit of production so there was little physical separation between childcare and productive work. Evidence suggests that during early industrial transition, the participation of women in new production processes was high, but this was because of the continuing domestic base of production: as Hobsbawn says "The obvious way of industrial expansion in the eighteenth century was not to construct factories but to extend the so-called domestic system"[61]. Many of these "putting-out" processes were characterised by very high female participation rates - as indeed was agricultural labour, which underwent a similar expansion up until the middle decades of the nineteenth century.

However, once industrialisation gathered pace, there was a contraction
and a narrowing of work opportunities for women, particularly amongst
married women[62]. Even within the textile industry, if the gains are
balanced against the losses of work for women in all branches of the
industry, the net consequence was, as far as it is possible to calculate,
to reduce female participation. The cotton industry was the first industry
to pull in women and children as unskilled factory labour and is often
cited as an example of an increase in employment opportunities which the
industrial revolution is supposed to have offered women. On closer
examination of these workers, however, it appears that more than half the
numbers of both sexes were under fourteen and no more than a sixth of the
female workers were married women. In the woollen mills also, the
Factory Commissioners' Reports showed that more than 50% of women left
the mills at the age of twenty or twenty-one and that of the women over
twenty-one employed, very few were married. The majority of the cheap
labour drawn into the mills was certainly female, but this workforce was
mostly made up of children and young unmarried girls. Furthermore, the
proportion of male workers in the textile industry was in fact higher
amongst factory operatives than it had been in the days of hand labour
when women spinners outnumbered all other types of textile worker[63].

In most other developing areas of the economy in the early nineteenth
century, the labour force was male dominated. As Pinchbeck says:

> "... the occupations open to men, always more numerous than
> those available for women, were increasing in number and extent
> throughout the whole period of the industrial revolution, as
> a result of developments in industry and transport".[64]

Women were not employed in any significant numbers in the main sectors of
the economy such as engineering, the building trades, ship-building, the
docks, and other transport areas, public utilities and, after 1842, they
were excluded from the mines[65].

Employment opportunities for married women contracted sharply during the
course of the nineteenth century. The 1851 Census returned 25% of
married women and widows as occupied. This figures includes those
returned as assisting their husband's labour, e.g. the wives of boot
and shoe makers, but is probably an underestimate of those actually
occupied. By 1901, including those returned as working at home, as few
as 13% of married women and widows were returned as occupied (this
figure again includes those returned as assisting their husbands)[66].

As new industries and industrial processes developed, it was male workers who were employed in the better paid occupations and who dominated most industries. The largest number of women workers (37% of the female workforce in 1881) were employed as indoor domestic servants, an area of work left almost entirely to women by the end of the nineteenth century. Another 36% of women were concentrated into the textile and clothing industries where in 1901 they made up 16% and 17% of the total workforce in these industries. Agriculture had been a major source of employment for women in the early and mid-nineteenth century but by 1881 it accounted for only 2% of women workers. Not only did the nineteenth century see a reduction in women's participation in productive activity but their work opportunities were limited to a smaller range of industries and occupations than were the work opportunities of male workers.

2.  Women and girls, almost universally, did different jobs from men and boys and the jobs which they did paid lower wages than the jobs done by men and boys. To illustrate this sexual division of labour, the following four tables (Tables 3.7 - 3.10) list the jobs done by men and women in the cotton industry, the brass and allied metal trades, the laundry trade and in shirts, blouses and underclothing manufacture.

It will be seen from these tables that in each of the trades men and boys were generally engaged on different work from women and girls and that the men's occupations attracted higher wages than those of women. Boys also being paid more than girls.

In the cotton industry equal piece rates were paid to men and women but it will be seen from Table 3.7 that even where men were employed on the same number of looms as women they still earned more. The average woman's wage in the cotton industry was 62.2% of the average man's. The table demonstrates that men were employed in the highest paying categories of work in the cotton industry from which women were excluded. Table 3.8 illustrates how in the brass and allied metal trades, women and girls were employed as lacquerers, burnishers and polishers, whereas men were engaged on the higher paid types of work. The average woman's wage in the trade was 37.6% of the average man's and it is also worth noting that apprenticeships were confined to boys. In the laundry trade (Table 3. 9) the development of steam laundries was accompanied by the employment of men in the higher waged jobs of foremen, washers, vanmen and enginemen. Women's wages were on average only 47.4% of men's. It will be noted that in this trade, men and women were both employed as foremen/women and as washers. However, forewomen only received on average, 63% of

86

Table 3.7   Net Earnings of Workpeople Employed in the Cotton Industry in the Last Pay-week of September 1906.[1]

|  | Average Earnings | |
|  | Time | Piece |
|  | s. d. | s. d. |
| MEN (of and above twenty years of age) | | |
| Foremen and Assistant Foremen | | |
| - Preparing Dept. | 38.5 | 43.2 |
| Spinning Dept. | 40.4 | 42.5 |
| Weaving Dept. | 38.6 | 43.10 |
| Mixers            time only | 21.5 | |
| Scutchers         "      " | 25.8 | |
| Grinders or card room jobbers | 29.3 | |
| Spinners (self acting mules) | | |
| Counts below 40s     piece only | | 38.5 |
| Counts 40s - 80s     "     " | | 42.10 |
| "      above 80s | | 45.11 |
| Big piecers | 18.4 | 20.8 |
| Twiners | | 36.10 |
| Ball warpers | 31.7 | 39.3 |
| Sizers, tapers or slashers | 42.1 | 44.7 |
| Warp dressers | | 35.0 |
| Twisters-in | 25.9 | 24.8 |
| Drawers-in | 28.4 | 30.1 |
| Weavers          piece only | | |
| 2 looms | | 21.8 |
| 3 looms | | 19.5 |
| 4 looms | | 24.10 |
| 6 looms | | 32.10 |
| Fustian weavers | | |
| 4 looms          piece only | | 27.1 |
| Warehousemen and packers | 24.1 | 28.6 |
| Mechanics        time only | 35.0 | |
| Enginemen and stokers    time only | 31.0 | |
| General labourers | 20.3 | |
| Other men | 23.3 | 29.2 |
| ALL MEN | 29.4 | |

Contd./...

Table 3.7 (continued)

| | Average Earnings | |
|---|---|---|
| | Time | Piece |
| | s.d. | s.d. |
| **MEN UNDER TWENTY** | | |
|     Full-timers | | |
|       Big piecers | 16.6 | 17.5 |
|       Little piecers | 11.11 | 11.7 |
|     Weavers    piece only | | |
|       2 looms | | 12.4 |
|       3 looms | | 17.10 |
|       4 looms | | 23.11 |
|     Other | 9.5 | 13.2 |
|     Half-timers | 3.6 | 4.1 |
|     ALL | 11.6 | |
| - - - - | | |
| **WOMEN (of and above eighteen)** | | |
|     Drawing frame tenters | 16.2 | 20.2 |
|     Scubbing frame tenters | 15.1 | 19.5 |
|     Intermediate frame tenters | 14.6 | 18.11 |
|     Roving frame tenters | 16.10 | 18.10 |
|     Frame tenters (unclassified) | | 21.3 |
|     Ring spinners | 14.7 | 16.6 |
|     Reelers | 12.3 | 12.10 |
|     Winders | 13.1 | 14.7 |
|     Doublers | 12.11 | 13.1 |
|     Beam warpers | 17.2 | 20.6 |
|     Weavers    piece only | | |
|       2 looms | | 13.7 |
|       3 looms | | 17.6 |
|       4 looms | | 23.4 |
|       6 looms | | 30.7 |
|     Fustian weavers | | |
|       2 looms | | 12.11 |
|       3 looms | | 18.2 |
|       4 looms | | 20.8 |
|     Other female | 13.1 | 15.2 |
|     ALL FEMALE | 18.3 | |

Contd./...

Table 3.7 (continued)

|  | Average Earnings | |
|---|---|---|
|  | Time | Piece |
|  | s.d. | s.d. |
| GIRLS (under eighteen) | | |
|     Full-timers | | |
|       Reelers | | 9.6 |
|       Weavers   2 looms | | 11.7 |
|               3 looms | | 17.1 |
|               4 looms | | 22.2 |
|       Fustian weavers  2 looms | | 12.1 |
|                    3 looms | | 17.9 |
|       Other | 8.5 | 9.7 |
|     Half-timers | 3.0 | 2.6 |
| ALL GIRLS | 10.0 | |

1.    REHE (1909) Vol.I PP1909 (Cd.4545)

Table 3.8    Manufacture of Brass and Allied Metal Wares - Net Earnings of Workpeople in the Undermentioned Occupations in the Last Pay-week of September 1906.[1]

| Occupation | Average Earnings | |
|---|---|---|
| | Time | Piece |
| | s.d. | s.d. |
| MEN | | |
|     Foremen | 44.5 | |
|     Casters | 30.9 | 40.11 |
|     Dressers and finishers | 27.7 | 32.7 |
|     Fitters and toolmakers | 34.2 | |
|     Turners | 28.1 | 28.5 |
|     Warehousemen and packers | 28.1 | |
|     Enginemen and stokers | 31.8 | |
|     General labourers | 21.7 | |
|     Other men | 27.8 | 30.7 |
|     ALL MEN | 30.10 | |
| | | |
| APPRENTICES (all ages) and lads and boys (under twenty) | | |
|     Full-timers | | |
|       All occupations | 10.1 | 10.9 |
|     ALL | 10.2 | |
| | | |
| WOMEN (of and above twenty) | | |
|     Laquerers | 11.11 | 11.5 |
|     Burnishers and polishers | 12.4 | 14.6 |
|     Other | 10.11 | 11.8 |
|     ALL | 11.7 | |
| GIRLS (under eighteen) | | |
|     Full-timers | | |
|       Laquerers | 6.7 | |
|       Burnishers and polishers | 7.0 | |
|       Other | 6.11 | 6.9 |
|     ALL | 6.10 | |

1.    REHE (1906) Vol.6   PP1911 LXXXVIII (Cd.5814).

Table 3.9    Laundries (Factory) - Net Earnings of Workpeople Employed
            on the Employer's Premises in the under-mentioned
            Occupations in the last pay week of September 1906.[1]

| Occupation | Average Earnings | |
|---|---|---|
| | Time | Piece |
| | s.d. | s.d. |
| WOMEN (of and about eighteen) | | |
| Forewomen | 21.5 | |
| Washers | 11.3 | |
| Calenderers | 9.11 | |
| Hand ironers   -   suit | 13.4 | 14.1 |
| finery | 13.0 | 13.2 |
| Body linen | 11.0 | 11.3 |
| Other | 11.2 | 12.1 |
| Machine ironers | 11.11 | 13.4 |
| Receivers, markers, sorters and packers | 12.11 | |
| Other | 10.11 | 13.5 |
| ALL | 12.4 | |
| | | |
| GIRLS (under eighteen) | | |
| Full-timers | | |
| Washers | 6.8 | |
| Calenderers | 5.11 | |
| Hand ironers | 6.5 | 7.8 |
| Machine ironers | 6.11 | 8.11 |
| Receivers, markers, sorters, and packers | 6.7 | |
| Other girls | 6.1 | 7.10 |
| ALL GIRLS | 65 | |
| | | |
| MEN (of and above twenty) | | |
| Foremen | 33.10 | |
| Washers | 25.0 | |
| Vanmen | 24.2 | 27.5 |
| Enginemen and stokers | 28.11 | |
| Other | 25.8 | 32.1 |
| ALL | 26.0 | |
| | | |
| LADS AND BOYS (under twenty) | | |
| Full-timers | | |
| Van boys | 7.1 | |
| Other | 10.11 | |
| ALL | 8.7 | |

1.    REHE (1906) Vol.8, PP1912-13, LVIII (Cd.6556).

Table 3.10    Shirts, Blouses and Underclothing - Net Earnings of
              Workpeople employed on the Employer's Premises in the
              Under-mentioned Occupations in the Last pay-week of
              September 1906.[1]

| Occupation | Average Earnings | |
| | Time | Piece |
| | s.d. | s.d. |
| --- | --- | --- |
| MEN (of and above twenty years of age) | | |
|     Foremen | 40.6 | |
|     Cutters | 30.4 | 35.9 |
|     Warehousemen and packers | 25.5 | |
|     Other | 25.10 | 24.0 |
|     ALL MEN | 29.8 | |
| | | |
| LADS AND BOYS (under twenty) | | |
|     Full-timers | 8.11 | |
|     All occupations | | 8.8 |
|     Half-timers | 2.0 | 3.0 |
|     ALL LADS AND BOYS | 8.9 | |
| | | |
| WOMEN (of and above eighteen years of age) | | |
|     Forewomen | 21.7 | |
|     Cutters | 14.8 | 13.8 |
|     Machine sewers - Hand or foot | 13.2 | 14.0 |
|                 Power | 12.4 | 12.6 |
|     Hand sewers | 11.9 | 11.5 |
|     Starchers and ironers | 11.4 | 12.2 |
|     Boxers and wrappers-up | 11.5 | 11.6 |
|     Other | 12.6 | 12.2 |
|     ALL FEMALE | 12.10 | |
| | | |
| GIRLS (under eighteen) | | |
|     Full-timers | | |
|         Machine sewers - power | 5.7 | 7.10 |
|         Hand sewers | 5.3 | 6.2 |
|         Boxers and wrappers-up | 5.8 | 6.7 |
|         Other | 5.7 | 7.1 |
|     Half-timers | 2.2 | |
|     All occupations | | 2.6 |
|     ALL GIRLS | 6.7 | |

1.   REHE (1906)   Vol.2   PP1909 LXXX (Cd.4844).

of a foreman's wages, and women washers, 42% of a man washer's wages.
Similarly, in the shirt, blouse and underclothing trade, (Table 3.10)
although men and women were employed as foremen/women and machinists,
women's wages were only 53% of the foremen's and 49% of the male cutter's
wages.    Generally, however, in the shirt, blouses and underclothing
trades - as in the tailoring trade - women were employed in the lower
paid jobs of machining and ironing, and this accounts for their average
wage being only 43.3% of men's in this trade.

The division of labour demonstrated by these tables was common throughout
British industry, although the lines of demarcation between "men's work"
and "women's work" could vary within an industry according to specific
local conditions.    The existence of competition for male labour between
different industries was often an important factor in determining what
was locally considered "women's work".    For example, in Accrington,
where the development of engineering in the late nineteenth and early
twentieth centuries offered well-paid employment for men, women pre-
dominated amongst the weavers in the local textile industry and weaving
was considered "women's work".    In Nelson, on the other hand, where
there was no major competitor for male labour, men were engaged on the
better paid sections of weaving[67].    The comparison of the tailoring
trade in London and Leeds discussed in Chapter 2 also indicates that
local conditions of the labour market could affect the sexual division
of labour and the level of women's wages;    alternative local employment
opportunities for both men and women could affect the division of labour
and wage differentials within a particular industry.

3.    The jobs which women and girls were engaged on were almost always those
created by the breaking up of the production process into more detailed
tasks and/or those created by the mechanisation of the production process.
As such they had little or no control over the work tasks which they did,
in the way that craft workers and industrial workers categorised as
"skilled" had at least some control over their pace and conditions of
work.    In the textile industry, the women workers with the most status
and the highest paid, the weavers, were by the end of the century, engaged
on doing little more than "machine minding" the mechanised looms, unlike
the male foremen, assistant foremen mechanics and even the male weavers,
who all exerted some autonomy in that they had at least some influence
over the pace of work, albeit a minimum of influence, through their role
of organising the work of other workers and of mending and setting the
pace of the machines.

In the clothing industry, women machined the garments cut out by men
and were brought in to do more and more of the machining as the making
up process was split into more detailed tasks.   Even the women who made
up garments throughout - e.g. the waistcoat makers and the women
machinists in the West End dressmaking trade - had a subordinate status,
in terms of the division of work, to male foremen, cutters and machinists.
Even the journeymen tailors who complained of being downgraded to mere
"hands" as a result of the dilution of labour earlier in the nineteenth
century, had authority over the women who stitched the button-holes and
carried out other parts of the finishing process.

Another example of the relationship between the employment of female
labour and the dilution of labour skills was to be found in the metal
and engineering trades which were developing rapidly around Birmingham
in the 1890s and 1900s[68].   Their expansion was based on the introduction
of

> "every variety of automatic or semi-automatic machinery-
> capstan, press, milling, drilling, grinding, polishing,
> screwing, gear-cutting"[69]

and it was the women who were brought into the workforce to perform a

> "whole series of operations of a light 'repetition' character
> and [who passed]  freely from one trade to another as 'lathe'
> or 'press' hands".[70]

The general absence of women in positions of authority in factories was
commented upon by observers at the turn of the century[71] as was the sometimes humiliating results of women's subordinate position.   For example,
in 1911, a woman Factory Inspector reported of a factory where

> "over 500 women are employed, each woman had to hand in her
> tally to a male timekeeper as she entered the lavatories,
> receiving it back as she came out.   The time she had taken was
> recorded and forwarded to the manager at the end of the month
> if she had exceeded four minutes".[72]

Another example was conveyed to Margaret MacDonald from a worker in the
Leicester shoe trade who, on reporting of the increased mechanisation and
employment of women machinists in the trade, revealed that the machinists
were locked into the factory during the working day laid down by the
employer[73].

The evidence demonstrates, therefore, that women were generally employed
as "semi-skilled" or "unskilled" labour and had a subordinate status in
the workplace.   This subordinate status and lack of influence over their
working conditions is an important factor in any consideration of the
determinants of women's low wages.

94

4. There was a larger proportion of younger women amongst the female work-force than young men amongst the male workforce; according to the 1901 Census returns, there was almost double the proportion of young women (31%) compared to young men (18%). This characteristic of the female labour force acted as a downward pull on the average woman's wage as there was to be found in most trades a division of labour according to age as well as the sexual division of labour discussed above. An increasing proportion of younger women employed in an industry indicated employers' success in introducing new production processes with the accompanying cheapest of cheap labour. The larger proportion of young unmarried women also illustrates the decreasing employment of older married women discussed above.

5. Women workers were less likely to be the sole breadwinner in a household than a male worker, although there was a significant number of women who were the sole household breadwinner (and these women caused particular concern to social reformers). It has been calculated that in 1911 only 9% of households were dependent solely on a female breadwinner whereas 41% were soley dependent on a man's wage[74]. The subsistence needs of the average woman worker were therefore likely to be lower than those of the average male worker who was more likely to be supporting dependents. This point is also related to the high proportion of younger women in the female workforce who were likely to be contributors to a household income rather than its sole provider. This is not to give credence to the idea that a man's wage was a "family wage", a myth which will be discussed later in this chapter, but merely to draw attention to what, according to some theories of the determinants of wage levels is an important, if not decisive, factor - i.e. the lower subsistence needs of the average woman worker.

* * *

The above five factors are important to any consideration of the female labour force at the turn of the century. They do not, however, provide us with an explanation of why the payment of below-subsistence wages to women workers was such a widespread phenomenon, or why there was such a rigid sexual division of labour. The most common explanations offered at the end of the nineteenth century for the low wages of women workers put forward two main causal factors:

95

1.  That women's wages were low because they were almost universally
    supplementary to a man's wage[75];

2.  that women's wages were low because they were generally engaged
    on unskilled work and were therefore unlikely to have received
    any training and were generally less efficient than most male
    workers[76].

The view that women's wages were low because they were supplementary to
men's was a widely-held view and was most succinctly expressed by the
economist, J. Hobson.   He maintained that most women did not have to
support a family out of their wages and, furthermore, were often themselves partially supported by a husband's or father's earnings (or by
charity and outdoor poor relief).   This factor, according to Hobson,
has a profound effect on the lowest wage paid within a trade.   He stated:

> "In so far as they [women] do receive assistance from one of
> these sources, enabling them to accept lower wages than they
> would otherwise have done, it should be clearly understood that
> they are presenting the difference between the commercial and
> the uncommercial price as a free gift to their employer, or in
> so far as competition will oblige him to lower his prices, to
> the public, which purchases the results of their work ...
> [women's wages are therefore] almost incredibly low, because
> there is an artificially large supply of women able and willing
> to take work at these low rates".[77]

The theory that women's wages are low because generally supplementary to
a man's was based on the assumption that normally a man's wage was a
"family wage" - i.e. the minimum wage for a male worker was a function of
the subsistence needs of a family.   This assumption, and its supposed
implications for women's wages, is subject to three major criticisms
based on evidence available to us.

Firstly, evidence of wages of male manual workers at the beginning of
the twentieth century indicates that for a significant number of men,
their wage was not adequate to support a family.   This was true, not
only for the casual male workers such as those discussed by G. Stedman-
Jones in his study of the London casual labour market, but also for many
workers regularly employed in all parts of the country.   Rowntree, in his
study of York in 1902 calculated the subsistence wage for the average
male worker to be 21/8d;   Cadbury in 1908 calculated it to be 25/-.   From
both Charles Booth's and B. Seebohm Rowntree's research, it was concluded
at the beginning of this century that

> "generally in the UK an unskilled labourer does not obtain a
> wage to enable him to keep himself and his family in a state
> of efficiency".[78]

Analysis of the Wages Census carried out in 1906 supports this view.

The following tables (Tables 3.11 and 3.12) indicate that a significant
number of men in some of the major areas of male employment earned below
these amounts.   In the cotton industry 27.2% of male workers earned
below 22/- per week and 14.4% between 22/- and 25/- per week;  in the
woollen industry, the figures were 28.7% and 19%.   The average male
agricultural labourer's wage (taking into account board and lodging, etc.)
was 18/4d per week in England.   In the metal, engineering and ship-
building trades which accounted for almost 12% of the male workforce,
20% of all men (over the age of twenty) earned less than 22/- per week[77a]
and another 10.6% between 22/- and 25/-.   In the building and woodwork
trades, which employed about 11% of the male workforce, 18.6% earned
below 22/- per week and another 11% between 22/- and 25/-.   The numbers
earning below a subsistence wage on the railways, in the textile
industries and in agriculture were even higher than this.   Chapter 2
has indicated that significant numbers of men in the clothing trade also
earned below-subsistence wages.

From an analysis of the 1906 Wages Census, it would appear that significant numbers of male manual workers at the beginning of this century
did not earn a "family wage".   We may therefore conclude that, although
women, because of the domestic division of labour, were less likely than
men to be continuously engaged in waged labour throughout their lives;
this does not mean that when they did work their earnings were unimportant.
As B.L. Hutchins puts it:

> "It is a special feature of women's employment that, unlike
> the work of men, who for the most part have to labour from
> early youth to some more or less advanced age, women's work
> is subject to considerable interruption, and is contingent on
> family circumstances, whence it comes about that women may not
> always need paid work, but when they do they often want it so
> badly that they are ready to take anything they get".[79]

Hobson is mistaken in his assumption that wives and daughters seeking
waged work were not urgently in need of the income;  the low wages paid
to men in a number of industries made additional income earned by other
members of the household a real necessity.   Under- and unemployment
amongst men also created a desperate need for other members of the family
to work.   Within the manual worker's family, the threat of destitution
was often only kept away by the earnings of the wife and/or children, and
this was particularly true as the male worker's ability to earn declined
with age.   Many women in these families took in washing, homework or

Table 3.11    Wages in Industries Which were Major Employers of
              Men, 1906.[1]

| | Industry | % of Men at each Wage Level | | | |
|---|---|---|---|---|---|
| | | Under 15/- | 15/- and Under 20/- | 20/- and Under 22/- | 22/- and Under 25/- |
| I | Metals, engineering and shipbuilding | 4.2 | 8.9 | 6.9 | 10.6 |
| II | Building and woodworking | 5.2 | 7.3 | 6.1 | 11.0 |
| III | Railways | | | | |
| | (a)  Electric | 31.4 | 7.4 | 9.2 | 14.7 |
| | (b)  Non-Electric | 3.4 | 18.3 | 11.8 | 16.4 |
| IV | Textiles | | | | |
| | (a)  Cotton | 2.5 | 14.0 | 9.9 | 14.4 |
| | (b)  Woollen and worsted | 3.0 | 14.7 | 11.3 | 19.0 |

1.    REHE Vol.1    PP1909, LXXX (Cd.4545)
             3    PP1010, LXXIV (Cd.5086)
             4    PP1910, LXXXIV (Cd.5196)
             6    PP1911, LXXXVIII (Cd.5814)

Table 3.12   Agriculture - Men's Wages, 1906[1]

Average weekly earnings of agricultural labourers (regularly employed) taking into account the estimated value of allowances in kind (e.g. board and lodging) -

|     |                    |   |        |
|-----|--------------------|---|--------|
| (a) | Ordinary labourers | - | 17/6d  |
| (b) | Horsemen           | - | 18/9d  |
| (c) | Cattlemen          | - | 19/1d  |
| (d) | Shepherds          | - | 19/7d  |

Average weekly earnings for all agricultural labourers (including estimated value of board and lodging and other payments in kind and excluding casual labourers) -

| England                   | 18/4 |
|---------------------------|------|
| Wales and Monmouthshire   | 18/0 |
| Scotland                  | 19/7 |
| Ireland                   | 11/3 |

1.   REHE (1906) Vol.5    PP1910, LXXXIV (Cd.5460)

went charing and were unlikely to appear on the Census returns as
occupied.   One piece of research has found a significant proportion
of women who made important contributions to the family income through
part-time work which varied from taking in dressmaking and laundry work
to opening shops in their parlours to sell home-made pies and cakes[80].

The desperate need of members of the household, other than the husband,
to bring in a wage, is demonstrated by the way that people tried to
evade the legislation restricting the waged work of mothers and children.
The Factory Inspectorate found many examples of women working right up
to the time of childbirth and returning to work immediately afterwards
in spite of the four-week ruling under the 1891 Act (see p.176).   They
also found many cases of parents forging or using other people's birth
certificates in order that children under 14 could be sent out to work[81].

Secondly, the assumption that a male wage was a "family wage" rests on
the myth that the average household was made up of a husband in employment, while the wife and children were not engaged in waged labour.
This was of course the norm amongst the Victorian middle class two-parent
family and any man who aspired to middle class status had, as a minimum,
to ensure that his wife did not need to go out of the home to work.   It
was not, however, the norm for the 1,246,407 women (7.4% of the total
female population) who were widows in 1901;   nor was it the norm for
the 2,650,273 women over the age of twenty-five who were unmarried in
1901 (16% of the total female population).   And for the majority of
families of manual workers, it was not the norm either.   The statis-
tician, A. Bowley, analysed the 1901 Census returns[82] and found that 48%
of manual workers' households were dependent on a combination of incomes
from husband, wife, siblings and children.   A further 9% were dependent
on a woman worker's wages alone.   Although Bowley calculated that at
the time of the 1901 Census 41% of households were solely dependent on
a male worker's wage, it is highly likely that at various times in the
life-cycle of these households, a wife's or children's income was
necessary to survival.

The final point to be made is that a higher proportion of women who were
engaged in waged labour were the sole breadwinners of a household
compared to the percentage of such women in the general population.
Charles Booth drew attention to the fact that of the 82,000 persons
engaged in the clothing trades in 1891 returned as heads of households,
30,000 were women.   This is an underestimate because it does not take account

of the fact that even when women were the sole breadwinners, the man still appears as the head of the family if he still lives in the same household. The figure of 30,000 women therefore only accounts for those who were widowed or deserted[83]. It is highly likely that amongst other groups of women workers, a significant number of the older women were sole breadwinners.

Proponents of the notion that a man's wage is, or should be a "family wage" also usually assume that a woman's wage does not need to be sufficient to support dependents. The evidence shows, however, that large numbers of women worked to support elderly relatives, unemployed husbands and/or children. Although these women were a minority of the female workforce, their need for a "family wage" was as great as that of the sole male breadwinner. However, their wages did not rise commensurate with their need and this must call into question the assumption that men's wages are so much higher than women's because a man's wage is a "family wage".

Hobson's assumption that the majority of women workers were wives of men earning a wage adequate for a family's needs is not borne out by the evidence.

The second type of explanation for women's low wages which was common at the end of the nineteenth century was put forward, in particular, by Sidney Webb. Webb accepted Alfred Marshall's theory of wages - i.e. that wages were determined by the efficiency of the worker and the social utility of the goods produced[84] and posited that women earned less than men because they were generally less efficient workers. He believed that men were more efficient than women because of

1.     men's greater physical strength, which, even if it is not directly required by a job, is nevertheless useful, particularly if long hours have to be worked;

2.     women's relative lack of industrial experience made them less useful. Even where women were occupied on skilled work, there was usually one part of it which they did not do, e.g. women weavers seldom tuned or set their own looms.

> "More commonly, women workers are untrained, or only partially trained, for their work and even if they learn to perform the lower branches of it well enough, they lack the masterly grasp which is required in the higher ranks of the industrial army".[85]

The first part of Webb's explanation may be taken as a biologically given factor. However, its significance is open to question when we consider that women's average weaker physical strength did not prevent their earlier employment in the mines and agriculture as little more than "beasts of burden". By the end of the nineteenth century women's employment in mines was prohibited and it was declining in agriculture but all the evidence is that many women worked very long hours and some were engaged in very heavy physical labour. Furthermore, technological developments in many industries made physical strength less and less relevant to the worker's ability to perform the work tasks. The importance of men's average greater physical strength as a determinant of low wages for women must be open to question.

The second part of Webb's argument contains the important recognition that women generally were not employed on those types of work considered as "skilled". There are two comments to be made here.

Firstly, recent research[86] has questioned the definition of "skill" and argued that

> "the classification of women's jobs as unskilled and men's jobs as skilled or semi-skilled frequently bears little relation to the actual amount of training or ability required for them".[87]

Braverman[88], in his discussion of the labour force in advanced capitalist society, stresses that the position of different sections of workers within the production process is a result not of conditions imposed by employers or of technological developments, but of a struggle carried on between employers and workers over the organisation of production. This approach is of primary importance to labour historians for it follows that it is the historical development of this conflict which is fundamental to any understanding of such vital questions as women's position in the workforce and the determinants of the sexual division of labour.

Far more research needs to be done on this question but there is evidence that the designation of a work task as "skilled" had more to do with whether the person who did it was a man or a woman than to do with any objective definition of skill. For instance, Ben Birnbaum's research[89] indicates that when machining was done by women in the clothing trade, it was classified as unskilled, whereas if it was done by men it was considered to be skilled.

The second comment is that even if Webb was right to assume that the

amount of training or ability required for a particular task was directly
related to the amount of wages received, an explanation is still
required of why "skilled" work was by and large not open to women and
how and why women were excluded from apprenticeships and training for
such work.    A clue to the answer is in fact to be found in Webb's own
recognition that women were moving into newly-created work brought about
by either mechanisation and/or the dividing up of the work process into
more detailed tasks.    Workers who earned adequate wages and exerted
some degree of control over their working conditions found that such
changes, in the production process were accompanied by employers' attempts
to introduce cheaper labour which usually turned out to be women, youths
and girls.    Where the men were organised they quite naturally fought
to exclude such workers in an attempt to maintain their jobs and level
of wages.    The question therefore has to be asked why were women and
girls such a frequent source of cheap labour for employers?    Sidney
Webb's explanation of low women's wages merely states the fact that women
were generally employed in jobs which did not require training or special
ability.    He does not explain how and why this came about.

Current explanations offered by economists of women's position in the
labour market do not really offer any major new theoretical developments
which would help us to understand women and work at the turn of the
century.    The main contribution has been the discussion on the concept
of a dual labour market.    The existence of a dual labour market, that
is

> "the stratification of the labour market into a primary
> sector - containing relatively well-rewarded and stable jobs;
> and a secondary sector - containing lower paid and insecure
> occupations".[90]

is said to arise for two reasons.    The first is employers' need to
promote employee stability in jobs which require manpower investment;
the second is in the necessity of reducing class conflict potential at
the workplace by weakening the unity of the working class[91].    Barron
and Norris identify women workers as falling into the secondary sector
and isolate five attributes of workers in the secondary sector, all of
which are exhibited by women workers - dispensibility;    easily identified
social differences which emphasise the relative inferiority of the
secondary group;    relatively low interest in acquiring valuable training
and experience;    relatively less concern with economic rewards for their
work;    a relatively low level of trade union or collective strength.

There are two major criticisms to be made of this analysis of women's position in the labour force.   The first is that the theory of the existence of a dual labour market rests on a functionalist and a one-sided analysis.   The existence of a primary and a secondary labour force undoubtedly assists employers' need for a stable workforce in certain areas while at the same time dividing the working class and therefore making united class action less likely.   What proof do we have, however, that these are the causes of the existence of a dual labour market? Division within the workforce, the status of different occupations, whether jobs are done by men or by women, are all part of a historical development where employers did not have the ability to unilaterally impose their wishes.   Trade union organisation was in the ring as well as employers and the outcome was and is the result of advances and defeats experienced by both sides of the struggle.

The reasons offered by Barron and Norris for the existence of a dual labour market are ahistorical.   A second criticism is that Barron and Norris do not really attempt any explanation as to why it is women who form the bulk of the secondary labour force in Britain today and their analysis is of very limited value in the context of the historical development of the female labour force.   The attributes of the secondary labour force which they identify and which are said to be exhibited by women are descriptive rather than explanatory.   The inadequacy of this approach is made particularly clear if we examine their treatment of one of these attributes, namely women's lack of trade union organisation. Barron and Norris state that "women have been notably less successful than men in organising themselves industrially", but although they intend "to suggest some of the reasons for this difference" they patently do not.   They claim that lack of trade union organisation reflects the work situation of women - low pay, scattered workplaces, high turnover and a high incidence of part-time and temporary jobs - and they claim that women are less concerned with economic rewards so are less motivated to organise.   They do not explain, however, why women are found in the jobs which make trade union organisation unlikely.   Furthermore, to ignore the historical development of the trade union movement and the central concern of organised labour to exclude workers whose entry into the workplace heralded a dilution of labour is to rule out any satis-factory analysis of women's position in the labour force.

An economic theory such as that of the dual labour market is useful in that the discussion gives us further insights into the position of women workers;   it is inadequate as a theory, however, as the explanation is essentially ahistorical and tends towards a very one-dimensional version of reality.

This is not a criticism which can be levied against the theoretical perspective offered by writers such as Sally Alexander and Michele Barratt[92], a perspective which also tackles the problems raised by the inadequacy of theories such as those of Sidney Webb and J. Hobson.  It is not my purpose to consider this theoretical perspective in depth but merely to draw attention to its relevance to the material presented in the first three chapters of this thesis.


We have seen that employment opportunities declined for women (particularly married women) during the nineteenth century and that where women were employed their status was subordinate to that of men in the workplace. Historians often cite the move of productive activity into the public sphere while child-bearing and rearing remained privatised as the reason for these developments.  Barrett and Alexander, however, both point out that this argument fails to take account of the fact that women also play a subordinate role in production in pre-industrial societies and that the sexual division of labour within the family unit of production had consequences for the position of women as workers within industrial production.  Alexander, writing of women workers in London in the mid-nineteenth century, states:

> "The sexual division of labour - both within and between the London trades - in the 1830s and 1840s had been established in the period of manufacture (roughly from the sixteenth to the eighteenth century).  It was predetermined by the division of labour that had existed within the family when the household had been the unit of production.  The epoch of modern industry, far from challenging this division further demarcated and rigidified it."[93]

The evidence is that in the pre-industrial economy women assisted and supplemented the work of men in the family production unit.  The majority of women worked on the land where their status and physical labour was not far removed from that of "beasts of burden"[94].  In the artisan class women and girls had an ambiguous status as workers and as a result did not serve the apprenticeships which would have made them into skilled craftswomen.  Such women usually worked for their husband or father and the borderline between the craft work which they carried on and their domestic work was blurred and shifting according to (a) childbirth and (b) fluctuations in the need for extra workers[95].  For all women in the pre-industrial economy their productive role was integrally linked

to their position as wives and mothers.   Women had the responsibility
of performing domestic duties for the male members of the household
and this division of labour was carried over into industrial society.

Women's position in pre-industrial society also had important consequences
when craft unions attempted to protect the status of skilled labour
against the development of a sophisticated division of labour and of
mechanisation and the demand by employers for a less skilled and cheaper
labour force.   In every industry where there was skilled and well-paid
work, craft unions fought to exclude unskilled labour.   The pressure
from employers was to split up the production process (usually made
possible by mechanisation) in order to increase productivity and profit
margins.   Skilled workers, in defending themselves against this dilution
of labour and the inevitable lowering of wages, excluded women (the chief
source of cheap labour because of their already subordinate position)
from their unions and when forced to accept them into the workplace,
negotiated specific jobs which were designated as "women's jobs", the
corollary being that male wages were protected as far as possible.

An example of this is to be found in the printing trade where as the
production process was split up into more detailed work tasks, employers
took on unskilled female labour.   Journeymen fought against the employment of this unskilled, unapprenticed labour and excluded women from
their unions.   The men were eventually forced to allow women into some
stages of the printing trade so their policy later became to confine
female workers to clearly-defined areas - which were then delineated as
"women's work" (e.g. paperfolding) and characterised by low wages and
unorganised labour.   An illustration of this development is the elaborate
agreement drawn up between the Bookbinding Trade Section of the London
Chamber of Commerce and the London Societies of Journeymen Bookbinders
whereby the unionists accepted unskilled female labour on certain
processes as long as the skilled work of bookbinders and their apprenticeship was protected.   Women workers were not consulted, nor represented
when this agreement was drawn up[96].

This exclusion of women from better paid work was common throughout
industry in the nineteenth century.   Employers seized any opportunity
to introduce cheaper labour while men's craft unions resisted to the
best of their ability.   The hostile attitude of the trade union movement
to women workers and their firm belief that women's place was in the home,
was not a surprising development in this context.

As Barrett points out, the subordinate status of women in industrial society was not an inevitable result of developments in the production process, but rather a result of a

> "long and uneven process, one element of which was a struggle between male and female workers in which the better organised, male craft unions succeeded in over-riding the interests of women workers, ..."[97]

## IV

The purpose of this brief discussion of various explanations offered for women's position in the industrial workforce was to illuminate the question of the sexual division of labour and suggest which type of approach is likely to be helpful to an analysis of women's low wages and which are not. We have found that an approach which focusses on particular characteristics supposed to be held by women workers is unhelpful in that it is unhistorical and tautological. Instead, the most fruitful consideration of the position of women in the labour force is one which recognises the historical development of the sexual division of labour in production, the relationship of this development to the domestic sexual division of labour and the part played by working-class organisations in excluding women from better-paid work against the background of employers' desire to bring about a dilution of labour skills and a lowering of wages in certain areas of industrial production.

The important conclusion of this chapter in respect of the analysis of sweated labour is that evidence relating to women's position in the labour force at the beginning of the twentieth century illustrates their subordinate position in terms of access to skilled, better-paid work. Women workers not only made up the majority of sweated workers in most of the sweated trades, as illustrated in Chapter 1, but the majority of women suffered from the major characteristic of sweated labour - below-subsistence wages.

Having established the nature of the problem to which those concerned with sweating addressed themselves, we will now move on to examine the role played by the various important interest groups in the building up of pressure for legislative action on the sweated trades. This examination will commence with an analysis of the relationship between sweated labour and organised labour, and of the attitudes of the trade union movement to sweated labour, their perception of the problem and the solutions offered.

1. House of Lords Select Committee on Sweating, 5th Report, PP1890, XVII (Cd.169), p.xlii.

2. A. Anderson, (1922), p.64.

3. Cadbury and Shann,(1908).

4. Anderson (1922).

5. Anderson (1922), p.64.

6. C. Meyer and C. Black, "Makers of Our Clothes, a Case for Trade Boards" (1909).

6a. Quoted by Anderson (1922), p.65.

7. Ibid., pp.65/66.

8. Ibid., p.78.

9. A. Report, 1900, pp.352, 400. The Annual Reports of the Chief Inspector of Factories and Workshops are referred to in this abbreviated fashion in the footnotes throughout this Chapter. Full references for the Annual Reports are to be found in the Bibliography.

10. Anderson (1922), pp.78 and 85.

11. J.A. Hobson "Problems of Poverty" (1895), pp.153-154.

12. A.R. (1905), p.60.

13. A.R. (1905), p.59.

14. A.R. (1902).

15. A.R. (1911), p.152.

16. Anderson (1922), p.28.

17. Ibid., p.39.

18. A.R. (1898), p.174.

19. A.R. (1897), p.106.

20. Anderson (1922), p.30.

21. A.R. (1908).

22. Anderson (1922), p.30.

23. A.R. (1913).

24. Cadbury and Shann (1908), p.37.

25. Ada Neild Chew, "Victims of our Industrial System, I Tailoresses" Young Oxford, Vol.II, No.18, March 1901.

26. British Association for the Advancement of Science, Report of the Committee on the Economic Effect of Legislation Regulating Women's Labour (1903), p.5 (the "Booth Committee").

27. A.R. (1900), p.386.

28. A.R. (1897), p.106.

29. A.R. (1898), p.174.

30. A.R. (1897), p.106.

30a. A.R. (1904), p.279.

31. A.R. (1896), p.38.

32. Anderson (1922), p.28.

33. Booth Committee (1903), p.5.

34. "Note on the Hours Actually Worked in an Ordinary Full-Time Week by Men and Women Before the War". Reconstruction Committee - Women's Employment Sub-Committee Collection: Document No.92. Box 2.

35. Anderson (1922), p.25.

36. The Booth Committee (1903), p.8.

37. Report of the Women's Employment Committee, Ministry of Reconstruction 1919, Cd.9239, p.1.

38. Ibid.

38a. Ibid., p.60.

39. See in particular, R. Samuel, "The Workshop of the World" in History Workshop Journal, Issue 3, Spring 1977.

40. Anderson (1922), p.43.

41. A.R. (1910), p.118.

42. A.R. (1892), p.194.

43. Anderson, p.65.

44. A.R. (1902), p.171.

45. A.R. (1906), p.208.

46. B.L. Hutchins, "Women in Modern Industry" (1915), p.58.

47. Ibid., p.59.

48. Ibid., p.184.

49. A.R. (1901), p.176.

50. A.R. (1908), p.146.

51. A.R. (1907), p.166.

52. Anderson (1922), p.40.

53. City of Westminster, Report of the Chief Medical Officer of Health, 1903, p.64.

54. Anderson (1922), p.110.

55. A.R. (1909), p.146.

56. Anderson (1922), p.81.

57. Departmental Committee, (1908), and earlier reports.

58. A.R. (1900), p.384.

59. This figure is arrived at by taking Sidney Webb's estimate of the average male and female wage from the REHE (1906), quoted in B. Drake, "Women in Trade Unions" (1920), p.44.

60. E. Richards, "Women in the British Economy Since 1700" in History, Vol.59 No.197, Oct. 1974; C. Collet, "Women in Industry" (1911); I. Pinchbeck, "Women Workers and the Industrial Revolution, 1750-1850" (reprinted 1968).

61. E.J. Hobsbawm, "The Age of Revolution 1789-1848" (1964), p.55.

62. C. Collet, "Women in Industry" (1911). Collet compares the participation rate of women in 1901 with that in 1851, using Census statistics.

63. I. Pinchbeck (1968), p.197.

64. Ibid., p.197.

65. See also S. Alexander, "Women's Work in Nineteenth-Century London; A Study of the Years 1820-1850" in J. Mitchell and A. Oakley, "The Rights and Wrongs of Women" (1976).

66. Collet, (1911), p.9.

67. UK Home Office: A Study of the Factors which have operated in the past and those which are operating now to determine the distribution of women in industry. PP1929, XVII (Cd.3508), p.9.

68. See the very interesting articles by Dr. A. Shadwell on the Midland Metal Trades in The Times, 8.1.1908 and 15.1.1908.

69. B. Drake, "Women in the Engineering Trades" (1917), p.8.

70. Ibid.

71. Anderson (1922), p.25; S. Webb, "The Alleged Differences in the Wages paid to men and women for similar work" in Economic Journal I (1891), pp.635-62.

72. A.R. (1911), p.138.

73. Letter from Catherine Smith (nd), Margaret MacDonald Collection, Vol.II.

74. A. Bowley, "Earners and Dependents in English Towns in 1911", in Economica 1921, No.2.

75.   J. Hobson, "Problems of Poverty" (1895) Chapter VII, The Industrial
      Condition of Women Workers.

76.   This is the viewpoint put forward by Alfred Marshall ("Principles
      of Economics" 1907 edn.) and Sidney Webb (in his 1891 article in
      the Economic Journal).

77.   Hobson (1895), pp.160-161.

77a.  The figure for those earning less than 22/- per week is presented
      as it is not possible from the Wages Census Analysis to assess the
      numbers earning 21/8d and under.

78.   Cadbury and Shann (1908), p.20.

79.   Hutchins, (1915), p.xiv.

80.   Elizabeth Roberts, "Working Class Standards of Living in Barrow
      and Lancaster 1900-1914" in EHR Vol.XXX No.2, May 1977.

81.   A.R. (1910), p.134.

82.   A. Bowley (1921).

83.   Booth (1902), Vol.7.

84.   S. Webb (1891).

85.   Ibid.

86.   H. Braverman, "Labour and Monopoly Capital" (1974).
      B. Birnbaum, unpublished manuscript "Women, Skill and Automation;
      a Study of Women's Employment in the Clothing Industry 1946-1972"
      (nd 1976?).
      A. Phillips and B. Taylor, "Sex and Skill" in Feminist Review,
      Issue 6, 1980.

87.   Taylor and Phillips (1980), p.79.

88.   H. Braverman (1974).

89.   See Note 86 above.

90.   R.D. Barron and G.M. Norris, "Sexual Divisions and the Dual Labour
      Market" in D.C. Barker and S. Allen (eds.), "Dependence and
      Exploitation in Work and Marriage" (1976).

91.   See D.M. Gordon, "Theories of Poverty and Underemployment" (1972).

92.   S. Alexander (1976).
      M. Barrett, "Women's Oppression Today:  Problems in Marxist
      Feminist Analysis" (1980).

93.   Alexander (1976), pp.74-75.

94.   See e.g. I. Pinchbeck (1969), P. Laslet, "The World we have Lost"
      (7651).

95.   Hutchins (1915), pp.15-27.

96.   J. Ramsay MacDonald, "Women in the Printing Trades" (1904), pp.7-8.

97.   Barrett (1980), p.165.

# 4  Trade unions and sweated labour

With this chapter we commence an analysis (which continues in Chapters
5 to 9) of how the Trade Boards Act came to be passed.   Working-class
pressure is commonly assumed to play an important part in the development
of social policy and we need to test this assumption in the context of
this particular piece of legislation.

In order to provide a background to the question of the role of the
trade union movement, we will first consider the relationship of sweated
labour to organised labour at the turn of the century.   Given the evidence
of the last chapter, we will then go on to consider the attitudes of the
trade union movement to women workers in particular and of the way in
which the male trade union leadership treated women workers as a separate
category of the workforce.   The final part of this chapter analyses the
solutions offered by the trade union movement to the problem of sweated
labour.

I

Sweated labour was identified as a terrible threat to the interests of
organised labour.   As the TUC declared in 1888,

> "One of the main features of trade combination is to contend
> against and to attempt to destroy the immoral system in the
> industrial world known as sweating"[1].

The more skilled and organised sections of workers were placed in jeopardy
by the dilution of labour in many industries.   As long as semi- and unskilled labour remained unorganised they were a seemingly never-ending
supply of cheap labour willing to work for the long hours, poor working
conditions and low wages which the trade union movement was fighting
against.   It could be argued, however, that it was the exclusion of
unskilled workers from the craft and "New Model" unions that provided
an added handicap to any attempt by such workers to organise and fight
low wages, and that skilled workers' vulnerability to the dilution of
skill and lowering of wages was one direct result of their own hostile
attitude towards unskilled workers.   Such a hostility was understandable
in the many situations throughout the development of capitalist industry
where skilled workers saw their jobs and livelihood threatened by what
was commonly seen as "blackleg" labour - workers brought in on lower wages
to perform the new tasks created by technological development and/or a

breaking down of the division of labour. Skilled workers excluded unskilled men and women from their organisations and unskilled workers'
organisation, when it came, was in the form of separate general unions[2].

Unskilled workers started to organise effectively in the late 1880s and
1890s but the workers who joined the "New Unions" were mostly men - the
dockers, public utility workers and the railway workers, etc. Women
workers, so often the source of cheap labour, remained largely unorganised with the exception of textile workers and the sporadic,
enthusiastic bursts of organisation by such groups as the London match-
makers (in 1888)[3] and confectionery workers in Bristol (in 1892)[4]. The
attempts of women to organise into trade unions are discussed in more
detail in Chapter 5.

The history of trade union organisation in the tailoring trade is a
particularly relevant example of how hostility between different sections
of workers helped to make united trade union action against low wages
unlikely. Skilled tailors, those who still retained control over the
making up of most of the garment, made up the majority of trade unionists
in the tailoring trade. Barbara Drake, an economist writing in 1912,
estimated that a large majority of the 2,000 trade unionists in the West
End trade were skilled tailors,

> "i.e. to some extent they resemble the old fashioned tailor
> in that he makes a garment almost throughout (with the
> exception of the cutting), or with the help only of a woman
> to fell the linings, and sew buttons and buttonholes".[5]

Tailors had been amongst the first groups of workers[6] to organise, the
first recorded striking taking place in 1721. The history of their
organisation illustrates their fight against a dilution of their skills
and attacks on their wages. The tailors' unions negotiated standard
wage rates, called the "time log" system[7] and were one of the first
groups of workers to attempt to negotiate national rate when the
Amalgamated Society of Journeymen Tailors (ASJT) struck in pursuit of
such a claim in 1867[8].

The development of a sophisticated division of labour from the mid-
nineteenth century (discussed in Chapter 2), saw the recruitment, by new
types of employers, of women workers to carry out fairly detailed tasks
and later to do most of the machining in factory production. The
skilled tailor had himself employed women (often his wife or daughter)
on the simplest tasks as his assistant. Access to the status of skilled

workmen was strictly controlled by the apprenticeship system and was not
open to women.   When women started to be employed in the trade on a
wider scale by the new wholesale and ready-made tailoring manufacturers,
they were easily identified by the skilled worker as the major source
of threat to the existing organisation of production and to the level of
wages.   The skilled tailors' unions did not admit to their membership
either these women workers, nor the Jewish workers in areas such as
London, Leeds and Manchester who were also closely involved in the
breaking down of the production process into many parts (see Chapter 2).

In 1867, when the ASJT in London struck for a national time log, they
sought the participation of women outworkers in the strike but they would
not allow them into the men's union.   An attempt was made to organise
them separately but it was not successful although the women had responded
to the call to strike[8a].   In 1877, the Amalgamated Society of Tailors
enlisted the help of the Women's Protective and Provident League to form
a separate tailoresses' union[9];   the male tailors were worried about the
effect of the women tailoring workers being unorganised but they still
would not allow them into their own union.

In Leeds, from 1855, the Jewish skilled tailors organised separately
from the English tailors, but together with the Jewish tailors'
machinists and pressers, because they were not admitted to the English
Amalgamated Society of Tailors (AST).   In 1886, the English and Jewish
skilled tailors amalgamated[10] while the Jewish machinists and pressers
(mostly workshop employees) continued to organise separately.   There
is evidence that the AST accepted Jewish tailors into membership in
London but that there was a separate branch set up for the Jewish
tailors - thus the Jewish Branch of the AST was represented at the
Conference for the Abolition of the Middleman Sweater in 1891[11].

Hostility between Jewish and Gentile tailors continued to create
divisions in the workforce, however.   This was recognised as a problem
by Lewis Lyons, a prominent Jewish trade unionist.   At the London
Conference in 1891, called to organise the boycotting of the "middleman
sweater", he regretted the fact that the Jewish and Gentile workers were
"being pitted against each other", in spite of the Jewish workers wanting
"to work in harmony with their English brothers"[12].

Factory machinists, Jew and Gentile alike, were excluded from the skilled
tailors' unions, and eventually started to organise separately.   In

Leeds they set up the Wholesale Clothiers' Operatives Union in the 1890s which then amalgamated with the Bristol Clothiers' Operatives to become the Amalgamated Union of Clothiers' Operatives (AUCO).

As the tailoring trade developed and particularly as the expansion of the trade brought with it intense competition between both employers and workers, there was great conflict of interest between the more skilled workers and those machinists, pressers, button-holers, fellers, etc. who did not enter any apprenticeship and who were only engaged on a minute portion of the garment.   This conflict and the exclusion of the unskilled and semi-skilled from the older skilled tailors' trade union severely handicapped any ability that the workers may have had to resist the downward pressure on wages.   As the official history of the clothing workers' unions puts it:

> "The division of interest between trained craftsmen and many
> other sections of the tailoring trade had been steadily growing
> and had become increasingly difficult to bridge.   That between
> those who claimed to be tailors, with all that this implied by
> way of tradition skills, and the new groups of semi-casual
> machinists grew wider and deeper"[13].

The organised tailors failed to help to organise the more vulnerable workers.   This is illustrated by the history of the Leeds AST who although they were well organised and their delegates dominated the Leeds Trades Council until 1891, made no attempt to help women machinists in the trade to organise.   It was only when the women in one factory them-selves struck against fines and deductions in 1889 that, with the help of a middle-class feminist, they secured representation on the Leeds Trades Council.   The Leeds Tailoresses' Union which was set up as a result of the strike sent delegates to the Leeds Trades Council for each year until shortly after they amalgamated with the male-dominated AUCO in 1900;  by 1904 there was no woman delegate from AUCO to the Trades Council[14].

The AST remained especially hostile to women workers in the trade but by the late 1890s they were forced to recognise that the threat posed by low paid women machinists was not going to disappear and the 1897 Conference instructed the Executive Committee "to formulate a scheme for female organisation".   They did not go so far as to offer women equal membership;  instead a separate "Female Section" was set up in 1900.

It must be stressed that the women were recruited as second class members; the highest subscription (and benefit) payable by a woman was equal to

the lowest subscription (and benefit) open to a male member of the Union.
Women's subordinate status in the workplace was therefore carried over
into the trade union organisation and it is probably not surprising that
the AST - fourteen years after opening its membership to women - had   not
made much progress in recruiting women before the First World War.  AUCO
also operated a similar policy of admitting women as second-class members
as Table 4.1 shows.

The history of organisation in the tailoring trade is one of conflict of
interest and division amongst the different types of worker.   Such conflict and division meant that there were huge odds against any effective
trade union action being taken to combat sweating in the industry.   Such
odds also existed in other industries where women were employed at the
end of the nineteenth century, one example being the Birmingham metal and
engineering trades.

As in the tailoring trade, the recruitment of women into the Birmingham
metal and engineering trades was accompanied by a dilution of skills and
a lowering of wages[15].   The Amalgamated Society of Engineers - a skilled
workers' union - promoted a policy of preventing women workers from
serving apprenticeships, even in the situation where women were engaged
on work which was classed as "skilled" when performed by a man[16].   The
ASE eventually opened its doors to the semi- and unskilled male workers
but still refused to admit women, the chief source of cheap labour.

Organised labour in the metal trades, seeing that the entry of women was
accompanied by the "degradation of the man's standard of living to a
'sweating' level"[17] - to the extent that the trades were included by
Mary MacArthur as amongst the worst sweated trades in her evidence to
the House of Commons Select Committee on Homework - strongly opposed
the employment of women.   The Amalgamated Society of Brassworkers was
one of the most vociferous opponents of women engaging in waged work and
their delegate spoke at many TUC Annual Congresses calling for legislation to exclude women from encroaching on the male-dominated sections
of the metal trades[18].

The male workers in the small metal trades were organised according to
their trade - the chainmakers, the nailmakers, nut and bolt makers,
bedstead makers, etc. - and having failed to exclude women from these
trades, tried to organise them separately hoping thereby to confine them
to specific types of work.   They failed however.   The general unions

Table 4.1

Terms and Conditions of Membership of the Amalgamated Union of
Clothing Workers, 1910[1].

| Contributions | Benefits |
|---|---|
| **MEN** | |
| 7d and 9d per week | Out of Work Pay:  Minimum of 9/- per week for six months |
| | Dispute Pay:  Minimum of 15/- per week |
| | Victimised Pay:  up to 25/- per week |
| | Sick Pay:  10/- per week for twelve weeks |
| | Funeral Benefit:  £10 (£5 at wife's death) |
| **WOMEN** | |
| 2d and 3d per week | Out of Work Pay:  Nil |
| | Dispute Pay:  7/6 per week |
| | Victimised Pay:  up to 12/6 per week |
| | Sick Pay:  6/- per week for six weeks |
| | Funeral Benefit:  £5 |

1.    AUCO Monthly Gazette, May 1910.

on the other hand, admitted women to membership with no restrictions and on equal terms as their male members, being semi- and unskilled workers themselves and having vested interest in particular trades. But these unions - primarily the Workers' Union and the National Union of General Workers - had limited power themselves for they had no monopoly on skill, established through an apprenticeship system, as had the skilled workers. Furthermore, women were slow to join the general unions and took no part in their management (until the National Federation of Women Workers started organising the women chainmakers in 1910) [19].

The Birmingham engineering and metal trades exhibited the same type of divisions amongst the workforce as found in the tailoring trade. There were conflicts of interest between skilled male workers and unskilled male and female workers. The main enemy of the skilled worker was seen to be the women workers who were employed to do many of the work-tasks created by the rapid development of the engineering and metal trades at the end of the nineteenth century. Trade union organisation amongst the workers reflected these conflicts of interests. The skilled male workers refused for a long time to open their doors to semi- and unskilled labour, spending much of their resources on fighting the employment of such labour [20]. Although they eventually were forced to accept that certain sections of their trade were now carried on by unapprenticed labour, they continued to fight against the employment of women [21].

The position of homeworkers and the hostility of organised labour to this most-exploited section of sweated labour in any trade meant that homeworkers found very few champions amongst organised labour. They were the lowest of low-paid workers, isolated, vulnerable and would have been a most difficult group of workers to organise - if any trade unionists had tried. The attempt in 1890 by a feminist in Bristol, Helena Born, to organise seamstresses who worked at home illustrates the difficulties: the women were scattered all over Bristol, working very long hours for very low pay and Helena Born had sometimes to tramp thirty miles in a day to maintain contact with them. Her attempt at organising them failed because although a number joined the union it consisted of "isolated and passive members and they did not find a means of acting effectively together" [22].

Not only did homeworkers face particular difficulties in organising but the stronger sections of the trade union movement did very little to help homeworkers to organise; male trade unionists were more likely to argue for the abolition of homeworking, as AUCO and the Scottish Tailors and Tailoresses Association did[23]. Their attitude was often that home-workers were primarily married women earning "pin money" and as such constituted unfair competition. The lack of organisation amongst home-workers thus created further barriers to united trade union action against sweating.

## II

We will now go on to discuss the attitude of organised labour generally to women workers. There were three types of response to women's work and wages amongst the trade union leadership at the end of the nine-teenth century. Firstly, the fear that girls and women were under-cutting their wages provided male trade unionists with a motivation for demanding the restriction or prohibition of women's waged work. This fear was expressed, for example, by George Keir, the Secretary of the Amalgamated Society of Tailors, in his evidence to the Royal Commission on Labour when he told the Commissioners that the employment of women lowered wages generally in the trade, as did, he believed, the employment of foreigners[23a]. The AST's Government Workers' Branch told the Select Committee on Homework some years later that women "flocking" into the factory had dragged wages down and also encouraged homework[24].

Evidence of the development of a sexual division of labour in the tailoring trade - as presented in Chapter 2 - would seem to justify these claims and there is no doubt that when women were brought into a particular industry, there was usually a lowering of wages, accompanied as their entry was by the development of a more sophisticated division of labour and/or the introduction of machinery. This blatant and some-times very real fear that cheap female labour would be used to replace men workers lay behind many of the TUC's demands in the mid-nineteenth century for the prohibition of female labour altogether.

However, with an increasing, though still tiny, number of women attending the TUC Annual Congress from 1875 onwards, speeches about the competition of female labour tended to be toned down somewhat. Mr. Juggins, a delegate from the Midland Trades Federation, was almost the only delegate (between 1888 and 1908) to be quite blunt about his wish to prohibit women from working altogether. In 1888, he seconded Clementina Black's motion "that in the opinion of this Congress, it is desirable, in the interests of both men and women, that in trades where women do the same

work as men, they shall receive the same payment". Miss Black proposed
the motion in terms of justice and equal rights; Mr. Juggins, on the
other hand, told the Congress that he supported the motion because he
had been told by an employer that when he had to pay women the same as
men, he would refuse to employ women. The motion was carried unanimously
and one wonders whether it was the proposer's or the seconder's argument
which carried the most weight amongst the male-dominated Congress[25].

In 1891, Mr. Juggins - this time as a delegate from the Amalgamated
Society of Nut and Boltmakers - again voiced his fear of female competition when he attempted to prevent women working in a better-paid
sector of his trade by moving that women and girls should be prohibited
from working iron or steel of more than a quarter of an inch diameter
into nails, spikes, rivets or bolts[26]. The Brassworkers Union also
wished to prohibit women working in certain sections of their trade and
this caused particular controversy at the TUCs of 1908 and 1909[27]. No
other delegate, however, said publicly that women should be ousted from
the labour force altogether, although a delegate from the Sheffield
Silversmith Society, in seconding a motion at the 1897 Congress prohibiting
a mother's employment until six months after childbirth, contended that
"married women should be altogether prevented from going into employments
in which they competed with men"[28].

This particular focus of attention on married women's work is of significance and in fact is indicative of the second type of response which
was more common amongst trade unionists in their attitude to women's
work. This response centred on a woman's role as wife and mother -
particularly her role as mother. Many male trade unionists subscribed
to the same ideas about the incompatibility of waged work and motherhood
as did those imperialists who were concerned about the quality of the
nation's workers. In the early 1880s, Henry Broadhurst (Secretary of
the TUC's Parliamentary Committee) argued in these terms in support of
an extension of factory legislation. Male trade unionists, he said

> "had the future of their country and children to consider
> and it was their duty as men and husbands to use their
> utmost efforts to bring about a condition of things, where
> their wives should be in their proper sphere at home, instead
> of being dragged into competition for livelihood against the
> great and strong men of the world".[29]

The fear of harm done to a woman's childbearing function and of harm done
to her children was an explicit reason for the TUC's support of the "four
weeks rule" - i.e. the prohibition of a mother returning to work until

four weeks after childbirth - and of the dangerous trades legislation. This fear often had moral overtones. For example, George Shipton, Secretary of the London Trades Council, told the Royal Commission on Labour that an increase in the number of women doing waged work had led to "social degradation".

> "I think [he told them] the man should be the breadwinner and be able to keep his wife or his children by his labour, instead of driving them at an early age onto the labour market. It must have a wholesale degenerating influence".[30]

However, by the end of the nineteenth century a third type of response to women workers was evident amongst trade unionists. This was a recognition of the need to organise women workers into trade unions and arose from three factors. Firstly, the older established craft unions were by now forced to accept that women formed a permanent part of the labour force and the threat which they posed to wages and conditions could only be met by organising them. For example, the Hanley District Secretary of the Amalgamated Society of Tailors, wrote in 1898,

> "Whilst deploring the effects of the competition arising from the introduction and extended employment of the machine, the female worker and the child worker, the bulk of the members of the Society have angrily clamoured for their elimination when they ought to have clamoured for their organisation".[31]

He applauded the decision of the AST's 1897 Conference to organise women workers in this trade.

Frances Hicks, herself a tailoress and also Secretary of the Women's Trade Union Association, attempted to organise women in other craft unions and found that in many instances the men "were very anxious" to organise the women[32]. The TUC gave official encouragement to the efforts of women to organise themselves into trade unions and gave formal recognition to organisations such as the Women's Trade Union League, which were primarily middle-class organisations set up with the aim of unionising working women. The explicit reason for this desire to get women into trade unions was to counteract their use as unorganised cheap labour in competition with organised male labour. Thomas Burt, President of the TUC, welcomed the fact that at the 1891 Congress

> "... we have the women of the country more largely represented than they have been before. Women need organisation even more than men. And wherever a woman does the same work, in the same quality and quantity as men, she ought to ask for the same pay as the men. And we ought to support her, not only on the grounds of justice and humanity, but on grounds of self-defence in asserting that claim".[33]

One of the main **reasons** that organised labour had supported protective legislation for women and young persons was to prevent such workers from undercutting and replacing male workers. The TUC was therefore very concerned about the failure of the Factory Inspectorate to enforce the regulations on protected labour (women and young persons). This concern was a recurrent theme at the TUC Annual Congresses at the end of the nineteenth century. The trade unions recognised that they had had more success in shortening men's hours and raising men's wages than the Factory Inspectorate had in protecting women workers from excessive exploitation. The Congress was told in 1892 that trade unionism amongst women must therefore be encouraged because it was trade unionism amongst men that had raised male wages and shortened hours[34]. Significantly the President's appeal for organisation amongst women was couched in terms of morality:

> "When we think of the miserable pittance paid to many of our factories and warehouses to the women workers, can we wonder at the vice and immorality so rampant in our midst".[35]

The second factor which prompted encouragement of organising women workers was the increase in unionisation amongst unskilled and semi-skilled male workers. These were men whose own employment was often casual, seasonal, insecure and low paid. They therefore depended upon a wife's wage to bring their own wage up to a family wage and to tide the family over during times of unemployment. Such workers could not afford to insist that women should not go out to work although of course many would ideally have liked to see their own wages increased thereby making it unnecessary for wives and mothers to work. Leaders of the "New Unions" were very much in favour of women joining trade unions to fight for better wages and conditions. For instance, Tom Mann, leader of the Dockers' Union (which set up women's branches of the union) successfully proposed in 1890 that women delegates should be admitted to the London Trades Council and a Sub-Committee was set up to investigate the position on women's trade unions and to help organise women workers[36]. Will Thorne, leader of the Gasworkers Union was also a strong advocate of organising women into trade unions and this union was open to women from the beginning.

Unskilled and semi-skilled male workers were also greatly threatened by the possibility of their replacement by cheap female labour and thus also had strong motivations of self-defence behind their encouragement of women's trade union organisation. Recognition of this encouragement is not to deny, however, that such trade unionists still had ambivalent attitudes to women workers - particularly to married workers.

It is also the case that, after their initial enthusiasm in the late
1880s and early 1890s, the general unions experienced such difficulty
in organising women workers that they tended to assert that legislation
was the only answer to the low wages and poor working conditions suffered
by women.    Will Thorne, at first eager to recruit women into his union,
recognised that "the double workload of women, home and work, left them
with little time or energy for organisation"[37].   In 1914, he told the
Webbs,

> "Our experience has been that women do not make good trade
> unionists and for this reason we believe that our energies
> are better used toward the organisation of male workers".[38]

Nevertheless, the Gasworkers Union had 5,000 women members by then[39] and,
in theory at least, the general unions remained committed to organising
women workers.

The third factor which forced upon male trade unionists the recognition
of the importance of women workers was the organisation of women themselves.    Although the female membership of trade unions remained a
very small percentage of the female workforce, their numbers did increase
from an estimated 36,900 in 1886 to 166,803 in 1906, textile unions
making up most of this membership.    It was the Matchgirls strike of
1888 which marked the beginning of organisation and activity of unskilled
and semi-skilled workers during the next few years.    Chapter 5 discusses
further the political and trade union activity of women between 1888 and
1908, but it is important to point to two factors here.    One factor was
the activity within the workplace and trade unions by women at the end
of the nineteenth century and beginning of the twentieth century;   the
other was the debates within women's organisation about women's status
and rights as workers.

The often spontaneous, industrial action taken by women frequently forced
the needs of women workers to the attention of male trade unionists.
Sheila Rowbotham in her book "Hidden from History" briefly outlines some
of the many disputes involving women workers during the "boom" period of
trade union activity during the years 1888 and 1892[40].    A later example
is what happened within the Leicester branch of the National Union of
Boot and Shoe Operatives in 1907.    Women's membership of the Union had
been dramatically increasing but a minimum wage had only been negotiated
for adult male workers, not for women.    A Women's Section of the

Leicester Branch had been set up in 1904 with 1,213 members and in 1907 the Secretary of the Women's Section - Elizabeth Wilson - led a break away from the main union brought about by dissatisfaction with the male leadership and their lack of representation of the women members' interests[41].

Other examples of women's industrial action which brought the attention of male trade unionists, employers, politicians and social reformers to the problems of women workers are easily found[42]; in 1890 Liverpool tailoresses were locked out after asking for a reduction in hours of work. They won their case with the help of Liverpool Trades Council; also in 1890 chocolate factory workers in London's East End struck against unjust fines[43]; in the well-organised textile trades women were known to go on unofficial strike when they felt the union hadn't represented their interests[44]. Examples like these can be found of women taking industrial action in almost all the trades in which women were employed, with the exception of domestic service.

Women may experience sometimes insuperable difficulties in organising themselves into trade unions, but this did not mean they took no industrial action. Such industrial action that they did take forced the attention of the trade union movement onto the problems of women workers.

The second factor, the controversy which existed within the women's organisations regarding women's status and rights as workers, brought the complicated nature of these questions to male trade unionists' attention - both within individual unions and at the TUC Annual Congress. The leadership of the TUC could no longer dismiss the rights of women to work for there, right under their noses, on the Congress floor each year, a fierce debate raged over how existing and future legislation and employers' practices affected women workers.

The middle-class women's organisations such as the Women's Trade Union League (see Chapter 5) tended to take the attitude that ideally women should not go out to work but that since for various social and economic reasons a large number of women had no choice, it was necessary for women to build the same protection for themselves as skilled male workers had, by organising themselves into trade unions. This attitude was summed up by Miss Emily Routledge when she spoke at a meeting held by the WTUL at the 1891 TUC, entitled "How trades unionism raises the social as well as the industrial position of women".   She was reported as saying that

> "the question of the employment of women and their industrial
> organisation bore upon the well-being of their husbands, their
> children and their homes.   They were often met with the remark
> that women were best in their own homes.   They believed that
> too;  but unfortunately, there were women who were not able to
> remain in their own homes and who were compelled to work".[45]

When it came to the question of legislation protecting women workers from
undue exploitation however, there was a division of opinion amongst both
middle-class and working-class women.   While many men supported trades
unionism amongst women and protective legislation in the hope that by
restricting female labour and raising women's wages, women could no longer
be used to displace men, many women workers feared this would result in
fewer jobs and clung to what they saw as their right to work for
starvation wages.   The arguments tended to get thoroughly confused for
the women who feared for their jobs put the same case as those politicians
and economists who, from a laissez-faire perspective, were against trades
unionism and any form of legislative protection for workers.   Some of
the women's organisations which campaigned for better wages and working
conditions for women workers were regarded with suspicion by women
anxious to hold onto their meagre earning power.   They had the support
of some middle-class women's organisations such as the Women's
Emancipation Union which in 1896 published a pamphlet opposing factory
legislation, declaring that

> "... any law which places full grown women in the position of
> a helpless, thoughtless, irresponsible child, who must be
> legislated for, has the effect of creating and fostering an
> opinion that women are helpless, irresponsible beings, in-
> capable of taking care of their own interests - an opinion
> which, untrue though it be in the present day, is yet so deeply
> rooted that it forms the chief hindrance to the emancipation of
> women".[46]

On the other hand, the WTUL, which by the 1890s, supported protective
legislation, pressed the TUC to agitate for the appointment of women
Factory Inspectors and for a more effective enforcement of factory
and workshop regulations.   Male trade unionists were in fact
quite eager to enforce and extend the Factory Acts and this
eagerness continued to be a source of much suspicion and bitterness
amongst some women trade unionists who were more concerned about their
rights as workers being eroded.   For example, when a new Factory Bill
was introduced in 1894 giving the Home Secretary the power to designate
a particular trade as "dangerous" and excluding women from working within
it, the delegate to the TUC from the Society of Women Employed in Book-

binding (Miss Whyte) objected very strongly.   She argued:

> "Let Parliament decide for women as it does for men.   At the
> present time women are treated like children;   indeed women
> and children are always associated in Acts of Parliament".[47]

The contradictions in the position of some women trade unionists were
revealed by the rest of her speech.   She objected to any restrictions
on women's hours of work and to the TUC's insistence that women should
be paid the same as men.   In these circumstances, she argued, men would
be preferred by employers and women would find themselves out of work:

> "... women had a perfect right to work if they could and hard
> work and even risky work was better than starvation".[48]

Debates such as this, and in particular the activity of the WTUL, meant
that the TUC could not ignore the question of women's work and wages,
nor dismiss the problems of cheap female labour by merely recommending
a prohibition on women working.   Women workers posed a problem for male
trade unionists concerned to improve the wages and conditions of their
members.   By the beginning of this century, it was obvious that that
problem was not going to go away.

### III

Against this background of divisions amongst workers in the sweated
trades and of the attitude of trade unionists to women workers, we will
now consider what solutions trade unionists offered to the problems of
sweating.

The main pressure that trade unionists put on government in relation to
sweated labour was in the areas of factory and public health legislation,
"alien immigration" and government contracts.   While women's organisations
played a decisive part in the campaign for a minimum wage for sweated
workers, the male dominated trade unions and the TUC played little part.

The TUC leadership at the end of the nineteenth century tended to view
proposals for legislation which would affect the adult working man's
conditions of work with a great deal of suspicion;   in contrast they
pressed for protective legislation for women workers.   As we saw in
Chapter 3, the trade unions had been very successful where they were well
organised in negotiating shorter hours and any attempt to bring the hours
of adult male labour under legislative control was strongly resisted by
many on the grounds that the workers would be better off if it was left
to the trade unions to negotiate with employers.[49]   The rather special

case of the miners[50], for whom an Eight Hours Act was passed in 1908, caused a lot of controversy, the main argument being over whether those miners who had managed to negotiate a seven-hour day would have their working hours increased as a result of eight-hour legislation.

When it came to legislation affecting women workers, however, the TUC was very much in favour of restrictions on the hours, conditions and extent of female labour.    From the 1830s, the trade union movement had looked to legislation rather than organisation to deal with the long hours and poor working conditions which many women workers had suffered[51]. Even the leaders of the new general unions who were more sympathetic to the organisation of women workers and whose unions admitted women into membership, tended, when faced with the difficulties of organising women, to conclude that legislation was the only answer[52].

Perhaps because of this enthusiasm for protective legislation for women workers, the TUC in the 1880s and 1890s placed more stress on the enforce-ment and extension of the Factory and Workshops Act than on anything more innovative.    Its Parliamentary Committee urged the House of Lords Select Committee on Sweating to adopt the TUC's recommendations of making a large increase to the staff of the Factory Inspectorate[53] and the President's address that year recommended amendments to factory legis-lation which it was thought would be adequate to deal with sweated trades, for example the repeal of a clause which prevented Factory Inspectors entering homeworkers' premises.    In 1889, a motion was adopted by the TUC which stated

> "This Congress is of the opinion that the present evils of
> the 'sweating system' have been brought about mainly by the
> inadequate way the Factory and Workshop Act has been
> administered"

and went on to urge the Government to appoint working men and women as Factory Inspectors[54].

The 1890 Congress accepted a motion from Lewis Lyons (delegate from the Tailors' Machinists and Pressers' Union) calling for the registration of Factories and workshops and for the inspection of factories and work-shops within six days of registration[55].   The Factory Inspectorate at that time (as before and since) was understaffed.   The Government, however, continued to reject proposals to increase their numbers, although the TUC was successful in getting working men and women appointed as Factory Inspectors.   Congress also called again and again for the full inclusion of laundries and domestic workshops under factory legislation, for example the motion so moved by James MacDonald of the Amalgamated Society of Tailors at the 1891 Congress.

The tailors' unions were in the front of the fight for more effective factory legislation. They were particularly concerned about the unrestricted and unrestrained competition amongst outworkers and were bitterly disappointed that the section of the 1895 Factory and Workshop Act dealing with outworkers was so weak. Under this Act, the giver-out of work was made responsible for the conditions under which his work was done, but the legislation was permissive and trades were only covered if specified by an order of the Home Secretary. Enforcement was difficult: the Inspector could give notice that work was being done in a place injurious to the health of the people employed and if after a month the work continued, the employer was liable to a fine of £10. The fundamental vulnerability of the position of the outworker is revealed in James MacDonald's objection to the 1895 Act. As Secretary of the Amalgamated Society of Tailors, he pointed out that

> "all a giver-out has to do under this Section of the Act is to go on sending his work to the place which has been condemned as insanitary for a month after receiving notice, and then transfer it to another place equally insanitary. There is no obligation on the giver-out to improve the condition of the place to which he is sending the work. The only sufferer is the outworker who must leave or lose his work".[56]

The AST put three amendments at the Committee stage of the Bill which attempted to make it more difficult for outwork to be done in insanitary premises. The strongest amendment was that advocating a licensing arrangement by which all workshops, including domestic workshops, must be licensed (on sanitary criteria). The amendments were defeated.

The TUC and particular trade unions such as those in the tailoring trade hoped to alleviate the problem of sweating by calling on Parliament to tighten up the restrictions on working conditions and to introduce new restrictions on homeworking. Trade unionists generally seem to have felt that homework in particular should cease to exist altogether. The 1888 Congress unanimously called on the government to implement the clause in its contracts which stated that none of the work must be done in the home of the worker. The same Congress also passed a resolution calling for licensing of homework which would mean that no work could be done in a dwelling-house unless a licence had been granted.

There was also widespread support in the late 1880s in the TUC for

restrictions on "alien immigration" as it was felt that by decreasing
the number of unskilled Jewish workers coming into the country, the
intense competition amongst workers in the sweated trades would be
eased.    These Jewish immigrants were considered to be a threat to
levels of wages, working conditions and employment.    The following
motion was proposed at the 1888 TUC Annual Congress by the delegate
from the Scottish National Operative Tailors Trade Protection and
Benefit Society and seconded by Keir Hardie who felt it didn't go far
enough:

> "That such an amendment upon the laws affecting immigration
> shall be made as will prevent indigent persons or paupers
> being landed in this country unless they can show that they
> are skilled workers or capable in some form of earning their
> living by manual labour at the date of their arrival".[57]

The motion was carried unanimously.

Apart from these attempts at persuading Parliament to pass legislation
which it felt would ease the situation of sweated labour, the trade
unions put forward two other solutions;   these solutions were based on
political and trade union action rather than parliamentary action.    One
was an attempt to combat the system of sub-contracting and the associated
payment of below-standard rates of wages;   the other was an attempt to
organise women workers and to fight for higher wages for women workers.

Most trade unionists insisted on a causal connection between subcon-
tracting to outworkers and the payment of very low wages.    Some outworkers attempted to get taken on as indoor workers.    For example, in
the London boot and shoe trade demands were made from the late 1880s for
the abolition of the sweating system and a resolution was passed by the
London Metropolitan Branch of the National Union of Boot and Shoe
Operatives in 1889 calling for all lasters and finishers to be brought
"indoors" and the manufacturers were given six months to provide workshops for them.    The outworkers failed in their demand but by 1894,
Northampton employers had agreed to abolish outwork and other major
centres of footwear manufacture soon followed[58].    Outworkers in the
clothing trade also demanded to be brought "indoors" but with little
success for, unlike boot and shoe manufacturing, mechanisation did not
make large-scale factory production inevitable[59].

The TUC urged the Government to discourage sweated labour on the work
generated by Government departments by prohibiting the sub-contracting
of work[60].    Harry Quelch, a dockers' representative, moved in 1890

that direct labour was the only solution since sweating was inseparable
from contract work[61].

The issues of direct labour and of municipal contracts were also taken
up by trade unionists at the level of local government.  In 1888, the
London Society of Compositors put up a candidate (A.G. Cook) for the
London School Board with the intention of getting the Board to impose
trade union rates on its contractors.  His successful candidacy and that
of others with him resulted in a public body imposing trade union rates
for the first time[62].  From the 1888 municipal elections onwards, there
was an increase in the number of trade unionists on municipal bodies.
In 1891, the London Trades Council called upon its affiliated bodies to
participate in the vestry elections either by putting forward trade
union candidates or by supporting those who were in favour of trade
union wages and hours[63].  In 1892, the "Labour bench" on the London
County Council adopted the following programme - eight hour day, labour
exchanges, free school meals, trade union rates and conditions to be
imposed on contractors[64].

The policy of imposing trade union rates on contractors was adopted by
many municipal bodies in the 1890s and in 1891, the House of Commons
passed a Fair Wages Resolution.  This Resolution was, however, rather
vague, stating merely that every effort should be made "to secure the
payment of such wages as are generally accepted as current in each trade
for competent workmen".  Investigations into government contracts
showed that firms receiving such contracts frequently paid very low
wages and indeed investigations revealed the low wages paid at the
government's own clothing factory in Pimlico.  Trade unionists often
found it difficult to keep track of municipal contracts when the contract
did not go to a local firm.  For example, the Nottingham branch of the
AST claimed that, although the local firm receiving the contract for
police clothing had been forced to pay standard rates, when in 1897 the
contract was given to a Bristol firm, below standard rates were paid[65].

The other solution to the problem of sweating which was put forward by
trade unionists was the organisation of women workers and the negotiation
of higher wages for them.  For the various reasons discussed above, by
the end of the nineteenth century trade unions had come round to recognising that if women workers were not to be a never-ending source of
cheap labour, they must be organised.  Having recognised this, however,
their support for women as trade unionists was usually half-hearted, as

is illustrated by the tendency to only allow them second-class membership. Male trade unionists' support of equal pay for women was prompted by self-interest and many women were justified in viewing with suspicion and mistrust their attempts to negotiate higher wages for women, for they were often motivated by a desire to restrict women's employment. An example is the attempt by the Oldham Amalgamated Society of Tailors to negotiate an equal wage for men and women which was accompanied by a demand that the proportion of male to female workers should be fixed[66].

One further solution to sweating was tried but had no real chance of success. The TUC formally supported a scheme for "trade union labels" to be put inside garments and other goods that were made by trade union (and by implication, non-sweated) labour. The idea was that the public - and especially other trade unionists - should not buy goods which did not have a trade union label. For example, the Federated Conciliation Board of London Tailors suggested in 1907 that a trade union label should be sewn into garments produced under conditions approved by the Board. This idea had the approval of the Anti-Sweating League[67]. The problem was that such a scheme was almost impossible to enforce, relying as it did on public opinion boycotting goods sold without a trade union label. A Consumers Association tried to promote the idea but without success[68].


                                    IV

These then were the solutions put forward by the organised trade union movement to the problem of sweating. The main proposals fell into two categories: one, pressure for parliamentary action in the form of (a) legislation further restricting women's hours and working conditions and restricting homework and (b) immigration controls; the second, industrial and political action in an attempt to (a) restrict sub-contracting and raise wages, and (b) to organise women workers. The trade unions did not initiate a demand for a statutory minimum wage for sweated workers and although they supported the demand for Wages Boards when it was made by the Anti-Sweating League, their support was only in response to pressure from, in particular, Mary MacArthur of the NFWW[69]. The impression is that left to themselves the trade union movement would have failed to mount a major campaign for legislation on low wages and would have restricted themselves to support for the solutions discussed above. Later, in Chapter 9, we will analyse in more detail the reasons for the trade unions' lack of initiative on sweating.

References - Chapter 4

1.   TUC, Annual Congress, 1888, p.13.

2.   E. Hobsbawn:  Labouring Men (1964), p.275.
     See also H.A. Clegg, A. Fox and A.F. Thompson, "A History of
     British Trade Unions Since 1889" Vol.1 (1964).
     H. Pelling, "A History of British Trade Unionism" (1963).

3.   See R. Beer, "Matchgirls Strike 1888" (National Museum of Labour
     History Pamphlet no.2 (n.d.).

4.   See Webb Trade Union Collection, Section 4, Vol.47 for this and
     other examples.

5.   B. Drake, "The West End Tailoring Trade" in "Seasonal Trades" ed.
     by S. Webb and A. Freeman (1912), p.75.

6.   F. Galton "The Tailoring Trade" (1923).

7.   The "log" system was based on the designation of a certain amount
     of time taken to make a garment.  Negotiations therefore took
     place, not only on the payment per hour, but on how much time was
     allowed for the making of a particular garment.

8.   M. Stewart and L. Hunter, "The Needle is Threaded - A History of
     the Clothing Industry" (1964).

8a.  Stewart and Hunter (1964), p.91.

9.   B.L. Hutchins, "Women in Modern Industry", (1915), p.122.

10.  Leeds Trades Council Annual Report, 1887.

11.  "Conference for the Abolition of the Middleman Sweater" 1891.

12.  Ibid., p.7.

13.  Stewart and Hunter (1964), p.116.

14.  See Leeds Trades Council Annual Reports.

15.  B. Drake, "Women in the Engineering Trades" (1917).

16.  Ibid., p.11.

17.  Ibid., p.12.

18.  TUC Annual Congress, 1908, 1909, and see below, pp.120-121.

19.  S. Boston, "Women of the Trade Unions" (1980), p.66.

20.  J. Hinton, "The First Shop Stewards' Movement" (1973), p.56.

21.  See also Boston (1980), p.88.

22.  S. Rowbotham and J. Weeks, "Socialism and the New Life" (1977), p.71.

23.	Report of the National Conference on Sweated Industries, 11 and 12 October 1907, held in Glasgow under the auspices of the Scottish Council for Women's Trades;  Women's Trade Union Review, April 1905.

23a.	Royal Commission on Labour, Digest of the evidence taken before Group C of the Royal Commission, Vol.II.  PP1892, XXXVI (Cd.6785-III), p.31.

24.	Report of the Select Committee on Homework, PP1908, VIII (Cd.246) p.109.

25.	TUC Annual Congress Report, 1888.

26.	TUC Annual Congress Report, 1891, p.57.

27.	TUC Annual Congress Report, 1908 and 1909.

28.	TUC Annual Congress Report, 1897.

29.	Quoted in B. Drake, "Women in Trade Unions", (1920), p.14.

30.	House of Lords Select Committee on Sweating, Fourth Report;  with the proceedings of the Committee, Minutes of Evidence ... PP1889, XIV Pt I (Cd.331), Q32174.

31.	Journal of the Amalgamated Society of Tailors, Vol.I, No.I, April 1898, p.16.

32.	Webbs Trade Union Collection, Section A, Vol.47, Item 11.

33.	TUC Annual Congress Report, 1891, p.33.

34.	TUC Annual Congress Report, 1892, p.28.

35.	Ibid., p.28.

36.	"London Trades Council:  A History", (1950), p.74.

37.	Quoted by Boston (1980), p.56.

38.	Webb Trade Union Collection, Item 42.  Letter from W. Thorne dated 30.3.1914.

39.	Ibid.

40.	S. Rowbotham, "Hidden From History" (1973), see especially Chapter 12.

41.	A. Fox, "A History of the National Union of Boot and Shoe Operatives, 1897-1957", pp.309-311.  (Oxford, 1958).

42.	Webb Trade Union Collection, Royal Commission on Labour, reports of various Trades Councils, etc.

43.	Webb Trade Union Collection, Section A, Vol.47.

44.	Ibid., Item 63.

45.	TUC Annual Congress Report, 1891, p.33.

46.	Jane E. Brownlow, "Women and Factory Legislation", paper read at a

London Conference, 14 October 1896 - published by the Women's Emancipation Union, p.6.

47.   TUC Annual Congress Report, 1894, p.56.

48.   Ibid., p.56.

49.   Eight hours legislation had been supported by the 1890 TUC under pressure from the eight hours movement (initiated by socialist trade unionists) as a remedy for unemployment.   When it became clear that, in manufacturing industries at least, productivity was not reduced by a shortening of the working day and that more jobs were not therefore created, the mainstream trade unionists lost enthusiasm for such legislation although socialists continued to urge for shorter hours as an improvement in working conditions. J. Harris, "Unemployment and Politics" (1972), pp.58-73.

50.   See Pelling, (1971), pp.106 and 134.

51.   Boston (1980), p.27.

52.   Ibid., p.56.

53.   TUC Annual Congress Report, 1888, p.12.

54.   TUC Annual Congress Report, 1889.

55.   TUC Annual Congress Report, 1890, p.53.

56.   G. Tuckwell, "Women's Work and Factory Legislation:  the Amending Act of 1895", (1895), p.14.

57.   TUC Annual Congress, 1888.

58.   Alan Fox, "A History of the National Union of Boot and Shoe Operatives, 1874-1957" (1958), Chapter 12.

59.   See Chapter 2.

60.   TUC Annual Congress, 1888, p.39.

61.   TUC Annual Congress, 1890, pp.43-44.

62.   London Society of Compositors, Annual Report, 1889.

63.   London Trades Council, A History, p.78.

64.   P. Thompson, "Radicals, Liberals and Labour in London, 1880-1900" in Past and Present, 27, (1964), p.88.

65.   Journal of the AST, Vol.I, No.3, June 1898, p.42.

66.   TUC Annual Congress Report, 1901, pp.55-57.

67.   Jewish Chronicle, 3.5.07.

68.   C. Black, "The Consumers' League" (1887).

69.   TUC Congress Report, 1907.

# 5  Women's organisations and sweated labour

The problem of sweated labour was essentially a problem affecting women workers.  Organised labour recognised that sweating was a threat to their interest but did not take a very aggressive approach to improving the conditions of the largest group of sweated workers, namely women. As we have seen, the trade union movement, although supporting trade unionism amongst women workers, did so for rather confused reasons.  The representation of women's interests through the trade union movement was of course hampered by the fact that the extent of trade union organisation amongst all women workers, except the textile workers, remained very limited at the end of the nineteenth century.  Only 123,195 women out of a total of 4,171,751 women workers were in a trade union in 1901[1].

In this situation a number of middle-class women's organisations who attempted to recruit women into trade unions and who also put themselves forward as representing the interests of women workers were an important factor in the building up of pressure to tackle the problem of sweated labour.  This chapter first examines briefly the difficulties that women had in organising and then goes on to discuss the three most prominent middle-class women's organisations who played an important part in bringing about legislative action on low wages.

II

The, as yet, inadequately documented, history of women's trade unionism indicates that in many cases it was often not for want of trying that women remained unorganised and low-paid workers.  Particularly spectacular strikes such as that of the match girls in 1888 are fairly well documented[2].  But all over the country women workers at the end of the nineteenth century and the beginning of the twentieth century were taking action against their working conditions.  This action was very often spontaneous and organisation came only after they had commenced a strike; as such it was extremely disruptive to the employer but was usually doomed to failure.  There are records of quite impressive solidarity between different groups of workers;  for example, £43 was collected by box-makers in Bethnal Green (most of whose wages would have been below 10/- per week) and given to the striking women at Bryant and Mays in July 1888; the boxmakers were women homeworkers who were thrown out of work by the strike[3].

The increasing popularity of "women's history" helps to dispel the myth that women workers very rarely took collective industrial action. We only have to look at local newspapers of the time, which were full of reports of women in many different trades taking action against their working conditions. Many of their strikes attracted a lot of public sympathy and anger against unscrupulous employers. Research by Sheila Rowbotham[4], Sheila Lewenak[5] and Sarah Boston[6] has brought to light some of these events; there is also an increasing amount of local history research being done which goes some way to documenting the history of collective action taken by women workers[7]. However, it remained the case that women, for a variety of reasons, found it difficult to organise and that even when they were well organised, it proved difficult to raise their wages above subsistence level; for example, the Female Cigar Makers Protective Union had a membership in Leicester of 380 out of 500 workers but wages stuck at 14/- per week, high for a woman's wage, but still below that needed to support herself or a family[8]. The similarly well-organised Upholstress Union in Liverpool could not achieve more than a rise from 10/- per week to 12/- per week[9].

As was indicated in the previous Chapter, women faced the barrier of the often hostile attitudes of male trade unionists and the reluctance of well-established trade unions to admit women to membership or at least to full membership.

It is also the case that the majority of women workers were in trades and working situations in which any worker, male or female, would experience difficulty in organising. 30% of women workers were employed as indoor domestic servants in 1901 and their vulnerability and isolation made trade union organisation almost impossible; there is evidence of a London and Provincial Domestic Servants Union in 1896 which was very feebly supported[10] and in 1910 a Domestic Workers' Union of Great Britain was formed but it only had 191 members[11]. Women who were employed as homeworkers were unlikely to be organised as discussed in Chapter 4 (p.119). Furthermore, many women worked part-time (e.g. as charwomen) or were engaged in seasonal work, such as in the food and allied trades and in the clothing trades. The working situations of all these types of workers, together with the accompanying low wages, were not conducive, to say the least, in trade union organisation.

An enquiry conducted by the Women's Trade Union League in 1900 into the problems of organising women found four main reasons for women's lack of trade union organisation[12].

1.   Women were primarily low-waged workers and suffered all the handicaps that such workers come up against when trying to organise.

2.   Whereas  men were free after their day's work, women had domestic duties and thus would find it particularly difficult to attend meetings.

3.   There was a continuing antagonism on the part of men workers as they regarded women workers as cheap and "blackleg" labour.

4.   As Isabella Ford (then Secretary of the Leeds Society of Work-women) put it:

     "Trade unionism means rebellion and the orthodox teaching for women is submission ... society encourages selfish indifference amongst women, in that it considers a woman's home must make her sacrifice to it everyone else's home and all public honour"[13].

The second reason found by the WTUL for women's difficulty in organising, namely the problems of attending meetings on top of waged work and domestic work must not be underestimated.  The following description of a woman jam-maker's working day was not an uncommon experience and illustrates the additional handicap that almost all married women workers faced as a result of the sexual division of labour inside the home:

     "I rise at 4.45, sweep the place a bit and get my husband his breakfast.  He must be off before six.  Then I wake and wash the children, give them each a slice of bread and butter and the remains of the tea and leave out the oats and sugar for Harry to prepare for the rest later on [Harry is ten years old]. I then open up the beds and take the baby to Mrs. T.  My own work begins at 7 a.m.  At 8.30 the firm sends us round a mug of tea and I eat the bread and butter I have brought with me. I used to come home in the dinner hour, but my feet are now so bad that I get a halfpenny cup of coffee in a shop and eat the rest of what I have brought.  At 4.30 I have another cup of tea and get home a little before 7 p.m.  I do the hearth up, get my husband his supper, and make the beds.  Then I get out the mending and am usually in bed by 11.  On Saturday, I leave work at noon so as to take the washing to the baths"[14].

The male-dominated trade unions had their middle-class supporters and sponsors but the organisation of women workers in the late nineteenth century probably owed even more to the activities of non-working women and men. The difficulties that working-class women experienced in organising themselves left them particularly vulnerable to the imposition of ideas and methods of organisation by well-intentioned middle-class men and women. The result was a number of women's organisations, middle-class in origin although often employing working-class women organisers, which encouraged unionisation amongst women, helped in local struggles, and also campaigned on broader issues. Many of these organisations remained of very local influence, an example being the Manchester, Salford and District Women's Trade Union Council, but three, the Women's Trade Union League, the National Federation of Women Workers and the Women's Industrial Council, played a more important part in the development of a public awareness of sweated labour and in the debate on what measures were required to deal with the problem.


III

## The Women Trade Union League (WTUL) and the National Federation of Women Workers (NFWW)

The forerunner of the WTUL, the Women's Protective and Provident League (WPPL) was set up in 1874. Its leadership was dominated by middle-class men and women and their primary aim was

> "to acquire information which will enable friends of the working class to give a more precise direction than at present to their offers of sympathy and help".[15]

The WPPL disclaimed "any views of antagonism towards the employers of female labour as a class" and dismissed strikes as "rash and mistaken action". Wages and conditions of work, they said, should only be changed where

> "terms appear unreasonable and unjust to the dispassionate third party, the consumer ... [who] is certainly not interested in adding artificially to ... cost".[16]

Separate women's societies were formed and emphasis was placed on their provident function - the provision of various benefits, in particular sickness benefit[17].


The League opposed protective legislation on the grounds that this interfered with women's right to work and that

> "the way to improvement was not through paternalistic state action, but through the building up of trade unions strong enough to negotiate agreements with employers".[18]

B.L. Hutchins comments that the secretary of the WPPL, Emma Paterson, was influenced by

> "the narrow individualism characteristic of what may be
> designated as the Right wing of the Women's Rights
> Movement".[19]

It is true that the emphasis on a woman's right to work, to the detriment
of demands for an improvement in working conditions, was at that time
more appropriate to middle-class women who wished to be accepted into
the various professions than it was to the factory, workshop or homeworker.   It is also the case, however, that women were right to be
suspicious of men's eagerness for protective legislation for women workers,
as discussed in Chapter 4.

The League had a very limited success in organising women workers.   During
the time of Emma Patterson's leadership of the WPPL, something like thirty
or forty women's unions were established but most of them were very small
and few survived for long[20].   One historian of women's trade unionism
estimated that in 1886 the combined membership of these women's societies
was about 2,500 compared to the 30,000 women who were members of the
cotton trade unions[21].

The middle-class nature of the organisation never changed.   After Emma
Paterson's death in 1886, and throughout our period, it was dominated,
first, by Lady Dilke (wife of the Liberal MP, Sir Charles Dilke) and
then by her niece, Gertrude Tuckwell.   Three major changes did take
place, however.   At the 1886 Conference a motion was adopted which laid
down that

> "the best way to extend the work of the League is to lay
> stress on its Protective-Trade Union element, as distinct
> from the Provident element;  and further for the League to
> use its influence to support such action of an economic
> description as will tend to bring about a better distribution
> of wealth".[22]

This motion was opposed by a number of people who argued that the League

> "carried on its propagandist work by means of outside sub-
> scriptions given by well-to-do people.   If this resolution
> were carried many of these people would withdraw their support".[23]

However, it was accepted  by the majority that the League's attitude to
industrial action should change and in subsequent years the organisation
was generally sympathetic to strike action and indeed often gave a lot of
help to women workers who had come out on strike but were not in a union.
In that same year, 1886, the League changed its name to the Women's Trade
Union League.

The second change was that in 1889 the WTUL became a federation of trade unions admitting women members and instead of attempting to set up separate women's trade unions, placed more emphasis on urging men's unions to open their doors to women workers. In return for affiliation the WTUL supplied male-dominated unions with the services of a woman organiser, the aim being to recruit women into these unions. The promotion of separate organisation on the part of women was considerably decreased therefore, particularly as, when the WTUL responded to spontaneous industrial action by women workers, they had no funds on which to draw and relied on raising public donations and attempted to recruit the women into the appropriate union which was of course usually run by men.

The third shift in the WTUL's policy was the acceptance of the need for protective legislation for women workers and a greater concentration on campaigning for legislative reform than on organising women workers. During the 1890s and 1900s the WTUL campaigned vigorously for the extension of the Factory Acts. For example, Lady Dilke started a campaign to get the hours of laundry workers reduced; a campaign was launched to limit women and young persons' work in the potteries, where lead poisoning was a hazard; there were (unsuccessful) attempts to lengthen the four-week period after childbirth established in 1891 as the period during which a mother should not return to work.

This support of legislation to improve the conditions of women workers was partly a reaction to the difficulties of organising women workers. It was felt that legislation was necessary to bring about improvements which could not be won through negotiations between employer and trade union. The leadership of the WTUL also felt that an extension of protective legislation would make organisation amongst women workers easier[24]. It is however also the case that a strong motivation behind the demand for an extension of the Factory Acts was a set of firmly-held views on the duties and obligations of working-class mothers and the relationship of motherhood to work outside the home. The League deplored the way that many working-class mothers of young children were engaged in waged work although at the same time they recognised the necessity of this employment in order for many families to avoid destitution. Lady Dilke proclaimed that women's place was "at the hearth"[25], and there is no doubting the opposition of Gertrude Tuckwell (Secretary and later President of the WTUL) to mothers engaging in waged work. In a book published in 1894 she advocated

> "the gradual extension of labour protection to the point where mothers will be prohibited from working until their children have reached an age at which they can care for themselves".[26]

Her motivation for state intervention was clear -

> "The state should see fit to intervene more fully between the
> claims of the little ones and the demands of labour, to inter-
> fere for the protection of family life and to restore the
> children to their homes".[27]

This willingness of the WTUL leadership to consider the exclusion of at
least mothers from waged work and their campaigning for protective legislation for women workers generally, brought them into conflict with some
of the women who had first been organised by the WTUL.    Miss Whyte, for
example, the delegate to the TUC for many years from The Society of
Women Employed in Bookbinding (an organisation initially established by
Emma Paterson and the WPPL) vigorously opposed the attempts to exclude
women from trades designated as "dangerous", and also any suggestion
that the four-week ruling should be extended;  both of these being
demands for which the WTUL was campaigning during the 1890s.    The WTUL
had the best of intentions when making such demands but one can see Miss
Whyte's point when, in arguing against a proposal at the 1897 TUC that
women should not be employed for six months after childbirth, she said
that

> "before passing this resolution they should pass a resolution
> declaring that no man should marry unless he was able to support
> a wife.   She did not believe any woman should go to working in
> the mill unless she was obliged to".[28]

Although the WTUL became more sympathetic to strike action its leadership
was very wary of more radical political influences.    Lady Dilke wished
to prevent the organisation being involved in militant rank and file
activity and to this end she wrote to Henry Broadhurst, President of the
TUC, and who was himself resisting pressure from radical trade unionists
in the TUC, urging him to be on the WTUL's Executive Committee.    They
obviously had some common political concerns as they were both members
of the Liberal Party.    She wrote saying,

> "Personally, I should be extremely grieved to see the (WTUL)
> used for other than pure trade union purposes and I should
> feel that your presence would not only be a tower of strength
> to our party but also an act of the greatest kindness to myself".[29]

During the 1890s, the leadership of the WTUL took an increasing interest
in the problem of sweated workers.    The demand for legislation to raise
the wages of such workers seemed to grow naturally out of the demand for
legislation to deal with the conditions under which women worked.   It was
first supported in Parliament by Lady Dilke's husband, an influential
back-bench Liberal MP.    Sir Charles Dilke was said to have had his

attention first brought to the idea of minimum wage by John Stuart Mill, who apparently came round to supporting such a measure in the last years of his life[30]. Be that as it may, it was his close association with the WTUL which maintained and strengthened his interest in legislation to raise wages. Like the rest of the organisation he stressed the political significance of low wages -

> "he held the stability of the State itself to be menaced by the existence of an unorganised and depressed body of workers".[31]

He often quoted Mill's contention that sweated wages depressed all wages and there is some evidence that he would have liked to see a universal statutory minimum wage[32].

Many women - including, one suspects, Mary MacArthur who became secretary of the WTUL in 1903 - looked on the demand for minimum wage legislation as a recognition of women's right to work. This was not, however, an accurate reflection of the motivations of those such as Gertrude Tuckwell, Sir Charles and Lady Dilke. Their motivation for supporting a minimum wage for sweated workers arose from two assumptions: (1) that such legislation would raise the wages of male workers and thus make it unnecessary for their wives to engage in waged work; (2) that many sweated workers, in particular homeworkers, were "inefficient", would not be able to earn a minimum wage and would therefore be shaken out of the labour market by minimum wage legislation. "Inefficient" workers were said to be those who, owing to personal circumstances, were unlikely to be productive enough to earn an adequate wage. The type of personal circumstances talked of ranged from the worker who was "inefficient" through age or ill health to the homeworker who was supplementing a man's wage, was willing to work for a below-subsistence wage and who thus dragged down the level of wages paid to the detriment of the homeworker who was entirely reliant on her own earnings. Gertrude Tuckwell complained that, together with the supplementing of such wages by poor relief, charity or "the poor's help of the poor", this resulted in the perpetuation

> "of a system by which sickly, anaemic workers are rearing a still feebler generation, whose fight for work must be appreciably weaker, who soon inevitably swell the ranks of the unemployable and disappear into the abyss".[33]

"Inefficient" workers and married women workers would, it was thought, be shaken out of the labour market by minimum wage legislation. Married women, it was claimed, would particularly benefit from any raising of

men's wages as this would diminish their need to work. This view was
not only held by the WTUL but by other middle-class women's organisations
such as the National Union of Women's Suffrage Societies who argued that
a living wage for men would prevent pregnant women and mothers from
working[34]. Clementina Black, at one time Secretary of the WTUL, argued
that women's waged work did not have a detrimental effect on children and
family life, yet she also put the case to the Select Committee on Homework that a decent minimum wage for men would mean that wives would not
have to work at least while their children were young[35].

The WTUL was particularly concerned about the effect of homeworking on
children and thus the future generation of workers. The destitution
which often accompanied homeworking was illustrated by a press report in
1907, which Gertrude Tuckwell cut out and kept, of a tailor's presser
driven by lack of work to do homework and charged for begging with his
two young children:

> "Mr. Wills, the London County Council officer, said the
> defendent and his wife formerly lived and worked off the
> Mile End Road. They were exceedingly poor, and the wife
> was about to be attended from the London Hospital, and what
> would become of the children then, unless the authorities
> looked after them, he did not know. To provide food for the
> children, the parents had been known to sit up half the night
> finishing trousers, for which they were paid the handsome rate
> of 1¾d. per pair. They had then drifted to the slums of
> Spitalfields and had had to beg".[37]

Publications such as a book entitled "Baby Toilers" published in 1907[38]
decried the way in which children helped their homeworking mothers,
particular attention being drawn to the employment of children to assist
homeworkers in the Birmingham hook and eye carding trade and in the
Nottingham lace trade[39].

In the early 1900s, the WTUL took on a new lease of life, particularly
helped by its new Secretary, Mary MacArthur. More trade unions became
affiliated and these totalled sixty by the end of 1905. Mary MacArthur
enthusiastically set out to recruit women into trade unions but she found
that, although she had little difficulty in joining them up, it was an
uphill struggle to keep them in a union if their initial interest did not
bring forth immediate results in terms of better pay and conditions[40].
It was a vicious circle, she concluded,

> "Women are badly paid and badly treated because they are not
> organised and they are not organised because they are badly
> paid and badly treated".[41]

Faced with these difficulties in organising women, the leadership of the WTUL continued to emphasise the need for legislative reform to improve the conditions of women workers. However, the organisation was also subject to pressure from women workers themselves to put more resources into organising women into trade unions. The WTUL was often called upon to help women who had already taken a decision on industrial action but were not in a union. When Mary MacArthur, appointed Secretary of the WTUL in 1903, was asked for help in 1906 by Edinburgh paper bag-makers who came out on strike against a wage cut, she responded by forming a new general union for women workers, the National Federation of Women Workers[42]. The Edinburgh workers formed the first branch and other branches were set up in different parts of the country. By 1908, the membership totalled 3,000. However, while the NFWW was able to respond more immediately to spontaneous action on the part of women workers in that the organisation built up a strike fund, the rules were that all NFWW members must also join the appropriate TUC affiliated union if there was one[43]. The WTUL's preference for recruiting women into the already existing male-dominated trade unions remained the guiding principle of the new organisation.

However, Mary MacArthur did have a more radical approach to the question of women's work and wages; she was more inclined to emphasise the right of women to work rather than deplore the effects of mothers working. In response to the continued attempts by the brassworkers' union to exclude women workers from certain sections of their trade, she retorted

> "Man has never objected to women working. She has borne her share of the world's burden since history began. It is her wage-earning which distresses the masculine mind".[44]

The NFWW concentrated on the question of women's low wages and followed the WTUL in pressing for minimum wage legislation for sweated workers. Although a consideration of the two organisations as separate organisations is in many senses a false distinction (Mary MacArthur and Gertrude Tuckwell were Secretary and President respectively of both) the NFWW lobbied as a separate organisation, basing its credibility on its browing membership of unskilled women workers. Mary MacArthur went into the drawing rooms of upper and middle-class women and stirred them to indignation over the conditions of their working-class sisters, and in particular over the conditions suffered by children. For instance, she told them

> "how in the slums of Birmingham, babies of five, four and even three years old were to be found toiling far into the night at

the linking of hooks and eyes; she told them of the girls who
earned 2d. an hour in London for exquisite needlework on babies'
clothes; of the East End workers who got 6d. or 8d. for blouses
displayed at 25s to 30s in the windows of West End shops".[45]

Mary MacArthur had a profound impact on the Select Committee on Homework
when she told them that the average wage for all women workers was just
7/- per week and she was able, through her organising work with the NFWW,
to bring a number of homeworkers to give evidence in person to the
Select Committee.    She also used the organisational base of the NFWW
in her involvement in the Anti-Sweating League.    The role of the ASL
is discussed in Chapter 8 when we examine the campaign for a minimum
wage for sweated workers.


IV

## The Women's Industrial Council (WIC)

The Women's Industrial Council evolved out of the Women's Trade Union
Association which had been established after the 1888 dock strike as an
expression of middle-class concern and sympathy with exploitation of
women workers and with the aim of organising women into trade unions.
Sidney Buxton, MP, Ben Tillet, Tom Mann, David Schloss and W.C. Steadman
were amongst the men who outnumbered the women on the new organisation's
Committee.    The WTUA, like the WTUL, had close links with the Liberal
Party and it sent speakers on women's work and wages to many meetings
of local Liberal Associations[46].    Some employers also gave the WTUA,
and later the WIC, a lot of support.    An employer at a ropemaking
factory spoke at the 1893 Annual meeting of the WTUA, praising the

> "better work and better relations brought about by the
> [Ropemakers'] union and expressed his opinion that the Union
> was of an advantage to him as an employer".[47]

However, the wave of enthusiasm for trade union organisation amongst
women workers which occurred in 1888 and 1889 suffered several setbacks
and the WTUA organisers found they were showing little returns on their
efforts to get women into trade unions.    In 1894, the WTUA decided to
concentrate its efforts on "investigation, organisation, education and
agitation for legal reforms"[48] and set up the Women's Industrial Council,
at the same time disbanding the WTUA.

> "Trade unions for women cannot, at the present, be formed and
> maintained effectively amongst the poorer classes of women
> workers in London",

they concluded[49].    The answer must therefore lie in legislative action

145

and a special Parliamentary and Legal Committee was set up through which
the WIC would agitate for reforms. The WIC continued to have the
support of some employers (George Cadbury was a Vice-President) and of
many Liberals. The embryonic Labour Party also gave their support and
Margaret MacDonald (wife of the Labour Representation Committee's first
secretary) became one of the WIC's leading members.

Like the WTUL and the NFWW, the WIC played an important part in the
dissemination of information about the living and working conditions of
working-class women and in raising the question of what was to be done
to counter the poverty experienced by many families. The WIC carried
out an extensive investigation into homeworking. 400 homeworkers were
visited in thirty-five different trades and the findings were published
as a series of factual reports giving valuable detailed information on
the rates of pay in a number of different homeworking trades[50]. The
1897 Report concluded

> "How most of these workers do escape starvation is a constant
> marvel - of those, at least, who depend on these industries
> for their livelihood, lonely spinsters, widows, and deserted
> women, wives whose husbands are ill or out of work, often with
> aged people, invalids or children dependent on them ...
> Another continual puzzle is how they get through the slack
> times, when in busy times they hardly earn enough to keep body
> and soul together".[51]

The WIC also published information about women's low wages generally[52]
and a monthly journal, the Women's Industrial News (WIN) kept account of
the pressure applied to bring about an improvement in women's working
conditions. The organisation attempted to inform working women of their
rights under the Factory Acts and to this end a poem was published which
facilitated an easy understanding of the provision of the Acts. The
rhyme ended

> "Moral: Such are the rules which every day
> Are broken, one or other way,
> A thing the workers, if they knew
> Could quickly put an ending to;
> But some don't know and some don't care,
> And some are always in a scare.
>
> So overwork and underpay
> Go gaily on from day to day,
> And will, till those who work unite
> To see their own affairs put right."[53]

The WIC was responsible for drawing to the attention of the public and
politicians the unemployment suffered by women during the trade
depressions of 1903-1905 and 1908-1909. Parliament, when it discussed

unemployment at all, talked about male unemployment and the paltry
measures that were taken, such as the Distress Committees, dealt almost
entirely with unemployed men.   Margaret MacDonald carried out a survey
in 1904 of trade unionists and others asking them to fill in a
questionnaire about the rate of unemployment amongst women and what
action was being taken.   The reply from Middlesborough typified the
response to the question regarding what provision was being made for
unemployed women:

> "The public authorities are doing nothing - and other agencies
> can hardly be said to be doing anything more - in fact, agencies
> for helping young women and girls might be said to be con-
> spicuous by their absence here".[54]

The WIC complained of the Central Distress Committee that, although there
was a high unemployment rate amongst women workers,

> "that Committee did practically nothing for women and girls,
> although it received a deputation at last from the Council,
> but only after it had spent all available funds on men".[55]

Following further pressure from the WIC after the passing of the Unemployed
Workmen's Act in 1905, a Women's Sub-Committee was set up under Ramsay
MacDonald's chairmanship, which provided a garment-making workroom for
unemployed women and girls.

Largely thanks to the efforts of the WIC, there was some considerable
concern expressed about female unemployment during 1906 and 1907.   A
Conference called by the WIC in 1907 attracted 1,145 applications for
400 places.   Significantly, many of the speakers addressed themselves
to the problem of women's low wages and the relationship of women's
wages to male unemployment, men's low wages and casual work.   Clementina
Black said that women workers fell into two categories - one, the women
whose husbands' wages were inadequate to provide for a family and two, the
"women dependent on their own exertions who have almost always someone
dependent on a part of their income"[56].   The remedy for the first
category was to tackle the problem of male unemployment and the low
wages of many workers -

> "the case of a woman whose husband is out of work very often,
> and does not earn enough to keep a family is a sign of a
> disease in the body politic, a sign of something wrong in our
> civilisation".[57]

As for the second category, the WIC demanded

> "that widows with young children or women with sick or infirm
> relatives dependent on them, should also be removed from
> competition in the labour market by receiving adequate main-
> tenance from State or local funds on condition of attending
> fully to their home duties".[58]

Apart from this radical demand, the WIC concentrated its efforts on pressure for proper industrial training for girls. Concern was expressed that when girls left school they drifted into "the trade which is easiest to enter, urged by the prospect of small wages at once and a short training". And "the trades which are easiest to enter are those characterised by many serious economic and social disadvantates"[59].

The WIC collaborated with the WTUL and the COS in 1907 in a Conference on Industrial Employment of Girls and the WIC intended that its investigations into about fifteen different trades would reveal what training opportunities there were for women and girls. They also called on the Local Government Board to encourage better industrial training for women and girls. However, the WIC seems to have had limited ideas about what type of training was suitable for girls. Their main emphasis was on training for girls to be domestic servants or children's nurses. In 1902, the organisation carried out an investigation of nine London trades where women were employed, including electrical instrument-making, french polishing and printing; yet they only recommended training provision in one - artificial flower-making[60].

Their attitude towards training for girls was related to their concern about the quality of motherhood. At a Conference held in 1904 of "representatives of educational bodies and of organisations interested in the work of women", the high infant mortality rate was deplored and said to be "proof of the national importance of training the future mothers in the care and management of children". Furthermore, the middle-class would benefit - it was intimated - from such training as "the position of nurse is filled chiefly by girls from the working class". Accordingly, the Conference resolved that it was "impressed with the urgent need of providing training for girls of the industrial class in the care and management of children" and recommended that appropriate one year courses should be set up at Technical Schools[61].

The WIC, like the WTUL and NFWW, did a great deal to disseminate information about the conditions of women homeworkers. Public opinion was horrified by the descriptions such as the one which Margaret MacDonald quoted in a lecture on homework. It is worth reproducing here in full to illustrate the powerful nature of the information which organisations such as the WIC were disseminating. The description is of fur-pullers in Southwark.

"The picture of the women working is a haunting one; they are
scantily clothed in rough sacking - like dresses, open for the
most part, at the throat, and letting the flesh appear through
various slits and holes. This garment is matted with fluff
or down. The women work and eat and sleap in an atmosphere
thick with impalpable hairs and tainted with the sickly smell
of the skins. Everything round them is coated with fur, and
they themselves look scarcely more human than the animals
beside them, from the thick deposit of fur which covers them
from head to foot, and forces its way into the eyes and nose
and lungs of the miserable workers. The rabbit skins are given
to the out-workers in 'turns' of 60 skins to be cleared, i.e.
for the long, outside hair to be pulled off with the plucking
knife, and the fur reduced to the soft, silky down which grows
close to the actual skin ... The women suffer greatly from
chronic asthma, brought on by the fur penetrating to the lungs,
and by the acids with which the Colonial skins are cleaned; and
the rate of infant mortality in the homes of the pullers appears
to be abnormally high".[62]

Like the WTUL, the WIC was concerned about the effect of homeworking on
the family. Margaret MacDonald deplored "the utter drudgery and lack of
homelife that [homework] entails" and condemned the system as "degrading
and lowering"[63].

There was, however, disagreement between two prominent members[64] of the
WIC on whether a minimum wage was the solution to the problems of homeworkers. Clementina Black argued in favour of Wages Boards on the
grounds that if a decent wage was paid to men then married women would
not have to engage in waged work either inside or outside the home[65].
Margaret MacDonald, on the other hand, argued that, although she had no
objection to the principle of Wages Boards, she believed that large-scale
evasion would be common and that this would make them ineffective[66]. She
maintained that homeworkers would be less subject to scrutiny under a
Wages Board system than factory and workshop workers and that therefore
more work may well be given to homeworkers as a result. She felt that
only a re-organisation of industry on a collective basis would solve the
problem of low wages and that in the meantime, the palliatives of
licensing of homework, of better provisions for the unemployed and of
proper relief for women with dependents were more likely to yield results
than Wages Boards[67].

On the other hand, she argued, a legal minimum wage was merely an attempt

"to regulate bargaining between profit-making capitalists ...
and wage-earners" and "the Australian workers tell you that
the employers always get the best of it in the long run".[68]

Margaret MacDonald carried the rest of the organisation with her and the

149

the WIC was responsible for a Bill for the regulation of homework along
the lines of the licensing system established in America.   In this Bill,
first introduced in 1898 but never accepted by Parliament, it was laid
down that a homeworker would have to obtain a licence from the Factory
Inspectorate and this would only be given if the premises were of
adequate sanitary and general standard and where there was no over-
crowding[69].   Although Margaret MacDonald denied that she or the WIC
wished to abolish homework, it is certainly true that the main male
supporter of the licensing of homework, her husband, was strongly in
favour of abolishing homework.   In supporting a licensing system, he
maintained that sweating was not actually a problem of low wages but a
question of the conditions of work "I will not recognise" he told the
National Conference on Sweated Industries in 1907, "the home as a proper
place for work being done, whether you get 5d. per hour, or 5 farthings
per hour, or nothing at all per hour".   He made his opposition to Wages
Boards clear

> "If you are in favour of homework, it is your duty to try and
> improve its condition and improve the prices for it, and so on;
> but if you are not in favour of it you should not tinker with
> it as those in favour of Wages Boards do.   You ought to put
> machinery into operation which will eliminate it".[70]

Margaret MacDonald also gave voice to the increased concern with the
conflict between the conditions of women workers and the health of the
future generation.   She strongly supported legislation preventing women
from returning to work immediately after childbirth -

> "However much it may interfere with the alleged liberty of the
> women worker, it is the undoubted duty of the community to
> protect through her the public health ... a woman's home
> duties are not only her own personal affair but they concern
> the welfare of the community.   The State is interested not only
> that she should bear healthy children but also that she should
> have time to attend to their needs, or those of any other
> members of her family afterwards, and so it is specially
> necessary that she should not have too long hours or too
> exhaustive work".[71]

Support for both Wages Boards and for licensing of homework was very much
a response to the difficulties of organising women into trade unions.   As
one speaker at the Glasgow Conference on Sweated Industries stated:

> "In view ... of the special difficulties in the way of
> organisation, we must abandon trade union effort as imprac-
> ticable of application to the homework trades and turn to
> the other remedy - regulation on the part of the State".[72]

This conclusion was applied not just to homeworkers but also to women
factory and workshop workers in the sweated trades.   An investigation

into the clothing trades, published in 1909, expressed the opinion that,
below a certain level of wages and conditions, it was impossible for
trade union organisation to be effective[73]. The same investigation
put the case for wages boards in a way which sums up the support
amongst middle-class women for minimum wage legislation:

> "Competition, especially on the lower levels, is intensified
> by the presence in the labour market of many married women
> absolutely compelled by economic pressure to add industrial
> toil to domestic cares that are already heavy enough. The
> employment of these women is in its essence a phase not so
> much of the underpayment of women as of the underpayment of
> men. It is because hundreds and hundreds of men in London
> are paid only enough to keep a person, not enough to keep a
> household, that these women have become wage-earners; and
> the proper way to save them from their own killing toil, and
> the self-dependent women from their competition, is to increase
> the pay of their husbands".[74]

## V

These then were the pressures for state intervention which came from the
three most important organisations which took it upon themselves to
represent working class women's interests. Although the WTUL/NFWW and
the WIC differed in their legislative proposals on sweated labour, they
shared three things in common - a recognition that the major problem
was women's low wages; an assertion of the relationship between men's
wages and male unemployment on the one hand, and the need for women to
work on the other; and a desire to see the elimination of the need for
mothers of young children to work.

References - Chapter 5

1. 16th Abstract of Labour Statistics of the United Kingdom, PP1913 LXXX (Cd.7131).

2. R. Beer (n.d.).

3. Webb, Trade Union Collection, Vol.47, Item 53.

4. S. Rowbotham, "Hidden From History" (1973).

5. S. Lewenak, "Women and Trade Unions" (1977).

6. S. Boston, "Women and the Trade Unions" (1980).

7. E.g. D. Russell and M. Tichelar, "Class Struggle in South London 1850-1900". Southwark-Lambeth History Workshop (1981) and other work associated with History Workshop Journal.

8. Webb Trade Union Collection, Section A, Vol.47, Item 47.

9. Ibid.

10. Booth, Vol.8 (1896), p.230.

11. Report of the Chief Registrar of Friendly Societies for the year ending 31 December 1911 - Part C, Appendix: Trade Unions.

12. See G. Boone, "The Women's Trade Union Leagues in Great Britain and the USA" (1942), p.28; B. Drake, "Women in Trade Unions" (1920) pp.41-42.

13. Quoted by Drake (1920), pp.41-42.

14. Anna Martin: "The Married Working Woman" (1911), pp.10-11.

15. WPPL Annual Report 1875.

16. Ibid.

17. See B. Hutchins, "Women in Modern Industry" (1915), p.121.

18. Lewenak, (1977), p.72; see also H. Goldman, "Emma Paterson" (1974).

19. Hutchins (1915), p.121.

20. G. Boone, (1942), p.25.

21. B. Drake, (1920), p.22.

22. Report of WTUL Conference on the best means of extending the work of the League, October 1886.

23. Ibid.

24. G. Tuckwell, "Women's Work and Factory Legislation" (1895).

25. E. Dilke, "Trade Unions for Women" (1892).

26. G. Tuckwell, "The State and its Children" (1894), p.161.

27. Ibid., p.162.

28. TUC Annual Congress, 1897, p.42.

29. Henry Broadhurst Papers, Letter dated 16 October 1889, Vol.III, Item 53.

30. Gwyn and Tuckwell, "Sir Charles Dilke", p.359.

31. Ibid., p.343.

32. R. Jenkins, "Sir Charles Dilke", p.396.

33. G. Tuckwell, Interview with the Morning Post, 10.12.1907.

34. A. Martin, "The Married Working Woman", 1911, p.45.

35. Select Committee on Homework, PP1907, VI (Cd.290) Q.2916.

36. Gertrude Tuckwell's collection of newspaper cuttings is deposited at the TUC library. For an account and analysis of the collection, see Jenny Morris, "The Gertrude Tuckwell Collection", in History Workshop Journal, No.5, Spring 1978.

37. Tribune, 30.8.1907.

38. By Mrs. Archibald MacKirdy.

39. G. Tuckwell Collection, Item 204, Child Labour; see also, G. Tuckwell, The Anomalies of our Factory Laws, in Labour Leader, April 1902.

40. M.A. Hamilton, "Mary MacArthur" (1925), p.36.

41. Quoted by Hamilton, ibid, p.23.

42. Lewenak (1977), p.115.

43. Drake (1920), p.182.

44. Report of 1909 TUC in Daily Sketch, 13.9.1909.

45. Hamilton (1925), p.62.

46. Women's Industrial Council Papers, Box 8, Annual Reports of the WTUA.

47. WTUA Annual Report, 1893, p.13.

48. WTUA Annual Report, 1893, p.14.

49. Ibid., p.14.

50. M. MacDonald. Coll. Notes for a Lecture on Homework, Vol.I, Item II, 33; WIC "Home Industries of Women in London", 1st Report (1897), Interim Report (1906), Third Report (1908).

51. Ibid., (1897), p.8.

52. WIC, "Women's Wages in the Nineteenth Century" (1906).

53. C. Black, "The Rhyme of the Factory Acts" (n.d.).

54. M. MacDonald Collection, Vol. II.

55. National Conference on the Unemployment of Women Dependent on their own Earnings, Report (1907).

56. Ibid., p.8.

57. Ibid., p.8.

58. Memorial to the President of the Local Government Board from the WIC; Conference Report 1907.

59. WIN, December 1903.

60. WIC Collection, Vol. C3, Report to the LCC Technical Education Board, 20 June, 1902.

61. WIC Collection, Vol. C6.

62. M. MacDonald Collection, Vol. II, Item 33, p.5.

63. Ibid., p.6, p.9.

64. See letter from Margaret MacDonald to C. Black (undated). M. MacDonald Collection, Vol. I, Item 24.

65. Select Committee on Homework, PP1907, VI (Cd.290) Q.2916.

66. Select Committee on Homework, 1907, Q.4390.

67. Ibid., QQ.4391-3.

68. Letter from M. MacDonald in Labour Leader, 3 January 1908.

69. Select Committee on Homework, 1907, QQ.4302-4358.

70. National Conference on Sweated Industries held on 11 and 12 October 1907 in Glasgow under the auspices of the Scottish Council for Women's Trades.

71. M. MacDonald Collection, Vol. II, Item 34, Notes for a lecture on women's work and legislation.

72. National Conference (Glasgow) 1907.

73. C. Meyer and C. Black, "Makers of our Clothes: a case for Trade Boards" (1909), p.181.

74. Ibid., p.183.

# 6 Employers and sweated labour

## I

This chapter examines the attitudes of three types of employer to the
sweated trades - the larger employers who were organised into associations
and represented through the Chamber of Commerce movement and the Employers'
Parliamentary Council, the employers' parliamentary lobby formed in 1898;
the employers in the sweated industries;  and the Quaker employers who
played an important role in the development of minimum wage legislation.
The first part of the chapter is taken up with an analysis of the
attitudes of employers in the sweated and non-sweated trades towards social
policy in general and minimum wage legislation in particular;  the second
part concentrates on the Quaker employers.

As J.R. Hay[1] has pointed out, there was at the beginning of this century
no single employer view on social reform.

> "Rather this was a period during which employers began to
> struggle towards common approaches in the face of internal and
> external challenges facing the British economy and society".

The level of wages was, of course, of vital concern to employers.   The
interests of capital were well represented amongst politicians and social
reformers in that many MPs were themselves employers, investors in
industry or land-owners, as were many social reformers.   During the early
years of the twentieth century, employers and their organisations made
clear their views on the rights and duties of labour.   The mining
companies withstood the pressure for shorter hours and a minimum wage for
miners until these were forced on them by the action of the miners' unions
and the pressure of government.   The railway companies refused to even
recognise the union to which an increasing number of their workforce
belonged and conciliation boards were only set up following government
intervention in 1907.   What, then, were the attitudes of employers to
minimum wage legislation for the "sweated" trades?

II

Evidence to the House of Lords Select Committee on Sweating and the
House of Commons Select Committee on Homework by employers tended to be
dominated by denials of workpeople's evidence and a defence of the

155

employers' position.  Many of these employers, however, were small contractors and were without political influence.  The value of their
evidence is that it indicates the "chaos of competition" (as Beatrice
Webb called it);  the desperate  struggle for survival which employers
as well as employees experienced and which accounted for the inability
of most employers in the  sweated  trades to raise wages.  Many of these
employers insisted that they were quite willing to pay higher wages were
it not for other employers in the same trade who would undercut them.
These claims were backed up by G. Askwith who, from his experience of
dealing with employers through the Board of Trade's conciliation function,
concluded "If somebody else was not paying or thought to be paying, a
less price, many employers would be prepared to pay higher wages"[2].  It
was for this reason that Askwith supported the idea of a minimum wage
for the sweated trades.

Most of the sweated trades, while characterised by a preponderance of
small business and sub-contracting, also had a few large companies, who
protested their inability to pay adequate wages because of the price-
cutting effects of chaotic competition.  Even George Cadbury, an
employer who, as we shall see, strongly supported minimum wage legislation,
maintained that he had to put the manufacture of cardboard boxes out to
sub-contractors because they were so much cheaper[3].  Some employers
felt that labour-intensive workshop and domestic production acted as a
brake on the capital investment in factory production and in the development of higher productivity and greater efficiency.

Well before the end of the nineteenth century the concept of there being
"good employers" and "bad employers" was widely accepted by politicians.
The term "good employers" tended to refer to those who were using the
most advanced technology, operating in modern factory premises and were
engaged in the largest production runs.  These employers often organised
sickness and medical clubs for their employees but even these employers
insisted and it seemed to be commonly accepted that there was a limit to
how "good" they could be in terms of offering better wages and conditions
in the context of a competitive economy.  As a Fabian Society pamphlet
put it

> "The employer has to sell his product in competition with all
> the other employers, and, if he does not keep his expenses of
> production down to the lowest point they can attain, he will
> be undersold and ruined".[4]

A recognition of the limited potential for private welfare schemes

contributed to the growing acceptance amongst employers of the necessity
for the State to intervene to promote the health and efficiency of
industrial workers[5].  Support for state intervention amongst some
employers went further.  Even before the 1906 Liberal Government, Sir
John Brunner, a chemical manufacturer and Liberal MP, urged the abandon-
ment of laissez-faire principles in favour of public investment in
technical education and the nationalisation of canals[6], and was supported
by a number of Liberal backbench MPs.  During the early 1900s a number
of large employers voiced their support for non-contributory old-age
pensions.  Two such employers were the Liberal MPs, Alfred Mond (founder
of ICI) and W.H. Lever (the soap manufacturer)[7].

Minimum wage legislation, however, involves a far more fundamental
interference by the State in the relationship between employer and
employee than the extension of private welfare schemes and this was
reflected in the ambivalence of the Chamber of Commerce movement towards
the notion of a statutory minimum wage for the sweated trades.  These
employers were far happier advancing the cause of setting up negotiation
and conciliation procedures and, as we shall see, the notion of minimum
wage legislation was regarded with a great deal of suspicion.  Yet in
many ways the demand for state action on wages arose out of the
experience that negotiation and conciliation procedures could not operate
effectively within the sweated trades.

The practice of setting uniform rates of wages was a popular one amongst
the more organised industrial and commercial interests at the end of the
nineteenth century.  The pioneer amongst employers of conciliation
procedures had also been a pioneer of the factory system, namely A.J.
Mundella, hosier and later a Liberal MP and Cabinet Minister for the
Board of Trade.  He had helped to set up a permanent Board of
Conciliation in Nottingham in 1860 to settle disputes and agree uniform
rates.

The advantages to employers of a body whose decisions both sides of
industry recognised were obvious.  The settlement of disputes without
strikes or lock-outs and the agreeing of demarcation lines and uniform
rates meant that trade disruption was minimised, under-cutting could be
prevented and the regularisation of production was promoted.  Most of
the commercial and manufacturing interests represented on Chambers of
Commerce throughout the country were very much in favour of promoting
structured negotiation procedures.  The dockers' strike in 1888 prompted

the London Chamber of Commerce to set up a London Labour Conciliation and Arbitration Board[8], and in 1891, the Association of Chambers of Commerce of the United Kingdom unanimously adopted a resolution in favour of Conciliation Boards[9]. A motion unanimously passed by the 1892 Congress of Chambers of Commerce of the Whole Empire sums up the fears about the disruption of trade caused by labour disputes. The Congress resolved:

> "That the frequent recurrence of labour disputes has caused and is causing great damage to the commercial and manufacturing interests of the Empire. That it is extremely desirable, in the best interests of both employers and employed, that the re-adjustment of the rates and the conditions of labour which from time to time is inevitable, should be brought about without the wasteful and calamitous results proceeding from strikes and lock-outs. And that this Congress strongly recommends the formation of properly constituted Boards of Labour, Conciliation and Arbitration in all important centres of industry and commerce throughout the Empire".[10]

The London Chamber of Commerce's Conciliation and Arbitration Board had equal numbers of employers and employees represented on it and its services were offered for "promoting the amicable settlement of labour disputes in the Metropolis"[11]. However, the success of attempts such as this to establish procedures which would diminish the risk of trade disruption were limited. It was very often difficult to get both sides to agree to use a Conciliation Board, let alone to agree to arbitration. Agreements when made were voluntary and could be, and were, broken by either side. In particular, where strong employer and union organisation didn't exist it was extremely difficult to get representatives around a table and to implement any agreement reached. It is significant that none of the trades covered by the Trade Boards Act were represented on the London Chamber of Commerce and that there were only two cases of the London Conciliation and Arbitration Board intervening in a dispute in such a trade[12]. The Master Tailors Association had set up an Arbitration Committee but there is evidence that it was not very effective[13].

The Conciliation Act of 1896 which followed the Royal Commission on Labour left conciliation procedures as voluntary and the Board of Trade was merely empowered to respond to requests for an arbitrator. British industrial relations remained based on voluntary negotiations between employer and employee. Usually, therefore, agreements could only be made and relationships stabilised when both employer and employee organisation was strong and stable. As Phelps-Brown[14] has pointed out, where such organisations were weak

> "all was strife and uncertainty, and where they did not exist
> at all, there was no generally accepted means of settling
> disputes".[15]

The sweated trades, dominated as they were by small employers, semi-
and unskilled workers and fierce competition, suffered particularly from
a lack of both employer and trade union organisation and there was little
possibility of a stable relationship between employer and employee.
Even amongst the skilled workers in the tailoring trade, where the "log"
system had been agreed between the trade unions and the employers, such
agreements were put in jeopardy by the rapidly-increasing number of unskilled workers who were not covered by such wage agreements.

The Chamber of Commerce movement's support for arbitration and conciliation
was very closely linked with their desire for a disciplined workforce
and a minimum of disruptions.  Amongst larger employers in the unorganised
trades there was likewise a distinct desire to exert greater control over
their workforce.  In the rapidly-expanding laundry trade, for instance,
employers told the Royal Commission on Labour[16] that they could not get
their women workers to work regular hours, a factor of particular
inconvenience to the new steam laundry proprietors.  Women apparently
often preferred working for smaller laundries because they could work
irregular hours and therefore fit their domestic work in more easily.
One employer tried to persuade his workers to be punctual by adding 10%
to their wages if they came to work on time  each day during the busy
months of April to July.  Many of the larger employers felt that an
extension of the Factory Acts to laundries would be beneficial to the
larger steam laundries[17], and the Principal Lady Factory Inspector
reported in 1903 that there was a

> "steady growth of a strong section of employers [in the laundry
> trade] who have set their minds on inaugurating a more rational
> system of employment in conformity with ordinary factory laws".

These employers, through a new periodical "The Power Laundry" pressed
for the further extension of the Factory Acts to laundries on the grounds
that proper regulation of hours would "raise the standards of work and
workers".

The President of the Master Tailors Association complained that employers
in the tailoring trade did not always agree to workers leaving the workplace for dinner "because they could not trust them to return"[18].  The
disruptive nature of strikes in the tailoring trade moved the Secretary

of the Association to suggest that a profit-sharing system was desirable
because, he said, it would "tend to settle the workman and to prevent
many of the strikes which occurred"[19].   Employers in the clothing,
laundry and other such trades were anxious for a workforce which came
to work on time, which was more productive and which did not indulge in
spontaneous walk-outs nor in long drawn-out disputes.   However, apart
from their attempts at conciliation, employers in these trades did very
little to promote a more disciplined efficient workforce.   Struggling
with fluctuating fortunes and fierce competition, employers in the
sweated trades found it difficult - and indeed sometimes undesirable -
to organise into employers' associations.   They were also not well
represented amongst the Chambers of Commerce movement or the Employers
Parliamentary Council, the employers' parliamentary lobby formed in
1898.   It is not therefore surprising that these bodies' main objection
to minimum wage legislation was the possibility of its extension to
trades other than the sweated trades and that no really strong opposition
was mounted by the employers' organisations against the Trade Boards Bill,
aimed as it was at four particular sweated trades.   In 1908, the
Manufacturers' Section of the Chamber gave evidence to the Select
Committee on Homework which was then considering the Sweated Industries
Bill,

> "with a view to preventing the application of the Bill to those
> industries which are carried on under reasonable and proper
> conditions",[20]

and when the Trade Board Act was passed in 1909, the Chamber objected to
the clauses which allowed the Act to be extended to trades other than
the four specified by the Act[21].

Of course, those few employers in the sweated trades who were organised
were obviously very worried about having to pay a minimum wage.   The
Londonderry Chamber of Commerce, representing as it did the Londonderry
shirt and collar manufacturers who relied heavily on homeworkers,
vigorously opposed the recommendations of the Select Committee on
Homework[22], with some success in terms of the application of the Trade
Boards legislation to Ireland.   Some members of the Nottingham Chamber
of Commerce, together with the Lace Finishers' Association, also objected
to the Trade Boards Bill, in particular to a minimum rate being applied
to homeworkers[23].   This vocal opposition from employers was the
exception rather than the rule however.   Once the campaign against
sweating got under way in 1906, support for a minimum wage for sweated
workers swept the country and any opposition was definitely a minority

opinion, backed in Parliament by only a few MPs who adhered to an extreme laissez-faire ideology.

However, the part played by two particular employers in initiating and carrying on the campaign for minimum wage legislation was crucial and the next section examines their decisive intervention.


III

In the early twentieth century, some employers, together with other influential groups of people, were moving towards an acceptance of the view that State intervention was necessary to ensure the continuation and improvement of the existing social order. There was one group of employers in particular whose religious principles took them along this path more quickly than others and whose coincident business success and prosperity enabled them to effectively propagate their ideas.

The group of employers to whom I refer are the Quaker employers who were prominent in a number of industries at the end of the nineteenth century and who applied their religious principles to their business practices. This cannot be said of all Quaker employers, but two families of influential Quaker employers, the Cadburys and the Rowntrees, (both cocoa manufacturers) believed that the welfare of their employees was related not only to business efficiency but also to the wider health and stability of the community.

The Society of Friends were generally concerned about the material quality of life. Social reform and social work played a major part in their organisation for, unlike the Salvation Army, the Friends emphasised the relationship of material well-being to spiritual well-being. The Friends Social Union - which had two prominent Quaker employers as Chairman and Treasurer in the early 1900s - was set up specifically to pursue questions of social welfare. Percy Alden[24], the Organising Secretary of the Friends Social Union demonstrated their down-to-earth concern about poverty and inequality when he wrote:

> "Notwithstanding the immense improvement in the conditions of the working classes as a result of factory legislation during the last quarter of a century, it is still true to say that large masses of our fellow-men have not felt the rise in the standard of living, or the increase in wages which has been the more fortunate lot of the skilled worker. It is a sad reflection that with the unprecedented growth of the wealth-producing power of this country there is a poverty which

161

obsesses the imagination and compels the social reformer to regard it as almost irremediable. Never was Dives so rich and Lazarus so poor as today".[25]

The Quaker concern for social reform, however, was not merely based on their recognition of the poverty and suffering of individuals but also on the belief that the whole community would benefit from a higher standard of living for its less well off citizens. The general support that Friends gave to the idea of a minimum wage was based on the contention that merciless competition, in driving down wages and working conditions, "demoralises and degrades" people and thereby damages the whole community[26].

The Society of Friends had not always supported legislation aimed at bettering the condition of the working class. One of Lord Shaftesbury's most vociferous opponents when he was promoting factory legislation in the 1840s was John Bright, a Quaker cotton manufacturer, who, although he claimed to support the ten-hour day, maintained that the State should not interfere between employer and employee[27]. Bright defended his position by attacking the landed aristocracy and the low wages of their farm labourers (for example, Lord Shaftesbury's farm labourers) compared with the wages of his cotton operatives.

Quakers of a later generation were, however, rather ashamed of the way that the Society of Friends had embraced the principles of laissez-faire. A.S. Rowntree, for example, in his Chairman's address to the 1918 Friends' Conference of Employers, looked back to the nineteenth century and deplored

"the blighting atmosphere of laissez-faire, to which many Quaker employers, in common with others then yielded ...".[28]

By the beginning of the twentieth century, the Society of Friends was a staunch advocate of social welfare reforms, although even then Quakerism could not be said to be synonymous with support for social reform. Bryant and Mays (the employers involved in the 1888 Matchgirls Strike) were a very well-known example of a firm which shamelessly exploited its workers and allowed them to work in conditions extremely damaging to their health. There were also other Quaker firms which qualified for the description of "bad employer" - Barclay & Fry's was one, a box-making firm in Southwark whose women workers struck against wages of 9/- to 11/- per week in 1908[29]. However, two prominent Quaker employers, the Cadburys and the Rowntrees were influential advocates of social reform and George Cadbury in particular played a decisive part in getting the Trade Boards Act passed[30].

162

In the context of their own businesses, the Rowntrees and the Cadburys related business efficiency to the material well-being of their workers. This relationship had been recognised as early as 1849 when John and Benjamin Cadbury, together with other Birmingham businessmen had attempted to set up a "model village". Their main concern at this point, however, was to encourage teetotalism and it wasn't until later on in the century that a more sophisticated approach to encouraging a healthy and efficient workforce was developed.

At the end of the nineteenth century, both Cadburys and Rowntrees were rapidly expanding businessess and their owners' social status and influence increased through their involvement in movements for social reform, particularly through their acquisition of newspapers which were used as mouth-pieces for the pursuit of these reforms. In 1880, Rowntrees employed 100 people, in 1894, 1,893 and in 1909, 4,066. Cadbury's Bournéville factory, built in 1879, had trebled in size by 1899. This rapid expansion was accompanied by developments which the employers hoped would increase the efficiency of their workforce. Cadbury believed it was bad business to pay low wages and allow bad conditions in his factory -

> "He held that it paid his firm and would pay all firms to devote both attention and money to securing the safety, the health and even the pleasures of the workers employed".[31]

Joseph Rowntree declared:

> "Healthful conditions of labour are not luxuries to be adopted or dispensed with at will. They are conditions necessary for success. In keen international competition the vigour and intelligence of the workmen are likely to be a determining factor".[32]

Both employers set up medical and sickness clubs for their employees in the 1890s and introduced a shorter working week than was customary. They also concerned themselves with their workers' education - an education that would enable workers to perform what was seen to be their proper role more adequately. Continuation classes for men were set up at the Rowntree factory in mathematics, English and woodwork, while there was the 'Domestic School' for women and girls. Cookery classes were compulsory for girls under seventeen.

As the size of their factories increased, the Cadburys and Rowntrees directed their wealth and status towards the study of poverty and the movement for social reform. B. Seebohm Rowntree's study of poverty in York in 1899 defined poverty as income insufficient to provide the diet

necessary for physical efficiency at work.   In 1904, the Joseph
Rowntree Charitable Trust was set up to support education and research
into the causes of poverty.   Edward Cadbury, together with George Shann,
wrote one of the most influential accounts of the sweated trades[33] and
George Cadbury financed the Sweated Trades Exhibition held in 1906 and
also contributed half of the cost of the National Old Age Pensions League.

The Rowntree and Cadbury families set out deliberately to acquire newspaper interests in order to propagate their ideas.   In 1891, George
Cadbury bought four weekly Birmingham newspapers - the aim being "not to
make money but to bring an enlightened and public-spirited criticism to
bear upon affairs"[34].   When David Lloyd George, concerned at the lack
of opposition to the Boer War amongst the main national press, started
to organise a syndicate to take over the Daily News, he approached
George Cadbury who, in the event, took over all financial control of the
paper.   With the end of the Boer War, the Daily News became involved
in the development of the policies of the expected new Liberal Government,
particularly concentrating its attention on the problems of low wages,
unemployment and the poverty of those no longer able to work.

When Cadbury handed over the Daily News to his sons he spelt out his
motivations as a newspaper proprietor:

> "I want you to know that the money that I have invested in
> these papers would otherwise have been given to charities.
> I had a profound conviction that money spent on charities was
> of infinitely less value than money spent in trying to arouse
> my fellow countrymen to the necessity for measures to ameliorate
> the condition of the poor, forsaken and downtrodden masses which
> can be done most effectively by a great newspaper".[35]

Joseph Rowntree's interest in newspapers also arose from a political
concern.   In the early years of the twentieth century he was worried
that

> "anti-Liberal and perhaps war-mongering interests might
> finally conquer the last strongholds of the English press".[36]

He was also concerned about the decline of the provincial press so he
directed his resources to acquiring provincial newspapers.  The Rowntree
Social Service Trust financed the launch of a York and North Riding
edition of the Northern Echo and Rowntree also purchased the Westminster
Press Provincial Newspapers Ltd., which comprised sixteen newspaper
companies.   In 1907 he helped to finance The Nation, a weekly journal
founded by a group of Liberals, edited by H.W. Massingham and influential
in the development of the "New Liberalism".   Rowntree also owned The

<u>Star</u> and <u>The Morning Leader</u>, although both of these were taken over by
Cadbury in 1910.

The Cadburys and the Rowntrees played a vital part in the advocation of
reforms such as old age pensions, health insurance and a minimum wage.
Cadbury in particular could claim a lot of the credit for getting the
Trade Boards Act passed.   Although Charles Dilke and the WTUL had been
pressing since the early 1890s for a minimum wage for sweated workers,
it was George Cadbury's financing of the Sweated Trades Exhibition and
of the Anti-Sweating League, Edward Cadbury's research into the causes
of poverty amongst wage-earners and the <u>Daily News</u>' espousal of the
cause which placed minimum wage legislation on the agenda of the new
Liberal government.   In Chapter 8 we discuss in detail the campaign
for minimum wage legislation and the part played by the Cadburys.

The Cadburys and the Rowntrees and many of the supporters of wages
boards, were presenting the interests of employers when they argued for
such measures.   Their concern at the poverty of many wage-earners was
sincere but it was based on a concern about the implications for the
whole community of such poverty.


                                    IV

Employers such as Cadbury and Rowntree recognised that business efficiency
was directly related to the health of the workforce, and they therefore
attempted to provide a living wage and private welfare schemes.   There
was a limit however to how far individual employers could bring about a
healthy efficient workforce - particularly when a large number of people
were employed in trades dominated by cut-throat competition, small
employers and seasonal fluctuations.   Such trades were considered by
the more far-sighted employers as parasites on the more healthy parts of
the economy.   They believed that poverty attacked the family, the
healthy, hygienic home of the current and future worker.   Women who
were forced out to work because of their husband's low wage were unable
to properly perform their role as the wives of current workers and the
mothers of future workers.   Yet the efficiency of the workforce depended
upon the proper carrying out of domestic duties.

Homework was believed to keep down the wages of factory workers and at
the same time to create an undesirable environment for raising children.

The whole structure of wages was thrown out of balance by inefficient workers desperate for any kind of work, however badly paid. Edward Cadbury argued[37], like the Webbs, that it would be better for these inefficient workers - the old, the disabled, the chronically sick (and the workshy) - to be taken out of the labour market completely rather than be allowed to prevent otherwise efficient workers from earning an adequate wage. It was accepted, and in fact welcomed, that by imposing a minimum wage such inefficient workers would cease to be employed as their low productivity would deter employers from taking them on if an adequate wage had to be paid. Cadbury and others believed that such people would then be properly classed as "unemployable", identified as the true residuum and dealt with accordingly.

Whilst some employers closed their eyes to the failure of private enterprise to heal the cancer of poverty, the evidence is that a few employers recognised that for their social order to survive the state must step in to provide the minimum standards necessary.

We will examine that particularly important part played by one large employer in the passing of the Trade Boards Act in Chapter 8. Before doing this, however, we need to consider the state's response to the problem of sweated labour prior to the campaign for Wages Boards which was launched in 1907.

## References - Chapter 6

1.  J.R. Hay, "Employers' Attitudes to Social Policy" in P. Thane (ed.), "The Origins of British Social Policy" (1978), p.115.

2.  G. Askwith, "Industrial Problems and Disputes" (1920), p.205.

3.  Select Committee on Homework, PP1908, VIII (Cd.246) Q665.

4.  B. Webb, B.L. Hutchins and the Fabian Society, "Socialism and the National Minimum" (1909), p.13.

5.  K. Burgess, "The Challenge of Labour" (1980), p.125.

6.  J. Harris, "Unemployment and Politics" (1972), p.217.

7.  P. Thane, "Non-Contributory Versus Insurance Pensions 1878-1908" in P. Thane (ed.), "The Origins of British Social Policy" (1978), pp.101-103.

8.  London Chamber of Commerce, Annual Report, 1889, p.3.

9.  London Chamber of Commerce, Annual Report, 1892, p.64.

10. Ibid., p.64.

11. London Chamber of Commerce, Annual Report, 1903, p.18.

12. In 1892, the Board arbitrated a settlement between the Association of London Master Tailors and the Amalgamated Society of Tailors on the time-log rate for the West End tailoring trade (London Chamber of Commerce Annual Report for 1893).  In 1904, the Board offered its services in the dispute between the AST and Messrs. Phillips & Sons but the employers wouldn't accept the existence of either a strike or a lock-out.

13. Royal Commission on Labour, Digest of Evidence, Vol.II, PP1892, XXXVI (Cd.6795-III), p.30.

14. E.H. Phelps Brown, "The Growth of British Industrial Relations" (1959), p.177.

15. Ibid., see also I.G. Sharp, "Industrial Conciliation and Arbitration in Great Britain" (1949), p.5.

16. Royal Commission on Labour, Reports of the Lady Assistant Commissioners on the Employment of Women, PP1893-4, XXXVII Pt.I, (Cd.6894), pp.17-18.

17. Ibid., p.19.

18. Royal Commission on Labour, Digest of Evidence, Vol.II, PP1892 XXXVI (Cd.6795-III), p.30.

19. Royal Commission on Labour, Fifth and Final Report, PP1894, XXXV (Cd.7421), p.240.

20. London Chamber of Commerce, Annual Report, 1908, p.73.

21. London Chamber of Commerce, Annual Report, 1909.

22.  Northern Whig, 20.10.1908.

23.  Nottingham Guardian, 29.4.1909, although see evidence of representative from Nottingham Chamber of Commerce to Select Committee on Homework, Chapter 8, p.     .

24.  According to Jose Harris, Alden's views on unemployment insurance and labour exchanges had a significant influence on William Beveridge - see J. Harris, "William Beveridge" (1977), p.116.

25.  The Friend, 17 May 1907, Vol.XLVII, p.315.

26.  Ibid., p.316.

27.  P.H. Emden, "Quakers in Commerce" (1939), p.84.

28.  Report of Friends' Conference of Employers, 11-14 April, 1918.

29.  Labour Leader,  3, 10 and 17 January 1908.

30.  Both G. Cadbury and B. Seebohm Rowntree played a decisive part in getting the Old Age Pensions Act of 1908 passed.

31.  A.G. Gardiner, "The Life of George Cadbury" (1949), pp.79-80.

32.  A. Briggs, "Seebohm Rowntree" (1961), p.101.

33.  E. Cadbury and G. Shann, "Sweating" (1908).

34.  A.G. Gardiner, "The Life of George Cadbury" (1949), p.206.

35.  Ibid., p.221.

36.  A. Vernon, "A Quaker Businessman" (1958), p.161.

37.  Cadbury and Shann (1908), pp.127-128.

# 7 The political response 1890-1906

The last three chapters have shown how three particular groups of people reacted to the problem of sweated labour and the remedies they proposed. The purpose of this chapter is to examine how politicians and civil servants responded prior to the anti-sweating campaign set up in 1906. Their response to this campaign for Wages Boards is discussed in Chapter 8 when we detail the development and effect of the campaign.

## The House of Lords Select Committee on Sweating

The events leading up to the setting up of the House of Lords Select Committee on Sweating have been discussed in Chapter 1. The primary motivation behind Lord Dunraven's proposal to carry out such an inquiry was his concern that "foreign immigration" was flooding certain trades with cheap labour[1]. The Secretary to the Board of Trade, responding favourably to his proposal, claimed

> "If any satisfaction at all could be got out of so melancholy a subject as this, it was, perhaps, to be found in the fact that almost the whole of the unfortunate people engaged in this sweating system in the E. End were not our fellow-subjects, but were either Polish Jews or German, or people of other nationalities ... This contract system, so far as the British tailor was concerned, was practically extinct"[2].

The scope of the enquiry was extended to trades other than tailoring and to all parts of the country, and the evidence gathered showed how wrong this view of sweating was: low wages, long hours and insanitary conditions existed before the Jewish refugees fled to this country in any great numbers and were found to exist in 1888 in industries and areas of the country where Jewish immigrants were uncommon. How did the House of Lords respond to this discovery?

Duncan Bythell, in his study of the sweated trades[3] says that the Select Committee members

> "seem to have become either so confused or so dispirited by what they found that they were unable to suggest any effective solutions to the 'sweating' problem"[4].

Certainly the detailed evidence contained in their five long reports of an intolerable situation crying out for government action contrasts strongly with the final report's conclusion that, apart from the appointment of additional Factory Inspectors and an ironing out of anomalies in the Factory and Workshop Acts, the remedy lay in the encouragement of a moral responsibility by employers and "improved habits in the employed". They concluded

> "[we] can also strongly second the zealous and judicious efforts now being made to encourage thrift, promote temperance, improve dwellings and raise the tone of living".[5]

However, Bythell's approach to the Select Committee's recommendations is too superficial; the reasons for the Lord's rather pathetic conclusions lie in the arguments about state intervention which dominated the Select Committee. This conflict led to the Chairman, Lord Dunraven, resigning in early 1890, following the Committee's rejection of his draft report because of the

> "very considerable difference of opinion between the Chairman and the Committee as to the whole nature and character of the Report that is called for by the evidence that was given to the Committee".[6]

Dunraven maintained that the evidence had revealed that the causes of sweating were three-fold:

- the abuse of sub-contracting;
- the competition amongst employers;
- foreign immigration.

Accordingly, he moved a resolution in the House of Lords in June 1890

> "that, in the opinion of this House, legislation with a view to the amelioration of the condition of the people suffering under that system [i.e. sweating] is urgently needed".

He proposed that legislation should be brought in to prevent sub-contractors evading the regulations under the Factory Acts and that in particular there should be a limitation of foreign immigration -

> "... some check or, if necessary, a full stop should be placed upon the importation of this cheap destitute and unskilled foreign labour".[7]

The Select Committee's Report, on the other hand, maintained that sub-contracting was a consequence and not a cause of sweating. The Liberal, Lord Thring, who had taken over the chairmanship after Lord Dunraven's resignation, spoke also against immigration controls arguing that it was wrong for the state to interfere with the freedom of the individual in such a way and that in any case foreign immigration was

> "a small thing, having regard to the enormous quantity of female and other unskilled labour in the market".[8]

The Conservative government was reluctant to consider bringing in immigration controls and was further hampered from tackling the problem

of sweating by their opposition to protective factory legislation for
adult male workers.  The Secretary to the Board of Trade accepted that
protection was necessary for women and children because, he said

> "they were not in a position to help themselves, but he should
> be very sorry if anything was done ... to interfere with the
> means of full-grown men obtaining a livelihood in the severe
> struggle for existence".[8a]

The same type of opposition to any legislation placing limitations on
men's hours and conditions of work was expressed by both Liberal and
Conservative leaders under pressure from trade unionists for eight hours
legislation. ` For Gladstone, the leader of the opposition, it was "an
intolerable infringement of personal liberty to prevent a man working
for a long as he wished to work"[9] and the Conservative Home Secretary

> "could hold out no hope that the Government will support any
> legislation which has for its objects to impose restrictions
> upon the freedom of adult males in the disposal and management
> of their own labour".[10]

A reluctance on both sides of the House to introduce further state intervention was therefore at the root of the lack of response to the problems
of sweating revealed in the House of Lords enquiry.  It is also
significant that there was general agreement amongst both Conservative and
Liberal politicians that trades union organisation of sweated workers would
counter the disastrous effects of intense competition between unskilled
workers and was therefore to be encouraged.  As Phelps-Brown points out,
this follows the conclusion reached by those concerned with industrial
relations in general - namely that the "best practicable development ...
lay in the growth of responsible trade unions"[11].  The development of
the State's approach to industrial relations is discussed below.


## Developments in State Intervention, 1890-1906

In spite of the general agreement in Parliament against State intervention
on sweating, there were three significant developments in the next
fifteen years which extended the State's role in the relationship between
employer and employee.  The first was the acceptance by the Government
that in its role as employer and in contracting out work, certain minimum
standards should be laid down;  the second was the extension of the Factory
Acts to allow for better regulation of non-factory production;  and the
third was the development of the Board of Trade's role in arbitration and
conciliation procedures.

## 1. Government Work and "Fair Wages"

In 1891, following concern expressed in the House of Lords Report about
Government contract work, a Fair Wages Resolution was passed, without
a division, by the House of Commons -

> "that in the opinion of this House it is the duty of the
> Government in all government contracts to make provision
> against the evils recently disclosed before the Sweating
> Commission, to insert such conditions as may prevent the
> abuses arising from sub-letting, and to make every effort
> to secure the payment of such wages as are generally
> accepted as current in each trade for competent workmen".[12]

This Resolution was adopted following evidence about the low earnings of
outworkers engaged on army and navy uniforms, and was in various forms
also implemented by some local authorities, the London County Council
being the most aggressive in its attempts to lay down a minimum wage.
The "fair wage" was usually set as that negotiated by the trade unions
and organised employers in the particular trade. The idea of employers'
and employees' representatives coming together to agree on uniform rates
of wages was not a new one; the problem was that it was only in the
organised trades - and where not only employees but also employers were
organised - that such uniform rates could be agreed and kept to. The
1891 Fair Wage Resolution, by attempting to apply uniform rates to unorganised labour and employers, such as in the clothing trade and casual
building trades, went one step towards recognising that the state should
intervene in the situation where intense competition amongst employers
and amongst workers forced down wages and where neither side was well
organised[13]. Another significant development was when the London
County Council in 1894 stipulated that contractors undertaking council
work must not give any of that work out to be done in the home.

The Fair Wages Resolution attracted widespread support but the limitation
of the working day in government employment to eight hours was more
controversial. As mentioned above, any limitation to the adult man's
working day was at first opposed on both sides of the House but a con-
certed campaign outside Parliament forced a change of heart by a
significant number of Liberal MPs in 1892 - support for eight hours
legislation was made a condition of labour support in a number of
industrial constituencies and in the 1892 election, the point was driven
home, when, in spite of a national Liberal victory, several Liberal
opponents of legislation lost either their seats or significant numbers
of votes[14]. The motivation behind this labour support of eight hours
legislation had little to do with tackling sweating; it was proposed
as a means of creating more jobs and reducing unemployment. However,

when three Liberal MPs, who were also employers, introduced an eight
hours day following electoral pressure, they found that productivity was
maintained and there was no need to employ extra workers. Following
this demonstration of economic efficiency, and as a matter of political
expediency, the Secretary for War introduced an eight hour day into
all War Office factories - in spite of continuing opposition from
Gladstone - on the grounds that it would bring both "gain to the
employer" and "moral and physical benefits to the men"[15].

However, the practical effects of the implementation of an eight hour
day had robbed the labour movement of its justification and although
legislation for a shorter working day continued to be supported by some,
the reluctance amongst both politicians and trade unionists to bring in
legislative restrictions on the adult working man was more dominant.


## 2. Factory and Workshop Legislation

There was general public acceptance during the late nineteenth century of the
need, as The Times in 1874 put it, for factory legislation "to prescribe
conditions of existence below which the population shall not decline"[16].
There were, however, limits to this acceptance of state intervention;
adult men's hours of labour should not be interfered with and there were
strong arguments raised against the regulation of domestic workplaces.
The demand for the inspection of homeworkers and the better regulation
of domestic workshops arose out of the investigations of The Lancet's
"Sanitary Commission on Sweating and the Homework System and their
influence in Public Health" in 1876[17]. There was pressure to include
such regulation in the 1876 Factory and Workshop Bill but the Commission
on the Factory Acts reported that year that

> "all domestic employment ... should be left under the system
> at present in force in workshops, as we think it desirable to
> interfere as little as possible with the habits and arrange-
> ments of families".[18]

However, the fear of contagious disease, such as the outbreak of smallpox
in Leeds in 1888 prompted greater support for the sanitary inspection of
domestic workshops and, following the Royal Commission on Labour local
authorities were given greater powers to inspect such premises under the
1895 Factory Act.


Further pressure for the extension of regulation to workshop and domestic
production arose from complaints received by the House of Lords Select
Committee that the existing Factory and Workshop Acts encouraged non-

173

factory production because of the disparities of regulation of factories and workshops. One Factory Inspector even went so far as to claim that the trend towards mechanised production had been reversed in London because the anomalies in the Acts and their implementation meant that workshop production was encouraged to the detriment of factory production[19]. It is extremely difficult to assess whether this shift from factory to workshop production was actually happening. James Schmiechen in an article published in the Economic History Review[20] presents the argument that decentralisation was taking place in the London clothing trade as a result of the Factory and Workshop Acts, but, as discussed in Chapter 2, this is based on a rather superficial analysis of the development of the clothing trade. Nonetheless, the case was strongly argued at the end of the 1880s and politicians were undoubtedly swayed by it. The result was the 1891 Factory and Workshop Act which made the registration of all new workshops mandatory and enabled the registration of outworkers. Following a recommendation of the Royal Commission Labour four years later, another Act strengthened local authorities' responsibilities for the sanitary inspection of workshops generally as well as greater powers to regulate the domestic workshops mentioned above.

The size and scope of the Factory and Sanitary Inspectorates increased during the 1890s and early 1900s. This was related to two developments in particular; first, the appointment of women Factory Inspectors in 1893 and the establishment of a separate department of Women Factory Inspectors under a principal Lady Factory Inspector; and the second, the appointment by a number of inner city boroughs of additional Sanitary Inspectors to deal especially with the inspection of workshops and the keeping of the outworker register.

The appointment in 1893 of the first woman Factory Inspector heralded the introduction of regular annual reports of what became a department of women Factory Inspectors who reported each year on the particular conditions of women workers in various trades and industries. These Annual Reports were an extremely valuable source of government information on women's work and wages; they were far more detailed than the reports of the male inspectors and the women Factory Inspectors frequently enquired into the family situation of individual workers.

In 1896 a separate Department of women Factory Inspectors was constituted with five women Factory Inspectors; their numbers were rapidly added to

and by 1906 there were twenty-seven of them.    The working conditions
of women received greater attention as a result of the long, detailed
reports and the special studies that these women carried out.    The
findings of the Factory Inspectors had important implications for
politicians' views on how women's labour was considered as a problem and
what solutions were offered.    Moreover, the attitudes of the women
Factory Inspectors themselves were significant.

These women Factory Inspectors firmly believed in the value of mothers
staying at home to look after their children - May Abraham the first
woman Factory Inspector, told a meeting during the 1891 TUC that she

> "believed that the less work women did in a factory the better
> it would be for their home life, and she would like to see the
> men doing all the work outside their homes".[21]

They found, however, that such a state of things was just not possible
for many women.    It is significant that, charged with implementing the
"four week rule" on employment after childbirth, they yet reported year
after year that such implementation was impractical.    They found case
after case of women returning to work immediately after their child was
born but concluded

> "with work for women as easy to obtain as it has been of late,
> while the supply of unskilled labouring men is so much greater
> than the demand for their labour, one cannot blame the woman
> for doing what seems to her the only possible thing ...".[22]

Miss Paterson, one of the women Factory Inspectors reported that she was
sure women would welcome at least a month off work after a birth -

> "were it possible by some system of national or trade
> insurance to provide a fund from which she could draw.
> Unfortunately, it is just when she is least fit to work that
> she most requires money".[23]

In some cases, it would even seem that the women Factory Inspectors were
refusing to implement the four-week rule[24].

Although the women Factory Inspectors condemned the practice of mothers
leaving the home in order to work they recognised the need for such women
to work and that this need arose either from the inadequacy of a man's
wage or from the woman's role as sole breadwinner with dependents.    This
recognition prompted their opposition to more radical restriction on
women's right to work and their support for two alternative policies - a
minimum wage which would prevent male or female wage-earners from falling
below the bread-line and which would, they hoped, decrease the need for
women to work by raising male wages;    and the provision of relief/benefits
to aid the woman with dependents[25].

As a result of the increased responsibility placed on local authorities under the 1891, 1895 and 1901 Factory Acts, a number of local authorities appointed Sanitary Inspectors especially to deal with the inspection and regulation of workshops and the compilation of the outworker register. In boroughs such as Kensington, Poplar and Islington which all appointed additional Sanitary Inspectors in the late 1890s, the workshop and out-worker registers were kept up to date and all types of non-factory premises (including homeworkers' premises) were subject to close super-vision[26].

Statistics of workshops, domestic workshops and outworkers collected by the local authorities were collated by the Home Office and published[27]. These two sources of additional information increased politicians' and civil servants' knowledge of the sweated trades and also provided valuable ammunition for those who campaigned against sweating and on women's work and wages.


3.   The Board of Trade

The third development which opened up possibilities for the extension of state intervention was the development of the role of the Board of Trade.   In Chapter 6 we discussed the support amongst many larger employers for conciliation procedures.   Such a view also supported "responsible" organisation amongst workers without which uniform wage rates and working conditions could not be agreed upon and implemented. The House of Lords Select Committee had supported trade unionisation for this reason as had the Royal Commission on Labour when it reported in 1894.   A desire to see "responsible" organisations of both capital and labour was expressed by the civil servants of the new Labour Department of the Board of Trade.   Set up in 1893, this Department became increasingly important, firstly through its publication of statistics on wages, hours and levels of employment;   and secondly, through its role as intermediary in industrial disputes.

During the 1890s it was only those attempting to represent the interests of unorganised labour who strongly supported compulsory implementation of agreed wage rates (and they were really after a minimum wage). Politicians of all persuasions, civil servants such as H. Llewellyn-Smith and the representatives of organised labour such as Thomas Burt, and employers' representatives, opposed compulsory arbitration[28].   As a result the 1896 Conciliation Act left the Board of Trade's role based

on the voluntary principle. Nevertheless, as the Board of Trade
was called in more and more often as an arbiter in disputes, this
experience demonstrated that voluntary agreements did not work in trades
where employers and employees were unorganised - a major characteristic
of the sweated trades. The Board of Trade's chief arbitrator, George
Askwith, was won over to the principle of compulsion for such trades
as a result of this experience, even though his superior (Llewellyn-
Smith) and some of his colleagues (such as Clara Collet) remained
unconvinced[29]. Askwith came to hold the view that to eliminate
sweating, "good employers" in the sweated trades should be given the
backing of legal sanctions

> "Get those men together, let them fight the sweater themselves,
> and insist upon reasonable equalisation of minimum rates and
> they will be able to fix a price for their locality and possibly
> for the Kingdom".[30]

Askwith later played an important part in persuading the Select Committee
on Homework to recommend the setting up of Trade Boards (see Chapter 8).


IV

## Women and the State

At the end of the nineteenth century the only legislation which affected
women as waged workers was the Factory Acts. In many ways, the Factory
Acts were the forerunners of minimum wage legislation in the sense that
the Trade Boards Act was an extension of the precedent set by the
Factory Acts whereby the State intervened in the relationship between
employer and employee[31]. Both types of legislation also primarily
affected women workers.


The Factory Acts explicitly treated first children, then women, as
separate categories of worker, in need of protection by the State. By
the end of the nineteenth century, a rather complicated mass of factory
legislation existed (consolidated by the 1901 Factory and Workshop Act)
which primarily restricted women's and children's hours of work and right
to work. Women workers were subject not only to regulations determining
their hours of work but also as to whether, in certain trades, they could
work at all. Women had been excluded from working in the mines as early
as 1842. The 1891 Factory Act allowed the Home Secretary to designate
certain trades as "dangerous" thereby enabling the Factory Inspectorate
to lay down rules and regulations restricting employment in these trades.
Although the Act did not distinguish between men and women workers, the
1895 Factory Act enabled the Factory Inspectorate to prohibit the employ-

ment of categories of workers in trades deemed to be particularly
dangerous for those workers.   Thus women were prohibited from working
on some or all of the processes involved in the manufacture of paints,
electric accumulators, pottery, india rubber and in lead smelting and
brass casting.   This was because lead poisoning, a hazard of all these trades,
was found to "have a serious effect on the child-bearing function"[32].   The
1891 Factory Act prohibited women from working within four weeks of childbirth, although this proved to be almost impossible to enforce (see p.176
of this chapter).

By the end of the nineteenth century, therefore, the State had already
taken a specific interest in how women's work outside the home might affect
their role as mothers.

Throughout the second half of the nineteenth century opposition was
expressed by politicians and civil servants to women working because of
the effect on their children.   John Simon had stated in 1858 that
"infants perish under the neglect and mismanagement which their mothers'
occupation implies"[33] and his conclusions were echoed by a number of
influential people at the end of the century.   W.S. Jevons, for example,
wrote of a "great evil" arising from the employment of women of child-
bearing age -

> "In the case of infants who ought to be suckled, the result
> is usually disastrous.   Committed during the whole day to
> the care of inexperienced and uninterested nurses, they are
> fed on 'pap' - that is, bread and water - or some mixed food
> hardly more suitable to an infant's stomach.   A large
> proportion succumb, and those who, by any fortunate accident
> of more vigorous constitution or slightly better treatment,
> survive, are too often ruined physically and mentally, and grow
> up into a stunted and sickly generation.   Improvident marriages,
> too, are much promoted by the fact that the nother can earn her
> own living".[34]

At the end of the nineteenth century, it was assumed by most politicians
that married women's waged work was an undesirable phenomenon.   This
attitude was apparent throughout the parliamentary investigations in the
second half of the nineteenth century and was confirmed by instances
cited of the immorality and suffering of women workers, by cases found
of child-neglect and by high infant mortality rates.

The 1880s and 1890s saw an increasing interest amongst social reformers
and politicians in the position of women;   an increasing interest in
their role both as workers and as mothers.   In part, this interest arose
as a result of the growth of information available on living and working

conditions of the working class in general, revealing as it did the particular poverty of many women and their children. During the 1890s and 1900s, investigations of women's work could almost be said to be a "growth industry" - a number of such investigations appear in the Bibliography. The House of Lords Select Committee on Sweating in 1888 to 1890 had taken a certain amount of evidence on women workers, although most of the focus was in fact on specific trades. The Royal Commission on Labour in 1891 to 1894, however, commissioned a special report on women workers[35] and 1891 also saw the publication of an article by Sidney Webb in the Economic Journal on the wages of women workers. The fact that this was published in the first issue of what was intended to be an influential journal indicates the importance given to the question of women's work and wages.

Economists and intellectuals such as Marshall, Hobson and Webb, paid considerable attention to the question of women's work and wages. They addressed themselves to the widely-held belief that women were displacing men in many areas of manufacturing industry and to the question of why the average wage for women seemed to be about 10/- to 12/- per week. The general assumption was that women were a different class of worker from men - i.e. the fact that a worker was female had consequences which cut across divisions of skill, training or other characteristics.

There were two ways in which the focus of attention was brought to bear on women workers - one was the concern that cheap female labour acted as a downward pull on male wages and sometimes displaced male workers; the other was the concern at the damage that working mothers incurred to their children. Both types of concern were based on the moral assumption that ideally a man's wage should be enough to support a wife and children and that mothers should not have to engage in waged work. Marshall, for instance, maintained that anything that increased the employment of women in waged work was to be deplored as it tempted women

> "to neglect their duty of building up a true home, and of investing their efforts in the personal capital of their children's character and abilities".[36]

The opposition to married women's work was given a further boost by the growing concern in the 1890s with the health of the nation, and in particular, with that of its children. Two recent pieces of research[37] have indicated how

> "around the beginning of this century infant life and child health took on a new importance in public discussion reinforced

by emphasis on the value of a healthy and numerous population as a natural resource".[38]

Statistics showed a falling birth rate and a rising infant mortality rate and the State started to take a keen interest in the family. As Davin puts it, "child-rearing was becoming a national duty, not a moral one"[39] Both Davin and Lewis' research show that the solutions were mainly posed in terms of improving the standard of motherhood and such aims were very much part of exhortations to mothers not to engage in waged work. An influential book on infant mortality published in 1906 by the man who was to become the Chief Medical Officer of Health to the Board of Education, stated

> "... in towns where women are largely employed in factories, away from home, the disadvantages [of urban life] are enormously increased ... And the operations of this are threefold. First, there are the ordinary injuries and diseases to which women and girls in factories are liable; secondly, there is the strain and stress of long hours and hard work to the pregnant woman; and thirdly, there is the absence from home of the mother of the infant. It cannot be doubted that these are the factors in the relation between factory occupation of women and a high infant mortality"[40]

Yet the reality of the necessity of women's waged work remained - and government officials, politicians and social reformers all recognised this necessity.

This is apparent in what is perhaps the most well-known expression of concern with the health of future British citizens - the Report of the Inter-Departmental Committee on Physical Deterioration, a Committee set up in response to the poor health of British army recruits during the Boer War. Evidence was received of what were considered to be frightening statistics of infant mortality and the Committee concluded that they had

> "no doubt that the employment of mothers in factories is attended by evil consequences both to themselves and their children and they would gladly see it diminished if not altogether discontinued".[41]

However, the Committee also received evidence (in particular from Adelaide Anderson, the Chief Lady Factory Inspector) that many women were forced to go out to work through sheer economic necessity and they therefore declined to express the opinion that steps should be taken at that time to prevent women from working outside the home[42].

There had been concern expressed about the health of the nation before the recruitment fiascos at the time of the Boer War. This just brought it to a head. Indeed, the evidence and conclusions drawn by the 1904

180

Committee showed that a considerable amount of debate and thought had preceded the Committee's deliberations.   It would have been too easy for the Committee to draw hasty conclusions about denying married women the right to work.   The fact that they realised that such simplistic notions were unrealistic and unlikely to provide a solution is a reflection of the discussion on a woman's role as wife, mother and worker which had already taken place.   The Victorian middle-class ideal was a two-parent family where the husband earned enough to enable the wife to stay at home devoting herself to household duties and motherhood;   the reality for a significant section of the working class was very different, as we have seen in Chapter 3.

If married women were prevented from working in industry - as they were in many white-collar occupations, the poverty of the families of semi- and unskilled workers would have deepened and more deserted mothers and widows would have to be supported from the rates or charity.   Further- more, married women were an important source of cheap labour which employers could not do without.   Jevons, in the book referred to above, while he condemned mothers working, also admitted - in the introduction added to the 1894 edition - that their exclusion from the labour force was impracticable and suggested instead that crèches should be provided[43]. The ideal and the reality were incompatible and it was this incompatibility which encouraged an attempt to tackle the problem of women's low wages in the form of minimum wage legislation.

The necessity for mothers to go out to work was recognised by even the most vociferous critic of married women's work.   George Newman, in his book "Infant Mortality" quoted a Medical Officer of Health for a textile town where there was a high infant mortality rate:

> "A weaver's wages will not allow of the wife's remaining at home, considering the high rents and rates, and so both go - which is the rule - and a hand-to-mouth existence results even for them- selves, let alone the little ones, who are left in the intervals to the mercies of the nurse, who as a rule, takes in the babies to eke out her own husband's wages.   Much good may be done by hygienic tuition, but I am certain that the root of the whole matter with us is, as I have said, comparatively low wages and high rents and rates".[44]

Newman recognised that low male wages or unemployment were the reasons for married women's work and criticised others, for example, Chiozza Money, for calling for a legal prohibition on married women working.

> "However much [Newman said] the employment of married women is open to criticism, the fact of their employment remains, and appears under present circumstances to be, in many cases at

131

least, a necessary evil.  Hence the immediately practicable
measure must be applied rather to the protection and relief
of such women than to any attempt at prohibition".[45]


4.    Changing Ideas on Poverty

The studies of sweated labour carried out in the 1880s and 1890s opened
up a new perspective on poverty - the poverty of people who worked
desperately hard for very low wages.  This "discovery" provoked a
particular concern;  as Charles Booth put it, "where there is industry,
there ought to be no poverty"[45a].  Politicians and the middle and upper
classes generally could attempt to blame the poverty of the unemployed
or casual worker on the individual's failings, but the poverty of
sweated workers was more problematic.

These years also saw a growth of information available on the living and
working conditions of the working-class in general.  The increased
attention paid by government to gathering information on unemployment,
on wages and on the living and working conditions of the working-class
has been well documented by J. Harris[46] and G. Stedman-Jones[47].  The
setting up of a Labour Department at the Board of Trade focussed official
interest on gathering statistics on levels of employment and wages in
different trades.  The first Wages Census was published in 1886 and at
the same time information on prices and consumption made possible the
assessment of relative standards of living.  These government studies
and the investigations carried out by individuals such as Charles Booth,
helped to advance an awareness of the conditions of working-class life
and in particular they revealed the poverty in which many families lived
and the unsatisfactory conditions in which their children were born and
brought up.

As Stedman-Jones'[48] research shows, a new attitude developed towards the
urban poor in the 1890s and 1900s.  Previously, the tendency had been
to blame the individual weaknesses of the casual labourer for the persistence of a "residuum" in inner city areas and to prescribe charitable
activity based on self-help as the only solution.  The studies of those
such as Charles Booth, now pointed to the conclusion that poverty was
widespread amongst  the unskilled and semi-skilled workforce and that
the causes were mostly out of the control of the individual worker.
Although characteristics supposedly exhibited by the "residuum" continued
to be deplored, increasingly the stress was away from individual

inadequacies and towards a recognition of the structural reasons for
un- or under-employment and low wages.

Concern about poverty was enhanced by the recognition that such conditions
persisted in the face of a general improvement in living standards.
Amongst statisticians and economists there seems to have been a dominant
optimism about wages, prices and the standard of living generally of the
working class.   The statisticians G.H. Wood and A. Bowley differed in
their detailed analysis of the figures but both concluded that the
"standard of comfort" had increased dramatically since 1890[49].   This
optimistic picture was explained at the level of economic theory by the
argument that a law of increasing returns was now operating in manufacturing and in relation to the growth of population.   Alfred Marshall
and other influential economists believed that Britain's earlier
population difficulties had been overcome, new areas of trade were
opening up and the purchasing power of wages was increasing.   Ricardo's
concept of the "wages fund" with its pessimistic Malthusian assumptions
was overtaken by the development of an economic theory dominated by con-
cepts of social and economic progress[50].

Yet, during this period there was ample evidence that large numbers of
people were living in great poverty and in fact, in spite of the
generally optimistic tone of the economic orthodoxy which he dominated,
Alfred Marshall was aware of the problems of unemployment, low wages
and bad working conditions and claimed that most of his work was directed
at the problem of poverty[51].   Probably the most important contribution
that Marshall made to the study of poverty was the popularisation of his
theory of wages, which broke completely from the economic tradition of
Ricardo.   Fundamental to Ricardo's theory of wages was the notion that,
ceteris paribus, the worker would always command his/her "cost of
production" - i.e. cost of daily subsistence - and that labour value was,
apart from unimportant empirical variations, uniform.   The school of
economists to which Marshall belonged, however, held

> "... labour to be essentially variable, so that its value must
> be determined by the value of the produce, not the value of
> the produce by that of the labour".[52]

Thus wages would depend on the efficiency of the worker and the social
utility of the goods produced.   It was conceivable, therefore, that
wages of "inefficient" workers or of those producing very cheap goods,
would fall below subsistence level.   These assumptions had great significance when social reformers came to consider sweated labour in

general and women's work and wages in particular. If there was no
relationship between the worker's subsistence needs and his/her wages,
then it was conceivable that large numbers of "inefficient" workers
could earn very low wages and would not only fall into the abyss of
extreme poverty, not only take their children with them into this abyss,
but also act as a downward pull on otherwise "efficient" workers' wages
which would in turn bring them into the degrading conditions suffered
by sweated labour.

At the turn of the century the recognition of structural causes of
poverty was associated with and given further weight by the development
of new perspectives on the role of the state and of social reform. The
perspectives to which I refer are the development of ideas about
"national efficiency"[53] and the new Liberal philosophy of the need for
state intervention to promote social justice and social stability. The
content and importance of these ideas have been widely researched by
historians, some of whom have emphasised the ideology of national
efficiency and others the "New Liberalism". In practice, however, it
would appear that the two perspectives were inter-related and this is
evident in the way that the sweated trades and sweated workers become
more and more a subject of public concern. Of particular relevance to
this study is how the sweated trades and sweated workers were considered
to be damaging to the health and stability of British society at the
beginning of this century.

Evidence of low wages amongst workers in the sweated trades, of unhealthy
working conditions and of their effect on the future generations continued
to be published in the late 1890s and early 1900s. At the same time,
politicians were worried by Britain's difficulties of gaining victory in
the Boer War and of the country's relative decline in industrial
production compared to Germany and the United States. People such as
Asquith and the Webbs contended that the material conditions of the
working people were directly related to Britain's economic and military
standing. This was demonstrated by Asquith when he supported the 1901
Factory and Workshop Act through the House of Commons. He defended
previous factory legislation aimed at better working conditions -

> "What would Great Britain have been today as an industrial and
> producing country but for the labours of Lord Shaftesbury and
> those who have succeeded him in this factory legislation? We
> should have a stunted, sickly, ignorant population, wholly un-
> fitted to hold its own in the growing stress and strain of
> industrial competition ...".[54]

But further reform was necessary, he maintained -

"The regulations in the countries with which we are in acute
competition in the labour markets of the world are far more
drastic than our own, as regards the age and period of employment and as regards the standard of education required ...".[55]

The fear that a degeneration of large sections of the working class would
drag the whole nation down into economic, political and moral chaos and
the arguments in favour of social reform to promote "national efficiency"
were increasingly cutting across party lines. The language of "national
efficiency" was used by Liberal and Conservative politicians and also by
many labour leaders. An illustration of this is found in the appointment
of William Beveridge by the Conservative newspaper the Morning Post, to
take over responsibility for all articles related to social policy. The
Morning Post's editor was on the social imperialist wing of the Conservative
Party and was anxious to develop Conservative opinion on social policy[56].
Beveridge followed the desire of the New Liberalism to promote policies
which would foster social cohesion and avoid political conflict between
capital and labour, and the recognition that in order for the current
economic and political framework to survive, the working class must get
its fair share of both economic and political returns[57]. During 1906
and 1907, Beveridge, who was to become an official at the Board of Trade
in 1908, wrote a number of articles in the Morning Post sympathetic to a
legal minimum wage for sweated trades. These articles are important in
that they reflect many of the dominant ideas which were held by politicians
and civil servants about sweating and which were the motivations behind
both Liberal and Conservative support for the Trade Board Act.

In his articles, Beveridge defined sweating as work which does not pay
enough to feed the worker and involves such long hours that he/she
cannot get enough sleep.

> "Such work, [he wrote] involves a steady drain on the physical
> strength of the worker; it wears him out before his time and
> inevitably shortens his life. Industries supported by such
> work draw from the worker not only his labour in the present
> but also his labouring strength for the future. Though they
> prove commercially sound and profitable to individuals, they
> are emphatically unprofitable for the community whose members
> grow old before due season or out of weakness rear a degenerate
> posterity".[58]

Such industries, Beveridge thought, were not only damaging to the future
health and prosperity of the whole nation but were also parasites on more
healthy industries. Many of the workers in sweated trades were women

who, either as wives or daughters, were partially supported by a male
wage.   Therefore, Beveridge maintained, the industry which obtains
cheap female labour because of women's dependence on male wages is really
receiving an indirect subsidy out of the wages paid in some other industry
to the wage-earner on whom the woman is dependent.   Such sweated trades
were parasites.

Beveridge in fact disapproved of women and in particular married women
doing paid work outside the home.   A woman would usually, according to
him

> "be leaving other duties at home in order to work in the factory;
> in the case of a married woman this is more likely to be the
> case and undoubtedly accounts for a large proportion of the
> appalling mortality of today".[59]

These two contentions - that sweated trades were "parasitical" and that a
large number of sweated workers, namely women workers, should not be part
of the labour force at all - were important motivations behind the
support of politicians and civil servants for the notion of minimum wage
legislation for sweated trades.

                              *  *  *

We have seen that, at the time of the first major investigation into
sweated labour, there was a reluctance on the part of politicians to consider state intervention.   However, over the next twenty years a number
of developments took place which resulted in an atmosphere more favourable to legislative action.

This more favourable atmosphere arose out of the pressure from two types
of development.   Firstly, it arose from the expansion of the role of
Government departments, particularly that of the Board of Trade and the
Factory and Sanitary Inspectorates.   The activities greatly contributed
to the information available on the working class in general but
specifically on the inability of trade unions or employers' organisations
to establish adequate or stable rates of wages in the sweated trades.

The second type of development was that of the increasing concern about
the effect of poverty on the nation's future prosperity and, in particular,
the effect of married women's work on the health of the future generation.
The general assumption was that ideally men's wages should be enough to

support a family, yet there was growing evidence that for a significant proportion of the working class this was not the case. The consequent recognition of the need for many married women to work was accompanied by evidence of a continuing high rate of infant mortality - a rate which was thought to be indicative of the harm done by married women's work.

This Chapter has analysed the political response to the problem of the sweated trades before the 1906 General Election. We have shown that there were important developments in state intervention which had implications for the sweated trades but which did not solve the problem of sweating. This discussion has thus provided the political background to the campaign for Wages Boards which was set up in 1906, the analysis of which forms the subject of the next Chapter.

1.  House of Lords Debates, **28** February, 1598-1606.

2.  Ibid.

3.  D. Bythell, "The Sweated Trades" (1978).

4.  Ibid, p.232.

5.  House of Lords Select Committee on Sweating, Fifth and Final Report, PP1890, XVII, (Cd.169), p.301.

6.  House of Lords Debates, 24 March 1890.

7.  Ibid, 298.

8.  Ibid., 450.

8a. House of Lords, 28 February 1888, 1617.

9.  J. Harris, (1972), p.66.

10. Ibid.

11. E.H. Phelps-Brown, "The Growth of British Industrial Relations" (1959), p.199.

12. House of Commons Debates, 13 February 1891.

13. See Phelps-Brown (1959), pp.202-204.

14. Harris, (1972), p.66.

15. Ibid., p.70.

16. B. Hutchins and A. Harrison, "A History of Factory Legislation" (1907), p.xiv.

17. The Lancet, 29 January 1876, pp.175-6.

18. Report of the Commissioners on the Working of the Factory and Workshop Acts, Vol.I, p.ix, PP1876, XXIX.

19. House of Lords Select Committee on Sweating, 2nd Report, PP1888, Vol.XXI, Q.16706.

20. J.A. Schmiechen, "State Reform and the Local Economy" An Aspect of Industrialisation in Late Victorian and Edwardian London" in Economic History Review 2nd Series XXVIII, No.3, August 1975. For a criticism of his use of the sources, see Jenny Morris,"State Reform and the Local Economy" in Economic History Review (forthcoming).

21. The Women Factory Inspectors themselves had to give up their post if and when they married and there is no evidence of any objections being made to this.

22. Annual Report of Chief Inspector of Factories and Workshops. 1907, p.184.

23. Ibid.

24. 1909 Annual Report, p.159.

25. See A. Anderson's evidence to the Select Committee on Homework.

26. See J. Morris, ibid., EHR (forthcoming).

27. E.g. UK Home Office: Return as to the administration in each county
    and county borough during 1904, by the local authorities of the
    Homework provisions of the F & W Act 1901, as shown by the reports
    of the MoH sent to the Home Office under Section 132 of the Act.
    PP1906 CX (Cd.211).

28. See Davidson, (1971), p.142.

29. G. Askwith, "Industrial Problems and Disputes" (1920).

30. Ibid., p.285.

31. Indeed, Ernest Aves, sent by the Board of Trade to investigate the
    Victoria Wages Boards reported that they were looked upon as a
    natural extension of the Factory Acts (Report on the Wages Boards
    and Industrial Conciliation and Arbitration Acts of Australia and
    New Zealand, PP1908 (Cd.4167).

32. M.I. Crofts, "Women Under the English Law", (1925), p.67.

33. Papers Relating to the Sanitary State of the People of England
    (1858), p.82.

34. W.S. Jevons, "The State in Relation to Labour ... "(first published
    1882, 3rd edn. 1894), p.73.

35. Royal Commission on Labour: Reports of the Lady Assistant
    Commissioners on the Employment of Women, PP1893-4 XXXVII (Cd.6894).

36. A. Marshall, "Principles of Economics" (1907 edn.), p.685.

37. A. Davin, "Imperialism and Motherhood" in History Workshop Journal,
    No.5, Spring 1978; J. Lewis, "The Politics of Motherhood" (1980).

38. Davin (1978), p.9.

39. Ibid.

40. G. Newman, "Infant Mortality - A Social Problem" (1906), p.131.

41. Report of the Inter-Departmental Committee on Physical Deterioration,
    PP1904 XXXII (Cd.2175), p.47.

42. Ibid., p.48.

43. Jevons (1894), p.xiii.

44. Newman (1906), p.138.

45. Ibid.

45a. C. Booth (1902), Vol.5, p.293.

46. J. Harris (1972).

47. G. Stedman-Jones (1971).

48. Ibid, Chapter 18.

49. G.H. Wood, "Real Wages and the Standard of Comfort Since 1850", in Journal of the Royal Statistical Society, 1909, No.72, pp91-103. A. Bowley, "Wages" in Dictionary of Political Economy (1909 edn.).

50. See T.W. Hutchison, "The Marginal Revolution and the Decline and Fall of English Classical Economy" in History of Political Economy Vol.4, No.2, Autumn 1972.

51. A. Marshall, "Principles of Economics" (1907 edn.) pp.709-710.

52. W.S. Jevons, "Theory of Political Economy" (1888), pp.165-166.

53. See G. Searle, "The Quest for National Efficiency" (1971).

54. House of Commons Debates, Vol.95, 17 June 1901, pp.640-641.

55. Ibid.

56. J. Harris, "William Beveridge" (1977), p.62.

57. Ibid, pp.80-90.

58. Morning Post, 4.5.1906.

59. Morning Post, 22.3.19(ᶠ

# 8 The Trade Boards Act 1909

## I

In the last four chapters we examined the attitude of various important
groups of people to the problems of sweated labour.  Chapter 1 to 3 have
shown that below-subsistence wages were paid to some factory workers as
well as workshop and homeworkers in certain trades;  and that very low
wages were primarily a characteristic of women workers.  The majority
of workers in the sweated trades were women and the majority of all women
workers earned very low wages.  It is not surprising therefore that the
focus of attention on low wages was mainly on the low wages paid to women
and the attendant unsatisfactory working conditions.  In contrast, when
politicians and social reformers turned their attention to the problem
of unemployment and casual labour, they focussed on male workers.
Although the concern about the sweated trades was part of the general
concern about the social, economic and political consequences of the
continuing poverty of as much as a third of the working class, there was
an additional dimension to the pressure which built up in support of a
minimum wage for sweated trades:  there was a particular concentration
on women workers and how their waged work affected their role as wives
and mothers.

Before going on to detail the campaign for Wages Boards and the events
which led up to the passing of the Trade Boards Act in 1909, it will be
helpful to set the discussion in a theoretical context.  One important
question is - why was there such a delay between the identification of
the problem of sweating and measures being taken to deal with it?
Caldwell[1] in his discussion of the Trade Boards Act, maintains that it
was laissez-faire principles which prevented state action before 1909.
From an examination of the conclusions reached by the House of Lords it
would certainly seem that an opposition, in principle, to state intervention played an important part in the lack of support for innovative
legislation to deal with sweating.  What is more significant, however,
is what factors brought about the increasing support for legislative
action on the sweated trades during the course of the next twenty years.
It is not sufficient to merely stress, as Caldwell does, the erosion of
laissez-faire principles and the acceptance of a greater degree of state
intervention.  From the evidence presented in the foregoing chapters,

it appears that it was the identification of women as the main group of sweated workers and the perceived social consequences of female sweated labour which were primarily responsible for the passing of the Trade Boards Act.  Furthermore, I wish to argue that the concept of "social control" is crucial to an understanding of the support for the Trade Boards Act and in particular the support for such legislation by some employers.

Before going on to discuss the campaign for Wages Boards and the passing of the Trade Boards Act, we will first introduce the concept of "social control" in order that the subsequent presentation of evidence can be placed in a theoretical context.

## The Concept of "Social Control"

Until recently, historians of social policy have tended to assume that social reform has been part of general progress towards a better society brought about by a desire for a more equal society and has heralded an improvement in the conditions of the less well-off members of society[2]. The assumption of "progress" is not only held by the more orthodox school of historians but also, implicitly, by those Marxist historians who see social reform as concessions won by the working class from a reluctant State[3].  Both perspectives see the motivation of social reform as "progressive", albeit in different ways and both perspectives assume that the working class is better off as a result of social reform.

It is not only most historians but also politicians, administrators and the general public who generally assume that social reform is part of a continuum of progress, of "things getting better", of a movement towards a more just, more equal society[4].  The implementation of a minimum wage for workers who were recognised to be earning a below-subsistence wage could plausibly be said to be part of such a movement. However, the evidence is that such were not the motivations of those who pressed for a minimum wage.  Neither was the Trade Boards Act a concession won by the working class: the organised labour movement did not play a decisive part in the campaign for the legislation.  Instead, the primary motivation was the concern felt, particularly by some influential employers, about the harm that the sweated trades were doing to the quality of labour and to the existing social order.  In order to understand these motivations, it is necessary to introduce the concept of social control.  Before we do this, however, one further criticism of the traditional theories of social reform is relevant, namely that an analysis of the ideology of social reform has been singularly lacking. There has been very little consideration or questioning of what type of social and economic relationships social reform has sought to promote; in particular there has been little recognition of the way in which the ideology of social reform has reinforced a certain conception of a woman's role as wife and mother, nor of the way in which the maintenance of the family has played such an important part in the history of social policy[5].  One of the purposes of my research has been to remedy this omission with respect to one piece of legislation which particularly affected women workers.

J.R. Hay defines the term "social control" to

> "encompass the activities, actions and influence of the ruling class of Britain by which they attempted to retain the existing basis of social relationships".[5a]

> "Social control [he maintains] is a social process occurring continuously within capitalist society, and is a product of the class antagonisms of that society".[6]

J. Brown[7] further illuminates the concept by emphasising that the rights and entitlements in legislation (on which the T.H. Marshall school focusses) cannot be separated from its restrictions, obligations, and disqualifications.  "Social policy" he states, "is a series of statements and reinforcements of what is considered to be socially appropriate"[8].

Social policy, according to this perspective, is fundamentally influenced by the ruling class's concern to maintain the status quo and to enforce what is considered to be necessary for such a maintenance.  This is simplistically stated but it should not be assumed that such a perspective involves a one-dimensional functionalist theory of social policy;  nor does it subscribe to a "conspiracy theory" of the State.

The State does not merely respond to the wishes of the ruling class, which in any case does not speak with one voice.  Even within the different sections of the ruling class, there are divisions of interest;  for example, at the beginning of this century, employers were taking more of a positive interest in state intervention, but many of them remained adamantly opposed to the Liberal welfare reforms.  It must be recognised that, although essentially the State in a capitalist society acts in the interests of maintaining capitalist relations of production, the relationship between the State and the ruling class is a dynamic and changing one and the State itself has a degree of autonomy.  Some employers at the turn of the century looked no further than their own immediate self-interest, but others had definite ideas about how best to maintain - and improve - the existing social order.

Although in many cases working class organisations were also putting pressure on the State and sometimes in a different direction from employers, the interests of employers, the interests of capital were a major factor in the State's decision-making process. One purpose of this thesis is to demonstrate that the process by which the Trade Boards Act was passed is an illustration of the importance of the concept of social control to the development of social policy.

This is the theoretical perspective in which I wish to consider the campaign for and the passing of the Trade Boards Act. Having done this, we will then consider, in Chapter 9, the application of the concept of social control to this particular piece of legislation.

## II

Previous chapters have demonstrated that there was, by the beginning of the century, considerable concern about the sweated trades. However, despite this widespread interest in the question of sweated labour, the problem was by no means an important issue in the run-up to the General Election of 1906. Mainstream political interest in the early years of the century was concentrated on the issue of Tariff Reform, particularly when in 1903, Joseph Chamberlain, Salisbury's Colonial Secretary, left the Conservative-Unionist Government to campaign for the British Dominions and Colonies becoming a self-contained economic unit. The argument raged as to whether trade protection was the solution to Britain's economic problems and Tariff Reform was the major issue in the 1906 General Election campaign[9]. The trade unions and the Labour Representation Committee candidates concentrated on the legal status and liability of trade unions, following the decision made in the Taff Vale case and two subsequent House of Lords decisions in 1901. The LRC and Lib-Lab candidates set their sights on the reversal of these decisions and the restoration of legal immunity for trade unions[10] and the rest of their election programme differed very little from that of the "radical" Liberals led by Masterman[11]. These "radical" Liberals concentrated more on social reform than tariff reform during the 1906 election but tended to be vague about actual detailed proposals, while emphasising a general

commitment to wealth being "spread more evenly"[12]. The mainstream
Liberal Party, although concentrating on tariff reform, did make some
commitments to poor law reform and action on pensions, unemployment and
housing.  However, there were no promises made for legislation on low
wages by any of the political parties.

Following the Liberals' landslide victory in 1906, action on social
reform got off to a slow start.  The main legislation in Campbell-
Bannerman's first year of office was the Trade Disputes Act, the Workmen's
Compensation Act, the Education Bill and the Plural Voting Bill (both of
these last two being defeated by the House of Lords).  During 1906 and
1907, the Liberals suffered three by-election defeats at the hands of
Labour candidates and Asquith and Lloyd George became very worried about
the possibility of the Liberals losing significant working-class support
to the newly-formed Labour Party[13] Lloyd George's reaction was to attempt

> "to persuade the Liberal Party to go forward on the path of
> social reform and to persuade Labour to avoid 'Socialism', to
> work side by side with him for limited and respectable
> objectives".[14]

Campbell-Bannerman, overwhelmed by ill health, was finally replaced as
Prime Minister by Asquith in 1908 who proceeded to "rededicate the Liberal
Party to the cause of social reform"[15].

No promises had been made by the Liberal Party in the 1906 Election of
action to raise wages in the sweated trades.  Yet three years after the
Election, the Trade Boards Act was passed, with all-Party support.  We
will now go on to discuss how and why this came about.


                                III

The Campaign for a Minimum Wage

Sir Charles Dilke first introduced a Bill to provide for the setting up
of Wages Boards in sweated trades in 1898.  Wages Boards had been set
up in Victoria in 1893 and the British campaigners against sweating con-
sistently referred to the Australian experience in support of similar
legislation in this country[16].  Dilke's Bill was based on the Victoria
legislation and would have enabled the Home Secretary to set up, after
an enquiry, a Wages Board for any trade, with representatives of
employees and employers and an independent chairman.  The minimum rates
fixed by the Board would be binding on all employers and be enforced by
Factory Inspectors with the sanction of fines.  Dilke presented the Bill

each year until 1906 but it wasn't until 1907 that a similar Bill
received a second reading.    It was Dilke's close association with the
WTUL which prompted him to press for such legislation.    As we have seen
in Chapter 5, the WTUL's support for a statutory minimum wage was to a
large extent based on the views of those middle- and upper-class ladies
as to the duties and obligations of working-class mothers and their
desire that male workers should earn a "family wage" thus removing the
need for mothers to work.    Dilke shared this concern at the need for
many mothers to work owing to the lack of an adequate wage being earned
by a man in the household and he also shared their concern that severe
poverty was a threat to the stability of the State itself (see Chapter
5, p.    ).

In 1906, there were three groups who could have taken up the demand for
a minimum wage for sweated trades and have expected to make an impact on
government - the trade union movement, one of the political parties, or
employers.    The Women's Trade Union League had been pressing the demand
for some years but had little power to influence either a Conservative
or Liberal Government.    Of the three groups that did have this power,
the trade unions did not take the initiative, nor did any of the political
parties, although once the campaign for a minimum wage got under way it
received all-party support.    It was from the third group that George
Cadbury, a cocoa manufacturer, emerged to make a decisive intervention
in 1906 and his intervention demonstrates the importance of employers
(and the particular influence that they have) to the development of social
policy.    It will also become clear that Cadbury's motivations, and those
of most of the supporters of Wages Boards, arose from a desire to bring
about a particular state of affairs considered to be more conducive to
the maintenance and improvement of the existing social order.

As well as being a cocoa manufacturer, George Cadbury owned a number of
newspapers, the most important being the Daily News with a circulation
of 200,000 in 1906.    His motivation as a newspaper proprietor was

> "to arouse my fellow countrymen to the necessity for measures
> to ameliorate the condition of the poor, forsaken and down-
> trodden masses" (see p.165, Chapter 6)

In 1906, the Daily News set out to do just this in respect of the sweated
trades.

Cadbury was sufficiently concerned about the condition of women workers
to be a Vice-President of the Women's Industrial Council.    However, he
disagreed with Margaret MacDonald in her opposition to Wages Boards.    He

believed that it was bad business to pay low wages and that compulsory arbitration was necessary for the unorganised trades[17]. Cadbury was also a firm supporter of trade union organisation, giving sanction to an almost religious support of trade unionism voiced by the Daily News in an editorial which emphasised the "moral value of trade unions" and complained

> "If only the duty of labour organisation had been steadily preached from the pulpits large numbers of men would have allied themselves together to resist the oppression which denies a livelihood to families unless the mother and children join with the father in a combined effort to secure a living wage".[18]

Cadbury and the Daily News supported "responsible" trade unionism in the belief that social stability could only be advanced by the organised resistance of workers to the sometimes anarchic effects of free market forces.   Unrestrained exploitation of labour may have been profitable in the short-run but Cadbury believed the social consequences would be disastrous and that more far-seeing employers should take steps to mitigate the chaos of competition amongst themselves and encourage workers to become responsible trade unionists.   Trade unionists and employers together should try to stabilise production, and set adequate wages and working conditions in order to prevent the plummetting of workers into the abyss of poverty with the resulting danger to social stability.   As the quote in the last paragraph illustrates, one of the most deplorable features of the result of unrestrained competition was believed to be the necessity for mothers and children to contribute to the family income.

Cadbury gave financial support to the trade union movement - including strikes - and although a member of the Liberal Party all his life, he also gave financial support to the ILP and later the Labour Party[19]. He approached the Labour Representation Committee in 1903 offering his support to the labour movement "which I am most anxious to forward if possible"[20], and in 1906 he underwrote the Labour Party's Colonial Deputation to the extent of £500.[21]  In 1906 he offered to finance a Labour candidate against J.W. Wilson, MP for North Worcestershire, who although both a Liberal and a Quaker, supported the Boer War[22].

In his desire to draw public attention to the need for State action on the sweated trades, George Cadbury financed the Daily News Sweated Industries Exhibition in 1906.   This was an exhibition of homeworkers in forty-five sweated trades which was opened by Royalty at the Queen's Hall in Regent Street at the beginning of May and lasted for six weeks.

The idea of such an exhibition was not an original one; a small
exhibition of sweated industries had been held in Bethnal Green in 1903[23]
and the immediate impulse for the Daily News' exhibition had come from
the Berlin Sweated Trades Exhibition held earlier in 1906.   At the time,
the Daily News editorial had commented

> "That Exhibition is held in Protectionist Germany.   We also
> could hold just such an Exhibition in Free Trade England ...
> The exhibits would include match boxes fitted together for 2¼d
> a gross, paper bags folded for 2½d a hundred and scores of
> other articles made for wages wholly insufficient to provide
> adequate nourishment for the workers.   Human exhibits might
> also be included - the wretched women toilers, white and gaunt,
> with some of their half starved children".[24]

The Daily News set up a small Committee to organise a London Exhibition
and the involvement of Mary MacArthur and the NFWW ensured that homeworkers
from a wide variety of trades were persuaded to take part.   For six
weeks, 30,000 of London's upper and middle classes flocked to see these
workers and 20,000 copies of the Exhibition's Handbook were sold[25].   A
typical example of the workers "on display" was that of a Bethnal Green
household where

> "the mother makes waistcoats, the married daughter comes in to
> help her and the son also helps a little.   Mrs. G. does all
> the machining in the 'ready-made' waistcoat and makes the button-
> holes.   Each one takes her from 2 to 3 hours.   She is paid 8/-
> to 10/- per dozen but she also had to provide cotton, and silk for
> the button-holes.   Rate of pay works out at about 2½d - 3d per
> hour and a machine has to be bought and the work carried back and
> forward.   If the two women are on full work for a week they can
> earn between them, £1".[26]

The Daily News gave maximum publicity to the Exhibition, carrying articles
on the sweated trades, the lectures given at the Exhibition and discussions
of possible solutions throughout the six weeks.   An editorial on the
launching of the Exhibition had made the position clear -

> "This kind of industry [i.e. sweating] is not necessary to
> commerce.   It is contrary to commerce.   It produces a class
> which has lost all power to maintain a reasonable rate of
> consumption in the home market - a class which is on the verge
> of pauperism and which, therefore, contributes enormously to
> the burden of the ratepayer - a class which lessens the standard
> of living wherever it exists, which lowers the average of the
> nation's vitality and which lays up a heritage of degeneracy for
> those who will follow us".[27]

However, the editorial emphasised that homeworking should not be abolished
outright -

> "To issue an absolute prohibition against homework would be
> to aggravate, if only for a time, the very horrors which we
> are seeking to alleviate".

Gardiner (the _Daily News_' Editor), Cadbury and Mary MacArthur were clear that the solution lay in raising wages in the sweated trades and that legislation was required to do this. On the day that the Exhibition ended, Clementina Black, another member of the Exhibition Organising Committee, launched an appeal for the setting up of a "Living Wage League" which

> "though it may begin with a Liberal newspaper ... must be no party organisation. The desire to wipe out the national scandal of starvation wages belongs to no party or section".[28]

That day's editorial supported the appeal stating that

> "Our object has been to shock the public mind in order that we may obtain a remedy for an evil which is not only a national shame but a national menace. For there can be no social advance while there is this morass of industrial misery undrained, always widening its area and always depressing more and more the general standard of life and living".[29]

The Exhibition Organising Committee then set up the National Anti-Sweating League (ASL) for a Minimum Wage. It is interesting to note that, while Clementina Black had suggested a campaign for a "living wage", this phrase was not adopted by the organisation which was set up. The issue of whether the minimum wage being demanded was to be a subsistence wage was played down, and in the event the ASL accepted that - for the moment at least - minimum wage legislation must be related to "what the trade could bear" rather than what wage the worker needed for the necessities of life. As the people involved in the ASL were quite clearly concerned that wages in the sweated trades were below subsistence and that legislation was required to raise them to at least subsistence level, we can only surmise that the ASL decided that subsistence minimum wage legislation was too ambitious an aim at that time and would not attract sufficient support. The motivation was clear, however. The sweated trades were a threat to the existing social order, and the existence of homeworkers was particularly to be deplored. The abolition of homework was not supported, however, because such a move would not diminish the need for mothers to work nor solve the problem of the low wages which existed also in factory and workshop production in the sweated trades. The campaigners for a minimum wage hoped that state action on wages in the trades where neither workers nor employers were organised and where anarchic competition therefore reigned, would bring about a more healthy and efficient workforce, would encourage both employers' organisation and trade unionism, would help stabilise production and, by raising men's wages, would reduce the need for married women to work.

Up until 1906, the trade union movement and its political representatives
had showed little desire to champion state action on sweated labour.  The
ASL realised, however, that trade union support was important to building
public pressure on the Government.   They therefore organised a Conference
in October with the aim of getting the labour movement to take up the
demand for minimum wage legislation.   Letters were sent out to labour
movement organisations announcing that the National Anti-Sweating League
had

>"been formed as the outcome of the recent Exhibition of Sweated
>Industries organised by the Daily News.   The League is non-
>Party and its object is to secure by legislation a minimum wage
>in sweated industries".[30]

Three hundred and forty-one delegates attended, representing most sections
of the labour movement - the trade unions, co-operative movement, Trades
Councils, TUC, Labour Party, ILP and SDF.   George Askwith, the Board of
Trade's arbitration expert, told the Conference of the experience of the
Conciliation Act and of his support for Wages Boards;  Sidney Webb read
a paper on the economics of the minimum wage and Gertrude Tuckwell spoke
on sweating and trade unions.

The last day of the three-day Conference heard a great deal about the
Australian Wages Boards and a motion was adopted supporting legislation
along the same lines for Britain.   Objections were raised to this motion,
particularly by the SDF, and amendments were put urging more aggressive
action, asserting that Wages Boards were a mere palliative[31].   The
amendments were lost but a motion was passed asking the Executive Committee
to look at the question of abolishing outwork[32].   The Daily News
expressed its approval of the outcome of the Conference, urging support
for minimum wage legislation and the motivation of social control was
apparent in the following editorial:

>"If the industrial supremacy of Great Britain is to be maintained
>it can only be by the organisation of industry.   Trade union-
>isation has done much towards that end.   Factory legislation has
>done much.   But these palliatives alone have proved insufficient.
>Sweating is still as rampant as ever, and organisation is impos-
>sible among that sorrowful class which is the sweater's prey.
>The one remedy is for the State to step in and lift them out of
>the morass, not for any philanthropic purpose, but because they
>are a weakness and a menace to the State".[33]

The ASL had, in organising the Labour Movement Conference, set out
deliberately to involve the trade union and labour movement who had not
previously shown much enthusiasm for minimum wage legislation for the
sweated trades.   There was already widespread support amongst middle-class

organisations which concerned themselves with poverty.    This is
illustrated by the composition of the delegates to a Conference on
Sweating organised in Glasgow by the Scottish Council for Women's Trades,
which was also held in October of 1906.    Of the 200 delegates to this
Conference, which supported both licensing of homework and minimum wage
legislation, fifty-six were from church organisations, the largest
single group of delegates.    There was also significant representation
from the Charity Organisation Society, from Town and Parish Councils and
from the Women's Liberal Federation, as well as delegates from the co-
operative movement and the trade union movement[34].

The ASL had been set up with the single aim of getting the government to
bring in legislation on wages boards.    Their position was that there
was irresistible pressure on employers to cut production costs which, in
trades where both employers and workers were unorganised, tended to pull
wages down to below-subsistence levels.    The results of such low wages
were a threat to the existing social order and legislative intervention
was therefore necessary.

> "Unless the lowest point in the absence of organisation is fixed
> by legal aid, the downward pressure will assuredly assert itself
> to the ruin of the poor".[35]

The League had in mind a total of thirty-four trades where Wages Boards
should be set up;   most of these trades had mainly female workforces[35a].

The League organised the introduction of a Sweated Industries Bill - along
the lines of the Bill previously introduced by Sir Charles Dilke - by a
Labour MP in 1907, a Liberal MP in 1908 and a Conservative MP in 1909.
A direct result of the Sweated Industries Exhibition was the setting up
of a House of Commons Select Committee on Homework which reported in
1907 and in 1908.    The ASL ensured that witnesses were available to put
the case for Wages Boards and to counter the unfavourable report by the
Board of Trade on the suitability of the Australian legislation for the
British situation.    Mary MacArthur organised a number of homeworkers to
give evidence on their own personal experiences to the Select Committee.

At the beginning of 1908, the ASL increased its efforts to get the Wages
Board legislation adopted.    They organised a National Demonstration on
28 January, the day before Parliament opened, at which the speakers
included a wide variety of politicians and churchmen.    Two of the
speakers stressed the detrimental effect of sweating on mothers and

children.  Mary MacArthur claimed:

> "It is on behalf of the children that we are here tonight ...
> the overworked and undernourished women is the greatest menace
> to the prosperity of the nation as a whole ... we claim that
> we are the true imperialists [cheers].  No matter what our
> political opinions may be, if we are in earnest in our attempt
> to solve this problem of sweating, then indeed, we are the true
> imperialists.  It is because we believe with Ruskin that the
> nation is truly great which has the largest number of happy-
> hearted children, that we are here tonight".[36]

And the Bishop of Birmingham expressed his concern about the mothers who
formed a large proportion of sweated workers and condemned

> "... the diversion of the energies and capacities of the mother
> from her proper occupation as the manager of the family and
> mistress of the house and maker of the home".[37]


When the Sweated Industries Bill was introduced in February 1908 by G.
Toulmin (a Liberal MP), it attracted widespread support outside Parliament.
The Daily News understandably gave the Bill plenty of favourable publicity
but so did the Conservative newspaper, the Morning Post which criticised
the Government for not wholeheartedly supporting Toulmin's Bill.[38]  Even
The Times, while expressing opposition to any adoption of the principle
that Government should set a minimum wage,   cautiously welcomed the
attempt to deal with what it considered to be the special circumstances
of the sweated trades on the grounds that

> "Employers of the better class are glad to be themselves
> protected against a competition based upon inadequate payment
> of workpeople".[39]

Meetings were held up and down the country in support of Wages Boards.
Lord Milner had spoken at a Sweated Industries Exhibition in Oxford in
1907, defending the idea of Wages Boards on the grounds that this was

> "a proposition that the state should intervene to do for the
> weakest and most helpless workers what the strong organised
> trades already did for themselves".[40]

Now, throughout 1908, a wide variety of organisations held meetings on
sweating.   In London, the Liberal Colonial Club heard a speaker on the
Australian legislation[41];  in Aberdeen, the University Christian Union
discussed the problem[42];  in Worcester, the Social Reform League invited
Gertrude Tuckwell to speak[43];  in Cardiff, Mary MacArthur addressed an
ILP meeting on sweating[44].


Bishop Gore proclaimed from the pulpit against sweating and on the
"Christian idea of work and wages".   There were two great principles, he
said,

> "the duty of all to work, and the right of all to a sufficient
> wage to enable a man to support himself and a family when he

had reached the age of marriage, so that women would not work in factories but be in their true place as mothers of families".[45]


IV

The Select Committee on Homework

Although the House of Commons Select Committee on Homework[45a], set up in response to mounting pressure on the Government, intended to consider homework, it also received evidence about conditions and wages in factories and workshops.   The definition of sweating which the Committee adopted was a general one, resting on the phenomenon of low wages - i.e.

> "that work is paid for at a rate which, in the conditions
> under which many of the workers do it, yields to them an
> income which is quite insufficient to enable an adult person
> to obtain anything like proper food, clothing and house
> accommodation".[46]

The Committee heard evidence from employers, trade unionists, women's organisations, women Factory and Sanitary Inspectors, and from important individual supporters of Wages Boards such as George Askwith and George Shann (both of whom were involved in the Anti-Sweating League).   They also heard evidence from seven homeworkers who were brought before them by Mary MacArthur.   These homeworkers gave direct evidence of piteous rates of pay - one of them, a shirt finisher, was asked "How do you manage to live?" and replied "I have to go without food"[47].

The majority of witnesses, including the majority of employers supported the idea of Wages Boards.   The director of a Nottingham lace manufacturing company told the Committee how the Nottingham Chamber of Commerce had decided to set a (voluntary) minimum rate for lace-making which was agreed upon by 125 manufacturers out of 175.   He was in favour (although the Nottingham Chamber of Commerce was not) of both a licensing system for homeworkers and of a "compulsory Wages Board"[48].   Alfred Smith, representing a wholesale clothing manufacturers which had factories all over the country, recommended that the Committee support a proper system of licensing and registration, increased inspection and a scheme for a Central Wages Board and District Wages Boards.[49]   Both these witnesses particularly deplored the undercutting of prices and wages by middlemen which made it impossible to set standard rates of wages.

George Shann, close associate of the Cadbury family and a leading member of the ASL, spoke on the sweated trade of box-making.   He told the

Committee that although Cadburys made most of their own boxes because of competition, they had to put some out to contractors who paid lower wages[50]. He put the case for Wages Boards which would enforce the payment of adequate wages, arguing that in the long run this would decrease the cost of production because it would encourage more up-to-date factory production[51].

Representatives of trade unions in the tailoring trade spoke in support of Wages Boards. The organising Secretary of the Society of Tailors and Tailoresses gave evidence on the difficulties of organising workers in the tailoring trade and argued that in view of this failure of organisation and the accompanying downward pressure on wages, the only way to effectively control the industry was to set up statutory Wages Boards[52]. Speaking of the mantle-making trade he claimed that the competition between master tailors was responsible for the lowering of rates and deterioration of conditions and that the master tailors themselves had recognised this and had set up the Master Mantle Makers Organisation "in order to secure their position against what they called the greed of the manufacturer"[53].

The lack of organisation amongst workers in tailoring was deplored by the Secretary of the Amalgamated Society of Tailors' Government Workers' Branch. He told the Committee

"On account of the unorganised position of our workers on the municipal and government clothing contracts, and the large number of women who are employed there is a continual reduction of wages going on, until it is absolutely impossible to make a living at it".[54]

He gave three examples where the competition between contractors and sub-contractors for government work had led to a reduction of prices and where the lack of organisation amongst the workers had meant there was little resistance to the consequent reduction in wages.

Gertrude Tuckwell, President of the WTUL, and a leading member of the ASL, gave evidence in support of the scheme for Wages Boards which the WTUL had supported for the last decade[55], but Mary MacArthur made a considerable impression on the Select Committee with her intimate knowledge of the conditions of sweated women workers and her strongly-argued case for the state to intervene to bring about an improvement in their conditions[56].

Two dissenting voices were heard amongst the women giving evidence - both Clara Collet (a Labour Correspondent at the Board of Trade)[57] and

Margaret MacDonald[58] spoke against Wages Boards and insisted that a licensing system, along the lines of the WIC's Bill, should be implemented. The WIC's Bill was based on the Massachusetts legislation where a home-worker was required to obtain a licence to carry out work in his or her home.   The licence would be granted according to whether sanitary conditions were satisfactory and there was no overcrowding.   Margaret MacDonald argued that such legislation

"would discourage a good deal of casual homework;  persons would not trouble to get licences unless they really wanted rather badly to do the work".[59]

She objected to Wages Boards on the grounds that large-scale evasion would be common and that homeworkers would be less subject to scrutiny and therefore more work would probably be given to homeworkers in preference to factory workers who were easier to regulate[60].    Mrs. MacDonald was questioned very aggressively by Arthur Henderson, a Select Committee member who was Chairman of the Labour Party and a keen supporter of Wages Boards.   She admitted that low wages were in fact the greatest evil and that a licensing system would not have much effect on wages[61].

A number of individual witnesses made a strong case for Wages Boards and seem to have made a significant impact on the Committee.   The person who probably made the greatest impact was George Askwith, his evidence in support of Wages Boards having great significance because of his long experience of arbitration and conciliation procedures, and his senior position at the Board of Trade.   He told the Select Committee that

"Parliament stepped in with the Factory Acts to stop the exploitation of the individual by unlimited competition in the production of articles and that is exactly what the idea of these Bills [i.e. for Wages Boards] is with regard to people who have not been able to organise themselves and, in certain industries, to continue the policy of the Factory Acts".[62]

He was of the opinion that the enactment of a minimum wage would increase efficiency in a trade:  "If the workers are in a better condition they can generally do better work"[63].   From his experience, many employers wanted to pay a higher wage but didn't because of competition from less socially responsible employers and they would therefore welcome the Wages Board legislation[64].   He spoke of his involvement in voluntary Wages Boards which had been set up, for example in the boot trade, and of the way that these Boards had "averted a great many strikes"[65].   He emphasised that the cost to employers and the State of Wages Boards would be much smaller than the cost of strikes[66].

It is clear that Askwith believed that the effect of statutory Wages

Boards would be to drive some homeworkers into factories and some out of work altogether[67], and that this would be in the long-term interests of society; although he felt provision should be made exemptions of the enforcement of a minimum wage in cases of particular hardship[68]. This belief that most homework would disappear if a minimum wage was enforced was held by many witnesses to the Committee. The Factory Inspector, Miss Squire, expressed the opinion that most homeworkers' wages were subsidised by poor relief or charity[69] and George Shann agreed, saying that it would be better if such people were forced entirely onto the rates as there could then be a "more scientific treatment of the question of unemployment in general"[70]. Clara Collet asserted that the husbands of homeworkers lost the incentive to work and Miss Squire concurred -

> "I almost agree with the social worker who said that if the husband got out of work the only thing the wife should do is sit down and cry, because if she did anything else he would remain out of work".[71]

It was generally agreed that if the wages of men in the sweated trades were raised, this would diminish the need for their wives to work[72].

From the evidence submitted to them, the Select Committee concluded that

> "a very large number of people are unable to, or at any rate do not, earn more than a mere pittance, and consequently live under conditions which are conducive to anything but social, material and moral well-being ..."[73]

The Committee felt it was impossible to say whether the incidence of sweating had increased since the House of Lords Select Committee, but, they stated,

> "sufficient evidence has been put before us to show that sweating still exists in such a degree as to call urgently for the interference of Parliament".[74]

They found that the homeworkers who required state intervention to improve their situation fell into three main groups -

(a) single women, widows or deserted wives or separated, or whose husbands are ill or unable to work;

(b) wives who obtain work when their husbands are out of employment;

(c) wives and daughters of men in regular employment, who wish to increase the family income[75].

In spite of the evidence of how the very existence of these homeworkers was a social problem, the Select Committee could not support any attempt to abolish homeworking: they felt that some people could not work in factories or workshops "and undertake the continuous attendance and work which are there required" and that it would cause serious hardship to prevent such people from working at home[76].  The Committee were influenced in this by the evidence presented by a Police Court Missionary who had started a Homeworkers' Aid Association whose 1,000 members, he claimed, were working for their own living and not supplementing the wage of a husband or father, nor subsidised by charity or poor relief. This witness also, however, supported Wages Boards on the grounds that they would raise the wages of homeworkers[77].

The Select Committee rejected the licensing system proposed by Clara Collet and Margaret MacDonald on the grounds that (a) too many inspectors would be required, and (b) it would be too difficult for a casual homeworker to take in work when she needed to[78].  They made four recommendations, placing most emphasis on the fourth:

1.  a more effective method of registering homeworkers should be introduced;

2.  Section 9 of the Public Health Act 1875 - which related to factories and workshops being kept in a "cleanly state" and properly ventilated with no overcrowding,- should be extended to premises in which homework was carried on[79];

3.  that the full protection of the Truck Act should be secured to homeworkers;

4.  the Select Committee recommended that legislation should be introduced for the setting up of Wages Boards to set minimum wage rates for homeworkers in the trades of "tailoring and the making of shirts, underclothing and babylinen, and the finishing processes of machine-made lace".  They did this on the grounds that "No proposals which fail to increase the income of these people can have an appreciable effect in ameliorating their condition".[80]

IV

The Government's Response

By the beginning of 1908, when the Select Committee on Homework was still sitting, three major events had already driven home to the Government the need to tackle the problem of sweating.  These were, the Sweated Industries Exhibition in May 1907, the ASL Conference in October 1907 and the Demonstration in January 1908.  In February, H. Llewellyn-Smith,

the Permanent Secretary to the Board of Trade, instructed the Labour
Department to look at draft proposals for Wages Boards[81].   On 25
February, H. Gladstone, the Home Secretary, submitted a lengthy memorandum to the Cabinet on The Sweated Industries Bill, which had just
been introduced by Toulmin in the House of Commons, pointing out that
the widespread support for Wages Boards included many employers who had
given evidence to the Select Committee on Homework, the majority of
Liberal MPs, the Labour Party and "a large section of Conservatives
represented by the  Morning Post " [82].   Gladstone suggested that the
Bill be referred to the Select Committee.   The same Cabinet meeting
also considered a memorandum on "The Wages Board System in Victoria"[83].

Later in the year, an initiative was made by the Board of Trade to
introduce legislation for the setting up of Wages Boards.   Davidson[84]
suggests that this initiative did not come from the Home Office because
of their reluctance to do anything on Wages Boards.   However, from
Gladstone's Cabinet Memorandum and also from the fact that he was a
Vice-President of the ASL, it would appear that he was willing to
support such legislation and even made suggestions for a system of
inspection[85].   However, Churchill's wish, as the new President of the
Board of Trade, to make an impact[86], together with Llewellyn-Smith's
recognition that extra-Parliamentary pressure demanded a response, took
the initiative out of the hands of the Home Office.   In August 1908,
Llewellyn-Smith informed Churchill that he was considering proposals on
legislation to deal with sweating as the issue "will give ... trouble
next year"[87].

Churchill held the view that the establishment of Wages Boards was part
of the development of Boards of Arbitration rather than an extension of
the Factory Acts[88] and certainly, Askwith, the Board of Trade's Chief
Arbitrator, felt that the need for compulsory Wages Boards arose out of
the Board of Trade's inability to support efforts in the sweated trades
to impose standard wage rates with only voluntary conciliation procedures
at their disposal.   Llewellyn-Smith had initially opposed the idea of
compulsory Wages Boards, associating them with an attempt to impose
minimum wages according to subsistence needs.   His reaction now was to
draft legislation which would preclude any attempt to set minimum wages
rates according to measurements of what level of income was necessary
to meet subsistence needs.   Instead, his Bill, for the establishment of
Trade Boards in a small number of trades, was posed as an aid to
collective bargaining in trades where organisation by employers and

employees was hopelessly difficult to sustain.   The Conciliation Act
had been increasingly used to reach agreement between employer and
employee - in 1905 the Board of Trade dealt with fourteen cases;   in
the first eight months of 1908, forty-eight cases - and this extension
of the Board of Trade's role in collective bargaining seemed a natural
step to take.   Askwith had introduced minimum wage rates into the
awards that he arbitrated in 1906 and 1907 and his experience and
involvement of this procedure made him the obvious choice to fill the
post of Controller-General for "Anti-Sweating" which Llewellyn-Smith
created in March 1909[89].

The ASL kept up the pressure on Government with a deputation to the
Prime Minister in early 1909 and were invited to meet Churchill,
Beveridge, Askwith and Clara Collet at the Board of Trade to discuss
the Bill which was that session being introduced by a Conservative MP[90].
Churchill, influenced by the Fabian notion of a "national minimum"[91]
proposed that a line should be drawn across the graph of wages for all
industries that the Board of Trade had compiled at the point which was
considered a "reasonable wage".   He intended, he said, to ask Parliament
to give him power to deal with all industries where wages were below this
line - which would cover about a third of the workforce[92].   The ASL
rejected this plan as too ambitious - such a scheme would certainly never
have got through the House of Lords as it would have covered all agricultural workers - and pressed Churchill to lower his sights.

In the event, on 24 March 1909, Churchill introduced a Bill which,
drafted by Llewellyn-Smith with the help of Beveridge, Collet and Askwith,
established collective bargaining machinery for certain sweated trades
whereby once wages rates had been negotiated and agreed between employers
and employees' representatives with the help of an independent chairman
and three independent members, this rate would be ratified by the Board
of Trade (if it approved) and would be enforced by the levy of fines
for non-compliance.   Four Trade Boards were to be set up initially,
covering the paper-box trade, machine-made lace, ready-made blouse-making
and the ready-made and wholesale bespoke tailoring trade.   (Chain-making
replaced blouse-making when the Act was passed).   There was provision
for further Trade Boards to be established if proved necessary.

When he moved the first reading of the Bill in the House of Commons,
Churchill stressed the importance of encouraging organisation in the
sweated trades.   He said

"The principles on which we are proceeding are to endeavour to foster organisation in trades in which, by reason of the prevalence of exceptionally evil conditions, no organisation has yet taken root, and which, in consequence, no parity of bargaining power can be said to exist; to use these organisations when formed as instruments to determine minimum standards below which the wages paid ought not bo be allowed to fall; to rally to the side of these minimum standards all the healthy elements in the trade; and finally, if and when this has been achieved, to protect the good employers - and there are always good employers in the worst of trades - who are anxious to pay a proper rate of wages from being under-cut, and to protect them by compulsory powers which are no doubt far-reaching in their character ...".[93]

The ASL welcomed the fact that the Government was taking the issue seriously but was unhappy with the permissive nature of Churchill's Bill[94]. The Sweated Industries Bill, backed by the ASL, had been introduced at the beginning of the session by John Hill, Conservative MP, who now objected to the second clause of the Government Bill which said "The Board of Trade may establish one or more Trade Boards" and further objected to the lengthy procedure for applying a minimum rate. He believed that "... compulsion is the only remedy and nothing of a permissive character will succeed"[95]. The WTUL objected that whereas the Sweated Industries Bill laid great stress on "complete enforcement and complete inspection, Mr. Churchill's Bill savours too much of conciliation"[96]. Hill still pressed for a second Reading of his Bill, supported by the social imperialist wing of the Conservative Party[97]. However, at its second Reading, the Bill was talked out[98].

Dilke had been persuaded, that the Government's Bill would "not be found wanting" on the question of inspection and enforcement[99] and had been told by Askwith that a compromise along the lines of Churchill's Bill was the best that could be hoped for[100]. When the Trade Boards Bill received its second reading a month later, it was welcomed by most shades of political opinion in the House of Commons. This time H.J. Tennant, Parliamentary Secretary at the Board of Trade (and a member of the ASL), introduced the Bill and replied to accusations that the Bill was the thin end of the wedge and that wages would soon be regulated in all industries[101]. On the contrary, said Tennant,

"Our remedy is only intended to apply to a very limited extent. It is a remedy which has reference to low wages and does not deal with the question of whether state action can, or ought to control wages".[102]

The Bill was intended

"to be applied exclusively to exceptionally unhealthy patches of the body politic where the development has been arrested

in spite of the growth of the rest of the organism.    It is
to the morbid and diseased places - to the industrial
diptheritic spots that we should apply the antitoxin of trade
boards".[103]

Later in the debate, Churchill voiced strong opposition to any extension
of the Bill to the organised trades, but intimated that he thought there
were at least thirty other unorganised trades to which the Bill might be
extended[104].    This provoked strong opposition from Sir Frederick
Banbury, MP for the City of London, a director of the Great Northern
Railway Company and a vociferous supporter of free market forces.    The
Railway companies had their own problems with the railway workers' union
claiming a minimum wage and Banbury's opposition to Wages Boards had
been strengthened during the debate on the second reading of the Sweated
Industries Bill, when J.J. Clancy, Nationalist MP for North Dublin,
brought the House's attention to the "starvation wages" received by
Irish railway workers and demanded that minimum wage legislation be
applied to all railway workers[105].    Banbury now voiced the fears that
were also held by many landowners and demanded to know whether Churchill
intended the Bill to cover agricultural labourers.    He declared

"I believe that this is one of the most dangerous Bills
that have ever been introduced into the House of Commons".[106]

Banbury may have been right about the Bill having far-reaching and
radical implications if there had been any intention by the drafters
of the Bill to set up machinery which would implement a minimum wage
based on subsistence needs.    Although Churchill in his initial burst
of enthusiasm had clearly had this type of legislation in mind,
Llewellyn-Smith made sure that the Bill he drafted merely set up
procedures for collective bargaining in trades where collective
bargaining had previously been impossible because of lack of organisation
amongst employers and workers alike.    The ASL, in building a broad-
based campaign, had avoided the question of whether minimum wages should
be set according to some standard of living.    Such a measure would not
have gained the widespread support which was needed to persuade the
Government to take action on the sweated trades.    The reasoning which
won the day for Wages Boards may be summarised thus - fierce competition
amongst employers and workers in certain trades dragged down wages to a
level at which the health of the worker and, in a wider sense, the
health of society, was threatened.    In these trades there were "good
employers" who wished to pay adequate wages but were unable to because
of competition from less socially responsible employers.    The condition

of the workers and the fact that most of them were women, prevented
trade union organisation from raising wages.  It was therefore
necessary for the State to step in where employer and trade union
organisation had failed to make it possible for uniform rates of wages
to be arrived at and enforced.  The motivation was a concern with social
control;  the aim was to preserve the existing social order by attempting
to eliminate the cancerous phenomenon of unorganised, inefficient and
poorly paid workers struggling for survival.

This was the reasoning behind the government's support for the legislation;  some supporters went further and expressed the belief that
Wages Boards would squeeze sweated trades out of existence and that,
as Sir Thomas Whittaker, Chairman of the Select Committee on Homework
put it,

> "the nation should take upon itself the responsibility of
> maintaining the people thrown out in that way if they are
> unable to get employment in other directions".[107]

Much was made of the conditions of women workers in the sweated trades
and of the detrimental effect that their work and low wages had on their
children.   Chiozza Money, discussing the match-box-making trade carried
on mainly by widows and other women with dependents in the East End of
London, stated -

> "It would be good for society, good for the widows, and good
> for the children that they should be driven out of that trade
> and the work done by machinery, and that human fingers should
> cease to be employed at it at all.   You can make match-boxes
> better and more cheaply by machinery than by employing the
> poor widow.   If we are to have regard to the children and of
> the generation which is to follow that widow - and if we are
> to see that there shall be fewer of these degraded units of
> society - we shall do our best with hard heads as well as soft
> hearts to get rid of these conditions".[108]

One of the most influential studies of sweating concluded

> "A trade that does not pay a wage that allows for the
> maintenance of the health and strength of the workers, is
> detrimental to the welfare of the public".[109]

The Bill came up for its third and final reading in July.  George Barnes,
Labour MP, put an amendment, seconded by Keir Hardie, which would have
made the inclusion of other trades easier and quicker.    However,
Churchill and Tennant had come to an agreement with the Opposition
that the Provisional Order procedure - which allowed for maximum
discussion and examination of the setting up of new Trade Boards -
should be part of the Bill.   The amendment was therefore lost[110].   The
Bill received Royal Assent and came into operation on 1 January 1910.

References - Chapter 8

1. J.A.M. Caldwell, "Social Policy of Public Administration 1909-1911". Nottingham, PhD, 1956.

2. See, in particular, T. Marshall, "Citizenship and Social Class", Cambridge 1950; also M. Bruce, "The Coming of the Welfare State", 1961.

3. See the article by D. Thompson, in New Reasoner, Vol.1, No.4, 1957; V. George and P. Wilding, "Ideology and Social Welfare", (1976).

4. P. Thane refers to this as the "broad path to betterment" school of the history of social policy, P. Thane (ed.), "The Origins of British Social Policy" (1978), p.16.

5. See. E. Wilson's "Women and the Welfare State" (1977), who makes this point very effectively, and also remedies the omission with her analysis of the Welfare State.

5a. J.R. Hay, "Employers' Attitudes to Social Policy and the Concept of Social Control, 1900-1920" in P. Thane (ed.) (1978), pp.108-109.

6. Ibid., p.109.

7. J. Brown, "'Social Control' and the Modernisation of Social Policy, 1890-1929" in P. Thane (ed.) (1978).

8. Ibid., p.218.

9. A.R. Russell, "Liberal Landslide", (1973) p.66.

10. H. Pelling, "A History of British Trade Unionism, (2nd edn 1971), pp.123-128.

11. Russell, (1973), pp.65 and 81.

12. See Russell (1973), p.65, referring to Masterman's campaign in West Ham North.

13. F. Brockway, "Inside the Left" (1942), p.23; W.S. Adams, "Lloyd George and the Labour Movement" in Past and Present, Issue 3, 1953, pp.53-64.

14. Ibid., p.59.

15. S.J. Hurwitz, "State Intervention in Britain: A Study of Economic Control and Social Response, 1914-1919" (New York, 1949), p.9.

16. R.H. Phelps-Brown, (1959), pp.206-207; J.A.M. Caldwell (1953), pp.11-12.

17. A. Gardiner, (1949), pp.79-80, 215.

18. Daily News, 3 May, 1906.

19. See A.G. Gardiner, (1949).

20. LRC Papers, 6/112, G.C. to Ramsey MacDonald, 12 January 1903.

21. LRC Papers, 3/56, MacDonald to G.C., 9 April 1906.

22. A.G. Gardiner, (1949), p.56.

23. Stewart and Hunter, (1964), p.136.

24. Daily News, 1 February, 1906.

25. Daily News, 13 June 1906.

26. R. Mudie-Smith, "Sweated Industries: Being a Handbook of the Daily News Exhibition" (1906), p.59.

27. Daily News, 3 May, 1906.

28. Daily News, 13 June, 1906.

29. Daily News, 13 June, 1906.

30. LPGC Papers, 8/16, August 1906.

31. See M.A. Hamilton, (1925).

32. Daily News, 26 October, 1906.

33. Daily News, 27 October, 1906.

34. National Conference on Sweated Industries, 11 and 12 October 1906.

35. National Anti-Sweating League, "Sweating and Wages Boards" (nd).

35a. Getrude Tuckwell, Coll. Item 200 I.

36. National ASL, "Living Wage for Sweated Workers - Report of the Great National Demonstration", 28 January 1908.

37. Ibid., p.4.

38. Morning Post, 22.2.08.

39. The Times, 22.2.08.

40. G.T. Coll. Manuscript notes, Folder 216h.

41. Daily Chronicle, 22.2.08.

42. Aberdeen Journal, 21.11.08.

43. Worcester Times, 26.11.08.

44. South Wales News, 14.12.08.

45. Birmingham Daily Post, 11.11.08.

45a. Report and Minutes of Evidence of House of Commons Select Committee on Homework, PP1907, VI, Cd.290, PP1908, VIII, Cd.246.

46. Select Committee on Homework, 1908, p.iii.

47. Ibid., 1908, Q2095.

48. 1908 QQ1519-1769.

49.    1908, QQ932-1165.

50.    1908, Q665.

51.    1908, Q676.

52.    1907, Q3350-55.

53.    1907, Q3340.

54.    1908, Q2506.

55.    1907, QQ2331-2689.

56.    1907, QQ2690-2853;   1908, QQ1770-1787;   QQ2222-2270.

57.    1907, QQ640-858.

58.    1907, QQ4296-4606.

59.    1907, Q4330.

60.    1907, Q4390.

61.    1907, QQ4494-4496.

62.    1907, Q4294.

63.    1907, Q4281.

64.    1907, QQ3947-48.

65.    1907, Q4120.

66.    1907, QQ4112-13.

67.    1907, QQ3690-64.

68.    1907, QQ3965-70;   4195-4208.

69.    1907, Q1049.

70.    1908, QQ692-693.

71.    1907, Q1026.

72.  E.g. Clementina Black's evidence, 1907, Q2916.

73.    1908, p.14.

74.    1908, p.iii.

75.    1908, p.iv.

76.    1908, p.xi.

77.    1908, QQ274-357.

78.    1908, p.xii.

79. p.xviii.

80. 1908, p.xii.

81. Clara Collet Papers, M. MacDonald to Clara Collet, 20.2.08.

82. PRO, CAB 37/91, No.26, 25 February, 1908.

83. CAB 37/91, No.27, 25 February 1908.

84. R. Davidson, (1971).

85. CAB 37/91 No.26, 25 February 1908.

86. E. Halevy, "History of the English People in the Nineteenth Century" Vol.6, The Rule of Democracy (1905-1914) (1961 edn.) p.238.

87. M. Gilbert, Churchill Companion Volume, Part II, p.834. Llewelyn-Smith to Churchill, 11.8.08.

88. R. Davidson, (1971), p.211.

89. PRO BT 13/134, H. Fountain to Llewellyn-Smith, 13.3.09.

90. Stewart and Hunter (1964), p.140.

91. Harris (1972), pp.262-263, 264. See Nation, 7 March, 1908. W. Churchill to the Editor, pp.812-813.

92. Stewart and Hunter (1964), p.140.

93. House of Commons Debates, 24.3.09, 1791-92.

94. Daily News, 25.3.09.

95. Morning Post, 29.3.09.

96. Daily Chronicle, 31.3.09.

97. Morning Post, 26.3.09; 27.3.09.

98. House of Commons Debates, 26 March 1909.

99. Daily News, 25.3.09.

100. Dilke Papers, Add. Mans. 43921 f.3. Askwith to Dilke, 1.2.09.

101. See speeches by Sir Frederick Banbury during the debates on both first and second readings.

102. House of Commons Debates, 28.4.1909, 342.

103. Ibid., 344.

104. Ibid., 405.

105. House of Commons Debates, 26.3.09, 2079-2081; 2091.

106. House of Commons Debates, 28.4.09, 408.

107. House of Commons Debates, 26.3.09, 2120.

108. Ibid., 2096-97, 26.3.09.

109. Cadbury and Shann (1908), p.10.

110. House of Commons Debates, 16.7.09, 2430-2481.

# 9 Conclusion: the Trade Boards Act — an exercise in social control?

## I

The term "sweated labour" was used at the beginning of this century to describe long hours of work carried on in poor working conditions for very low wages. The emphasis was, as the support for Wages Boards indicated, on the payment of low wages, and the major concern was at how widespread very low wages were.

The first three chapters of this thesis have illustrated how the development of a number of industries in the late nineteenth century was characterised by the payment of very low wages. It can be argued that the very rapid expansion in such trades as the clothing trades, the metal industries, the food processing trades was, to a large extent, made possible by the availability of a supply of cheap labour. Sweated labour was not a residual characteristic of an earlier stage of industrial society. On the contrary, the payment of very low wages was found in some of the most "advanced" sections of many industries and was particularly common where women formed the majority of a particular section of workers. The detailed analysis of the tailoring trade illustrated quite clearly that very low wages were not only found in, what was considered to be, the more "backward" London bespoke trade, but also in the London and Leeds ready-made section of the trade. This widespread payment of low wages was primarily associated with the use of women and girls as cheap labour and the factors behind the existence of a surplus cheap female labour force were discussed in Chapter 3.

Homeworkers were the lowest paid of workers and worked in the poorest conditions, yet even they were not the residual phenomenon as is often assumed. A lot of the work put out to be done in the home was a direct result of the extra work created by the development of the ready-made and wholesale bespoke trades in tailoring and dressmaking. There were - and are - a number of causal factors operating to bring about the existence and persistence of homework in a number of trades; the fact that there are an estimated 250,000 homeworkers[1] at work in Britain today and that new areas of homeworking are still opening up (for example, with the use of visual display units) indicates that the phenomenon was not, at the end of the nineteenth century, merely a relic of an earlier industrial era.

Chapter 3 demonstrated that sweated labour was particularly a feature
of the female workforce. Women were concentrated into low-waged
industries and the sexual division of labour within each industry meant
that they were employed on the lowest-paying type of work. Chapter 3
also showed, however, that significant numbers of men received below-
subsistence wages and this was not confined to the trades designated
as employing sweated labour but also included agricultural labourers,
railway workers, and textile workers. The House of Lords Select
Committee on Sweating considered one important group of low-paid male
workers - the dockers - and could well have considered other groups of
unskilled men in their concentration on low wages. The fact that they
didn't and that subsequent investigations of sweated labour concentrated
on women workers is significant and can be explained by the focussing of
concern on the effect of married women's waged work on their children
and on the consequent harm to the wider society.

Chapter 3 also examined the way in which the extent of below-subsistence
wages amongst semi- and unskilled male workers brings into question the
assumption that a man's wage was sufficient to support a wife and
children. Then and now, women's low wages were often justified by the
contention that they did not have other people to support on their wages.
The evidence is that, on the contrary, a significant number of women
workers were either the sole breadwinner or an essential contributor to
the family income.

This then was the background to the action of the three key groups of
people which we discussed in Chapters 4-6. What were the motivations
behind the action taken on the sweated trades - or not taken - by the
trade unions, women's organisations and employers and how did these
motivations make their impact on the Liberal Government? By pulling
together the evidence presented, I intend to illustrate that the concept
of social control is vital to an understanding of why the Trade Boards
Act was passed. First, however, we will discuss various other possible
analyses of this particular development in social policy.


II

Some historians of social policy emphasise the pressure put on government
by the working class - either in the form of direct demands for social
reform or in the form of the threat of social unrest - and the determining
influence of this pressure in the development of social reform. In the

case of the Trade Boards Act, however - a piece of legislation which
signalled a fundamental interference in the relationship between employer
and worker, in favour of the latter - the organised working class played
little part.

Analysis of the position of the trade union leadership on sweated labour
has shown that they took little initiative on the problem of sweated
labour. We saw that cheap unskilled (particularly female) labour was
identified as a threat to the interests of skilled, organised (mainly
male) labour, and that sectional interests within the labour force
dominated to the detriment of class interests. Skilled workers
identified unskilled workers as their enemy; male workers identified
female workers as their enemy - as indeed in many cases of skill dilution
and mechanisation they were. Such a conflict of interests, having such
a strong material base, led - probably inevitably - to an exclusion of
unskilled workers from skilled workers' organisations. Even when
hostility between male skilled and unskilled workers was to some extent
overcome or temporarily put aside, the hostility between male and female
workers remained. Together with this division of interest and hostility
went a "ghettoisation" of women workers into the lowest paid, lowest
skilled jobs in industry brought about by the desire of employers in
some of the rapidly-developing sections of industry to employ the
cheapest labour possible.

We discussed how the trade union movement had a rather confused
attitude to women workers. There were obvious differences of opinion
between the labour aristocracy who were able to earn sufficient to
support a family and who insisted that wives' and daughters' primary
role was a domestic one, and the unskilled labourer who relied on his
wife's and children's earnings for family survival. The ascendency of
the general unions during the 1890s and 1900s and their questioning of
the way that men like Henry Broadhurst ran the TUC, meant that there
was a more sympathetic attitude to women workers and women organising.
However, this sympathetic attitude was severely handicapped by a failure
of male trade unionists to recognise the particular problems that women
experienced in attempting to organise themselves. These difficulties
were discussed in Chapter 5 and we found that they arose from (a) the
sexual division of labour within the workplace which meant that women
were almost entirely concentrated in the lowest paid, lowest skilled
jobs and experienced all the associated difficulties of unionisation;
and (b) the sexual division of labour within the home which meant that

a woman's participation in the workforce fluctuated according to child-bearing and rearing and that when she was engaged in waged work, her additional domestic responsibilities made union activity very difficult.

The general unions which organised semi- and unskilled workers were in the industries where the majority of workers were men - the docks, railways, the gas workers and municipal manual workers. These unions did try to press for a statutory minimum wage for public employees but met opposition from the leadership of the TUC - as did the miners, some of whom also demanded a legal minimum wage for mineworkers. Trade union organisation in the sweated trades (where there were more women workers) was very weak - the Amalgamated Union of Clothing Workers, for instance, had no power to push the TUC to take up the cause of clothing workers. There was thus little or no working class representation of the interests of women workers.

The views of the trade union leadership were in any case formed by factors other than the interests of women as workers. Labour aristocrats like Henry Broadhurst wanted more protective legislation to restrict the extent of female labour. He wanted this because he believed women should not have to engage in waged work. Will Thorne, leader of one of the largest general unions, was at first firmly in favour of women organising and fighting for better working conditions as men had done, but was driven, by experience of the difficulties of getting women to become active trade unionists, to also advocate protective legislation (although he would not have countenanced the exclusion of women from the workforce altogether) to counteract the way in which women were used as cheap labour and were believed to be displacing male workers, or at the least, acting as a downward pull on wages.

Both types of trade unionists were influenced by the Victorian ideal of womanhood and this helped to form their attitude towards women workers. The labour aristocrats subscribed to the Victorian ideal of womanhood as part of their wish to better themselves and their families. Socialist trade unionists, while more positive about women organising as trade unionists also "embraced the bourgeois ideal of the Angel in the House, the perfect Wife and Mother"[2] as part of their demand for better material conditions of life. The ambivalent attitude on the part of the trade union leadership of both skilled and unskilled workers to women on the one hand as workers and on the other as mothers, made it unlikely that they would seriously campaign for women's interests as workers.

A further reason for the trade union's lack of enthusiasm about Wages
Boards was their wariness of any state interference with the conditions
of work of the adult man; Wages Boards would of course cover men as well
as women. Trade unionists were aware by the end of the nineteenth
century that organisation and industrial action amongst male workers
had done more to bring improved conditions of work than protective
legislation had done for unorganised women workers. There was also
concern that state interference would bring a curtailment of trade union
activity; in particular, there was the possibility that compulsory
arbitration procedures such as the Wages Boards under discussion would
be accompanied by a denial of the right to strike[3]. A Bill, drafted
by Llewellyn-Smith at the Board of Trade, to amend the Conciliation Act,
would have prohibited industrial action until after conciliation
procedures had been exhausted. The Bill had to be dropped because of
trade union opposition[4].

The trade union movement, while identifying sweated labour as a threat
to the interests of organised labour, was handicapped from taking
effective action by divisions between skilled and unskilled workers and
in particular by the division between men and women workers. Although
by the end of the nineteenth century, many of the established trade
unions had come round to accepting the need to organise women workers,
this acceptance was in general half-hearted and there was little or no
attempt to confront the many practical difficulties which women
experienced when trying to organise. Instead, male trade unionists
reacted to these difficulties by claiming that legislation was the only
answer to unsatisfactory working conditions suffered by women. This
support for legislation was for legislation which would restrict women's
hours and ability to work.

An analysis of the pressures which led up to the passing of the Trade
Boards Act indicated that the trade unions were not a key factor. The
TUC leadership expressed support for the legislation when approached and
AUCO was involved in the ASL but no initiative had been taken by trade
unionists on the matter. The ASL felt that the support of the labour
movement was important so they deliberately set out to get that support,
but the decisive influence on government did not come from the trade
unions, or from the Labour Party. Neither was the government influenced
by a fear of social unrest, for sweated workers were not organised and
could hardly be said to constitute a threat of civil disorder.

It is quite common for the development of social policy to be seen in
the light of demands put on government by pressure groups representing
the interests of a particular social group.   In the case of the Trade
Boards Act, a superficial analysis of the evidence may suggest that
the WTUL/NFWW were representing the interests of working-class women in
the demand for Wages Boards and that, as a pressure group, the WTUL/NFWW
were successful in persuading the Liberal Government to act on the behalf
of sweated workers.   But this was not the case.

Such organisations that there were representing the interests of women
workers were dominated by middle-class women, who, although motivated by
the best of intentions, were primarily guided by the Victorian bourgeois
ideology of the way in which working-class women should be fulfilling
the role of wife and mother.   The employment of mothers of young
children was socially unacceptable.   Attention was drawn to the conflict
between the care of children and the demands of earning a living.
Although the two most active women's organisations (the WTUL and the
WIC) disagreed about the legislation needed to deal with the sweated
trades, they concurred in their analysis of the problem of women workers
and their recognition of the unfortunate necessity for mothers to work.
Women had to engage in waged labour either because of their husband's
inadequate wage or unemployment or because they were on their own with
no man to support them.   In the case of women on their own with
dependents, there was, on the part of the women's organisations, a
working towards the demand for income maintenance in the form of State
benefits;  this was voiced during our period not only by the WIC (see
p.   ) but also by the women Factory Inspectors (see p.   ).   In the
case where there was a male breadwinner but his wage was inadequate or
he was unemployed, the WTUL, NFWW and WIC all recognised that the
solution could only be tackled by raising men's wages and taking
measures against male unemployment for this would then remove the need
for married women to work.   The WTUL's particular reasons for supporting
minimum wage legislation were two-fold:  (1) to raise male wages in the
sweated trades and thus make it unnecessary for married women to work,
and (2) to shake out the "inefficient" workers who were unable through
their own inadequacies to earn a subsistence wage and who, together
with women who merely wished to earn a "pocket money" wage, acted as a
downward pull on wages.

It is undoubtedly the cases that the lives of working-class mothers

would have been made easier if they did not engage in wage labour.
This was not however the motivation of organisations such as the WTUL
and NFWW; their support for any measure which would make it less likely
for mothers to work was firmly based on ideas about what harm such
employment did to the children of these mothers and what consequences
this had for the future generation.   Furthermore, the WTUL/NFWW on
their own had little impact on government.   The WTUL had been campaigning since the early 1890s for Wages Boards and although they played
an important part in providing information and creating a debate on
the question of women's low wages, their influence on policy-makers was
small.   It was only through the ASL that these two organisations had
any influence and the strength of the ASL came from other sources - its
access to a popular newspaper and the support of influential employers
and politicians.

As we saw in Chapter 8, the ASL could not be said to be representing
the interests of working women; rather their concern was with the
interests of the wider society.   Although supporters of the ASL were
no doubt genuinely moved by the appalling conditions under which sweated
labour worked, their concern was with the harm done by the sweated trades
to the existing social order - and this was the justification for their
support of minimum wage legislation.   Again a superficial analysis may
at first suggest that the ASL as a pressure group was crucial to the
passing of the Trade Boards Act.   However, this would be to ignore the
role played by a section of the ruling class in the organisation - who
could hardly be described as a "pressure group".

IV

Davidson[5] explains the passing of the Trade Boards Act in terms of the
expansion of the Board of Trade and the influence of Llewellyn-Smith
and George Askwich.   Askwith's support for Wages Boards was certainly
important but, as we have seen, neither he nor Llewellyn-Smith were
either the source of the pressure for the legislation nor crucial to the
building up of support for a minimum wage.   It is however the case that
Llewellyn-Smith was largely responsible for the limitations of the
legislation in that he drafted a bill which was essentially no more than
an extension of the Board of Trade's arbitration and conciliation
activities and bore little relation to the type of minimum wage legislation subsequently passed in the USA, France and other countries,
where the minimum wage set was based on subsistence needs rather than
on "what the trade could bear".

224

None of the above explanations of social policy account for the passing
of the Trade Boards Act.    The legislation was not primarily the result
of working-class pressure, of the activities of a pressure group acting
on behalf of sweated workers, nor of the influence of civil servants
or government departments.    Instead, the explanation for the origins
of minimum wage legislation in this country lies in the concern of one
section of the ruling class with the maintenance of the existing social
order and their recognition of the harmful effect of sweated labour on
social stability.


V


Chapter 6 has shown that while the small employers in the sweated trades
viewed the prospect of a minimum wage with suspicion, there were a few
large employers who interested themselves in social policy and who
strongly supported a minimum wage for sweated workers.    Employers such
as Cadbury and Rowntree held clear views on the relationship between the
welfare of the working class and the health and stability of the whole
country.    They also felt that women should be in the home once they had
married.    At the same time, they recognised the inability of small
employers to do other than merely respond to cut-throat competition by
forcing down costs.    It was also felt that homeworkers pulled down
factory wages and that "inefficient" workers in general acted as a downward pull on wages.    Minimum wages for the unorganised trades would
solve these problems and by indirectly removing married women from the
labour force, help to promote more hygienic homes, happier and healthier
workers, the proper fulfilment of maternal duties and social stability
in general.


Chapter 7 outlined how, by the end of the nineteenth century, the State
had already taken an interest in the effect of waged work on women's
role as mothers and how the state was also gradually taking more
interest in the relationship between employer and employee.    We
discussed the concern felt by the Conservative Government and the
Liberal opposition alike about the way in which Britain had had
difficulty in defeating the Boers and was experiencing increasing
difficulties in competing in the economic field with German and American
competitors.    Some politicians and intellectuals, such as the Webbs
and the young Liberals influenced by T.H. Green's philosophy, concentrated their attention on the condition of the British working class:
the detrimental effect of poor housing and working conditions on the

health of the nation and thus on Britain's ability to compete in world
markets.    There was a particular concern about sweated trades being
"parasites" on the rest of society.    This concern was most coherently
expressed by William Beveridge when he condemned the way in which some
trades, by paying a below-subsistence wage were forcing their workers
to be dependent on either workers in another industry or on charity and
poor relief.    Such trades, it was felt, should be forced out of existence rather than continue as a drain on the rest of the nation.

During the years between the House of Lords Select Committee on Sweating
which reported in 1890 and the election of the Liberal Government in
1906, there was a significant shift in the attitude of key sections of
the ruling class to poverty and its causes and solutions.    It is significant that two of the most influential studies of poverty were
carried out by men who were themselves members of the capitalist class -
Charles Booth, who was a shipowner and B. Seebohm Rowntree, a member
of the Rowntree family of cocoa manufacturers.    Their studies had a
profound impact in that they illustrated that something like a third of
the working class lived in conditions of poverty which were demanding
the country's future prosperity.

Central to the concern about poverty was the idea that it was desirable
that mothers of young children should not engage in waged work.    The
research carried out by Davin and Lewis[6] demonstrates how at the turn
of the century increasing concern was expressed about the health of the
nation's children and the quality of the future labour force.    The
answer to the existing unsatisfactory state of affairs was felt to be an
improvement in the quality of child care given by the mother, who in
order to fulfil the standards held desirable, should certainly not be
employed outside the home, nor engage in homework.    A man's wage should
be a family wage, and in most cases, it was thought that his wage would
be enough to support a wife and children.

Studies such as Booth's and Rowntree's, however, illustrated that for
a significant section of the population, the ideal was not the reality.
Not only did many men not earn a family wage, but a large number of
women and their dependents did not have an employed man to provide for
them.    The response to the problem of poverty was very much based on
the assumption that the ideal state of affairs was where men did earn
a family wage and women devoted themselves to the home and child-rearing.
Furthermore, the response to poverty was also based on the assertion

that it was a man's _obligation_ to provide for his wife and children[7].
This was a central moral value underlying the Liberal's welfare reforms,
as was the more general fear that nothing should be done which would
diminish the individual's simple economic need to work.

Investigations had been carried out for more than twenty years on
sweated labour; concern at low wages, long hours and insanitary conditions had been expressed by all shades of political opinion and by
the 1906 General Election there was a fairly widespread concensus of
opinion about the undesirability but also the necessity of married
women's work. But the decisive intervention, when it came, was from
within the ruling class. It came from one particular type of employer,
who was also appearing in increasing numbers in Parliament and who saw
the long-term damage that the sweated trades were doing to society.
Fierce competition amongst small, insecure employers was believed to
have a detrimental effect on the general development and modernisation
of industry. Below-subsistence wages created an inefficient and a
potentially dangerously desperate workforce. The low wages earned by
men created a need for mothers to work which it was believed was
responsible for a high infant mortality rate and the poor health of
surviving children. Thus the motivation which was crucial to the
campaign for the Trade Boards Act arose from the perceived material
interest of one section of the ruling class. The motivation was one
of social control - the desire was to bring about more efficient
industry, to discourage homework and to create a healthier workforce.

## References - Chapter 9

1.    P. Townsend, "Poverty in the UK" (1979).

2.    E. Wilson (1976), p.26.

3.    <u>Labour Leader</u>, 10 and 17 January 1908.

4.    R. Davidson (1971), p.186.

5.    R. Davidson, "Llewellyn-Smith, "The Labour Department and Government Growth 1886-1909" in G. Sutherland (ed.) "Studies in the Growth of Nineteenth Century Government" (1972), p.227.

6.    A. Davin (1978); J. Lewis (1980).

7.    The opposition to the idea of state subsidies for children expressed the fear that such measures would withdraw the incentive from a man to support his wife and children.

# 10 Epilogue

The Trade Boards Act passed onto the Statute Book in January 1910.
What did the Act achieve?  This Chapter looks briefly at the immediate
operation of the Trade Boards Act and then goes on to outline how
sweated labour, and in particular homeworking, is attracting concern
today.

Within one year of the Act being passed there was a demonstration of
the support of some employers for the payment of adequate wages, and of
how a minimum wage could be implemented with trade unions, employers'
associations and the State acting together against those employers who
paid excessively low wages.

The chainmakers in Cradley Heath were some of the most exploited workers
whose conditions were brought to public attention by the ASL.   Chain-
making was one of the four trades covered by the new Trade Boards Act
and in 1910 the Chainmaking Trade Board set a rate of $2\frac{1}{2}$d per hour for
adult women workers - a rate which would not have yielded a subsistence
wage but which was still higher than that which was at that time paid.
The Cradley Heath employers attempted to delay the implementation of the
new wage rate and in response the National Federation of Women Workers
called a meeting of the women chainmakers  at which a resolution was
passed refusing to work at the old rates.   The Chainmakers' Association,
set up by the NFWW, quickly grew in numbers.   The resulting strike
attracted a great deal of public support and within a month the employers
who were members of the Chain Manufacturers Association agreed to pay
the new rates on the understanding that the workers would boycott non-
Association employers.   The action against the unorganised employers
was so successful that within another six weeks the majority of them
had been forced to agree to pay the new rates[1].

However, this is only one incident, and was, moreover, provoked by
action on the part of the workers.   In the other trades covered by the
Act, things moved much more slowly.   During the first six months after
the legislation was passed meetings were held in the areas where the

trades covered were carried on, at which Board of Trade officials
explained to workers and employers how the Boards would be set up.
W.H. Yates from the Board of Trade spoke throughout the country at a
number of meetings of workers in the tailoring trade, together with
representatives of AUCO, the ASL and the WTUL/NFWW.   He asked for the
names of proposed representatives to be sent to the Board of Trade who
would then select who they thought suitable to sit on the Trade Board[2].
The large employers in the wholesale trade held a national meeting in
order to select their representatives[3].

The first meeting of the Tailoring Trade Board was held on 14 December
1910.   There were four appointed independent members with two officials
from the Board of Trade acting as Chair and Secretary, twelve employers'
representatives of whom two represented sub-contractors, and twelve
workers' representatives, including Mary MacArthur, J. Young (Secretary
of AUCO) and J.J. Mallon (Secretary of the ASL).   The Chairman opened
the meeting by stressing how

> "anxious they all were not to interfere with the prosperity
> of the trade.   He said that employers and employees alike
> were interested that a fixed minimum rate of wages should rule
> in the trade both as a protection to the good employer against
> unfair undercutting by a competitor and also as a protection
> to the worker".[4]

The Board did not start discussing minimum rates until meetings of
District Trade Committees were held in seven centres of the trade where
local representatives aired their views on what the rates should be.
The first meeting of the Trade Board to consider minimum rates was held
in August 1911.   A clear division of interest emerged during the discussion on rates for adult women workers between the main employers
and the sub-contractors, who wanted a higher rate.   The employers
insisted on voting "by sides" so that the sub-contractors and the workers'
representatives could not form an alliance to carry the higher rate of
4¼d per hour supported by both[5].   Voting "by sides" meant that no
majority could be achieved without the votes of the appointed members
who used their votes to defeat both the higher rates proposed by the
workers' representatives and the lower rates proposed by the employers.
The only rate which received a majority was therefore that favoured by
the appointed members with the support of the workers' representatives -
3½d per hour for adult women workers (over twenty-one) and 6d per hour
for adult male workers (over twenty-three years of age), for a fifty-
hour week.   In the event, the rate for women approved by the Board of
Trade was 3¼d per hour.   In the case of both male and female home-

workers the rate was to be the same as for factory and workshop workers[6].
These rates yielded a minimum weekly wage of 13/6d for women and 25/-
for men.

It is of interest to note that this setting of such different rates for
men and for women institutionalised the sexual division of labour and
corresponding wage differentials which existed within the trade;  the
setting of rates was not done according to what job the worker was
doing, but according to whether they were male or female.

The three other Trade Boards also set their minimum rates by the end of
1911 and they too set the rates according to whether the worker was
male or female.

Within the tailoring trade, an hourly rate of 3¼d per hour was generally
higher than that which adult women workers were currently paid but the
crucial factor was whether fifty hours a week were worked.  Even if it
was, a wage of 13/6d was below the subsistence wage of 14/- to 16/- for
women calculated by Edward Cadbury (see Chapter 2, p. 30 ).  The adult
male rate set of 6d per hour, which yielded 25/- per week, would just
meet the subsistence wage for men but again the crucial factor was
whether fifty hours were worked each week.  As we have seen, the
tailoring trade in all its branches was subject to fluctuations.

The tailoring trade unions campaigned vigorously against the minimum
rates set, particularly against the decision that men under the age of
twenty-three were to be treated as "learners", and paid a lower rate.
As an AUCO branch official told a protest meeting, the union rate for
men was 9d per hour and the workers could therefore be worse off as a
result of the deliberations of the Tailoring Trade Board[7].  Tom Mann
addressed a meeting in Whitechapel called by the Amalgamated Society
of Tailors and Tailoresses, urging direct action;  the meeting passed
unanimously a resolution protesting against the minimum rate[8].  The
charge was levied against the Tailoring Trade Board that such low
minimum rates - particularly the 3¼d for women - would merely legalise
sweating rather than prohibit it;  a resolution was passed by the
Manchester and Salford Trades Council to this effect in April 1912[9].
The chairman of a mass meeting of tailoring workers held in Manchester
a few months earlier asserted that if Government wanted to do away with
sweating then they would have to legislate for a "fair living wage"[10].
But this was just what the Government had decided not to do;  the Trade

Boards machinery was geared towards setting a uniform rate which it was considered "the trade could bear", not a minimum wage necessary for the subsistence of the worker.   Nevertheless, there is general agreement that wage rates in the trades covered by the legislation did rise as a result of the Trade Boards' deliberations.   The Ratan Tata Foundation carried out research into the effect of the legislation on three out of the first four trades covered and each study concluded that wages, particularly those for women workers, increased significantly.   R.L. Bowlby,[11] drawing on D. Sells' research[12] on the industries which were covered by Trade Boards by 1937, concludes that

> "the increase in every category of regulated rates was greater than the increase in unregulated rates".[13]

and the increase was particularly striking for women workers.


Even the tailoring unions had to admit that in some parts of the country the increase in wages was significant;   for example, a survey by AUCO showed that nearly 60% of the low-paid workers in the Hebden Bridge trade received an increase as a result of the minimum rate set[14].   The official history of the clothing workers unions concluded that the largest benefit was to women workers in London and the South, but that throughout the country about a third of the female workforce received an increase[15].


In 1913, the ASL demanded that the Board of Trade set up Trade Boards in six other trades;   five were actually agreed, sugar confectionery, shirt-making, hollow-ware-making, linen and cotton embroidery and certain sections of the laundry trade.   This added another 140,000 (mainly women) workers to the half million already covered by the Act.


The Trade Boards system was further expanded after the First World War following the recommendations of the Reconstruction Committee's Sub-Committee on Women's Employment[16], which, concerned that the end of the war would see a drop in the real wages of unskilled workers, recommended that women workers should be protected by Trade Boards machinery.   This recommendation was echoed by the Whitley Committee[17] who felt that in the industries where there was little or no organisation, Trade Boards should be set up.   The 1918 Trade Board Act which followed made this possible and by 1921 there were a total of sixty-three Trade Boards covering three million workers, 70% of whom were women[18].


Further research needs to be done on this expansion of the Trade Boards

machinery and how the development of what are now called Wages Councils
has effected women workers' wages. The general opinion of current
campaigners on low wages is that the Trade Boards Wages Council system
has not increased unemployment or damaged the industries concerned but
that the wage rates set are too low[19]. There has, however, been controversy over whether Wages Council machinery discourages trade union
organisation and what implications this has for the workers concerned
and the trade union movement generally[20].

Those who initiated the campaign against sweating had a clear idea that
they wanted to promote the family social and economic relationship
where the father is the sole breadwinner earning enough to keep his wife
and children. In particular they wished to diminish the incidence of
homework. Criticisms can be made of these aims but suffice it to say
that the goal has not been achieved. The problem of low wages is still
with us; government estimates show that in 1979, 1.3 million men and
4.4 million women earned less than £60 per week before deductions.
Campaigning organisations on poverty, such as the Low Pay Unit and the
Child Poverty Action Group stress that the phenomenon of wage-earners
and their children living in poverty is still with us.

Moreover, homeworking is still the last resort of many women - at least
a quarter of a million of whom are engaged in working for wages in their
homes today. Homeworking is still an integral part of the clothing
trade; 13.5% of the clothing workforce in one London borough is
estimated to be made up of homeworkers[21]. Women are engaged in working
in their homes in a wide variety of trades. A report on homeworking
in South London concluded that "It is an integral part of many trades
and industries and not just the product of a few bad employers"[22].
Women homeworkers are engaged not only in the clothing trades but also
in trades such as electrical and plastic assembly work, packing, jewellery-
making, spot welding, printing, and clerical work[23]. The increasing
use of visual display units brought about by developments in micro-chip
technology have opened up new areas of homework.

One survey of homeworkers found that 31% were dependent only on their
own income. The following description of one homeworker (a deserted
mother of three sons) indicates how desperate the situation of such
women can be.

> "There is an absolute world of difference between going out to
> work and working at home. At home your work becomes your life,

it takes over, nothing else is so important.  In my case it
took up a great deal of room in the living room.  I couldn't
put it anywhere else, and even when I stopped working, which I
rarely did, there it was defying me not to start again.  All
the paraphanalia attached to the job, the varnish and its smell,
the glue that wouldn't wash out, the problem of having razor
blades around, the dust from the cork butts and the metal filings
from the rings were all extra problems.  I scraped my knuckles
so often with the file, smoothing the edges of often as many as
500 rings that even the prospect of having to do it brought me
near to tears.  The nylon thread had to be pulled very tight
and cut my fingers - deep cuts which took ages to heal and often
re-opened.  I once sprained my wrist turning a rod, but on I had
to go.  The close work in artificial light, to make sure that
sometimes intricate patterns of thread were accurate has damaged
my already none too good eyesight.  I seemed to work all the
hours God sent, from morning till late at night, often into the
early hours and sometimes through the night to meet deadlines.
I worked when I was ill, I wasn't entitled to sick pay.  My wages
averaged about £8 per week, £13.65 at the top and as low as
£3.14, it all depended on what was sent out.  If work was short
so were my wages.  I had to pay an insurance stamp of £2.00 as
I was considered self-employed."[24]

The proponents of Trade Boards had hoped that the system would encourage
not only higher wages but a stabilisation and modernisation of the
industries covered.  There is some evidence that in the years immediately
following the Act, factory production was encouraged in those trades
first covered by the legislation.  However, sweated labour is currently
becoming an issue again, particularly in relation to the clothing
industry, where in recent years there has been an increase in sub-
contracting.  The clothing industry had experienced a centralisation of
production and the growth of large companies during the 1950s and 1960s
and by 1970, 8% of the firms in the industry produced 75% of the output
indicating that a great deal of concentration of capital had occurred
and had considerably lessened the proliferation of small firms and much
sub-contracting which had dominated the trade at the turn of the century.
However, the last decade has seen the expansion of the outworking system
once again, as the large national and multi-national companies have lost
their hold on the market[25].  Large manufacturing retailers such as
Burtons, United Drapery, and Hepworths, are moving out of manufacturing
and confining themselves to retailing, as are medium-sized firms such
as Stirling Cooper[26].  At the same time, there has been an expansion of
small businesses, often family concerns, which now carry out orders for
the large retailers.  The large companies have not only brought about
this growth of small employers by their policy of moving out of manufacturing themselves, but have even helped, in some cases, to set small
businesses on their feet;  for example, when Burtons closed down their

Doncaster factory they gave away some of the most modern machinery to a clothing co-operative set up by West Indian women in Leeds Chapeltown area. In other branches of the clothing industry, particularly in the making of women's light clothing, the Asian[27] and Cypriot communities in Britain's inner city areas have, through a lack of other employment opportunities, taken the same kind of initiatives in setting up new businesses that the Jewish community did in the last century in the tailoring trade. This has been associated with an expansion of sub-contracting; the larger firms, instead of producing garments themselves are now contracting the work out and this may be sub-contracted out yet again. In this situation, particularly in the context of the difficulties that Asian and Cypriot women experience in obtaining employment outside the home, we may assert - as the TUC has[28] - that homeworking has increased, but it is in fact impossible to back this up by statistics. Homeworkers are to a very large extent "invisible". Increasing interest in their situation over the last few years has brought about more accurate estimates of their number but we have no comparable earlier statistics. It is likely that large numbers of these homeworkers earn below the minimum rate set for their work. All the research indicates that they are unlikely to even know of their right to a minimum rate and that even if they did, their vulnerable situation would prevent them from claiming that right. Many homeworkers believe that they should be paying national insurance and tax when they are not; in fact most of them are unlikely to be earning enough to do so. Homeworkers who are also claiming supplementary benefit are reluctant for obvious reasons to bring attention to their earnings. Homeworkers in Council property can fall foul of the planning regulations and their tenancy agreement - these and other reasons, together with the employer's ability to cut off the supply of work, mean that homeworkers are amongst the most vulnerable and exploited members of our society.

It is interesting that over the last few years there has been increasing concern about the situation of homeworkers. This started ten years ago when a study was carried out of lace workers in Nottingham[29]. The authors of the study found - as did the investigators eighty years ago - evidence of very low wages and of whole families, including children, being involved in the work. A campaign was launched which led to an increase of 32.3% in the hourly rate but the wages earned were still very low. Also in 1972, a Homeworkers Study Group carried out a survey of homeworkers in North London[30]. They found that the majority of homeworkers in their small survey were tied to the home with small

children.   A report published in 1974 by the Long Eaton and District
Trades Council found that it was not uncommon for homeworkers to be
working forty hours a week and earning £4.50.   In 1977, the Homeworkers
Association was set up by the Low Pay Unit, which has sought to bring
the attention of the public and politicians to the need for greater
protection of homeworkers[31].   Significantly, the TUC, which at the
beginning of this century wished to abolish homework, has recognised
that such an aim is not, in the current situation, defensible and is
instead pressing for legislation to improve the rights of homeworkers
while one of the largest trade unions, the GMWU, is attempting to recruit
homeworkers.

Under pressure, the last Labour Government agreed to extend the
Employment Protection Act to homeworkers, action which it was felt
would give homeworkers a stronger position from which to fight themselves for higher wages and better working conditions.   However, the
Government was only won over to such action at the end of its term of
office and failed to legislate before the general election of 1979.
The current political climate does not seem to hold out much hope for
legislation to improve the situation of homeworkers or other low-paid
workers.


IV

This thesis, whilst addressing itself to an explanation of social
policy, has also shown that sweated labour and homeworking at the
beginning of this century were not a residual characteric of an earlier
industrial era.   We found that the main characteristic of sweating -
the payment of below-subsistence wages - was a phenomenon of both
factory and non-factory production in certain trades.   The reasons
behind the existence of sweated labour were found in the dilution of
labour skills, brought about by developments in the organisation of
production, and in the ready availability of a supply of cheap labour
(mainly women and girls).   Below-subsistence wages and homeworking
were features of both the "anarchy" of capitalist relations of production,
and the desperate need for women to work (brought about by the lack of
a male "family wage" and the limited work opportunities for women).   The
purpose of the Trade Boards Act was to modify free market forces and to
counteract their harmful effect;   today, there is increasing evidence
that such problems are still with us.

References - Chapter 10

1. S. Boston (1980), p.66.

2. Yorkshire Post, 28.1.10; Daily Telegraph, 26.4.10.

3. The Times, 1.2.10.

4. Morning Post, 15.12.10.

5. Minutes of the Tailoring Trade Board 1910-1913 PRO LAB 35-355: 3rd Meeting, 2 and 3 August 1911.

6. Ibid., 5th Meeting, 18, 19 and 20 October 1911.

7. Daily Dispatch, 10.11.11.

8. Morning Post, 27.11.11.

9. Manchester Courier, 18.4.12.

10. Daily Dispatch, 19.12.11.

11. R.C. Bowlby, "The Statutory Regulation of Minimum Wages in Great Britain", PhD. University of Texas, 1958.

12. D. Sells, "The British Trade Boards System" (1923).

13. R.C. Bowlby (1958), p.121.

14. Stewart and Hunter (1964), p.146.

15. Ibid., p.146.

16. Reconstruction Committee, Sub-Committee on Women's Employment, PP1919, XXXI (Cd.9239).

17. Committee on Relations Between Employers and Employed - 2nd Report, PP1917-18, XVIII (Cd.8606).

18. Report of Committee appointed to enquire into the working and effects of the Trade Boards Acts, PP1922, X (Cd.1645).

19. F. Field (ed.), "Are Low Wages Inevitable?" (1976).

20. Report of TUC Conference on Wages Councils, 1969.

21. Islington Borough Community Plan 1975: Topic Paper No.6, Employment, p.1. Figures calculated according to a 1971/72 survey.

22. Borough of Lewisham: Corporate Planning Unit, Homeworking in London, 1980, p.2.

23. Ibid., p.3.

24. F. Field, "Seventy Years On: A New Report on Homeworking" (Low Pay Bulletin No.10/11, August-October 1976) p.10.

25. National Union of Tailors and Garment Workers, "Employment in Clothing - a Struggle for Survival" (nd 1977?) p.6.

26. B. Campbell, "Lining Their Pockets" in Time Out 13-19 July, 1979.

27. Samir Shah, "Immigrants and Employment in the Clothing Industry: The Rag Trade in London's East End". Report for the Runnymede Trust (1975).

28. TUC, "Homeworking" (n.d.), p.1.

29. Liberal Party, Study of Nottingham Lace Homeworkers (1972).

30. British Sociological Association, Working Paper to 1974 Conference, "Homeworkers in North London".

31. S. Crine, "The Hidden Army" (1979), p.5.

# Bibliography

Conferences and Reports

Conference for the Abolition of the Middleman Sweater (1891).

Friends' Conference of Employers, 11-14 April 1918.

Industrial Remuneration Conference (1885).

Industrial Remuneration Trust (1884).

Leeds and District Trades and Labour Council:  Annual Reports.

London Chamber of Commerce:  Annual Reports.

National Anti-Sweating League:  Annual Reports.

National Anti-Sweating League:  Living Wage for Sweated Workers.  Report of the Great National Demonstration (28 Jan., 1908).

National Conference on Sweated Industries.  11 and 12 Oct. 1907.  Glasgow. Scottish Council for Women's Trades.

National Conference on the Unemployment of Women Dependent on their own earnings:  Report (1907).

Report of the Proceedings of the Second National Conference on Infant Mortality, London 1908, (York, 1909).

Trades Union Congress:  Annual Congress Reports.

Women's Trade Union League:  Conference on the best means of extending the work of the League, Oct. 1886:  Report.

Women's Trade Union Association:  Annual Reports.

Women's Protective and Provident League:  Annual Reports.


Contemporary books, pamphlets and articles

W.S. Adams, "Lloyd George, and the Labour Movement", in Past and Present, 3, 1953.

Adelaide M. Anderson, "Women in the Factory:  An Administrative Advance 1893-1921" (1922).

Apprenticeship and Skilled Employment Association   "Trades for London Girls" (1907).

G.R. Askwith, "Industrial Problems and Disputes" (1920).

D.M. Barton, "The Course of Women's Wages" in Journal of the Royal Statistical Society 1919.

M.M. Bird, "Women at Work:  a study of the different ways of earning a living open to women" (1911).

Clementina Black, "The Consumers' League;  a proposal that buyers should combine to deal only with employers who pay their workers fairly - being the substance of an article published in Longman's magazine of August 1887."

C. Black, "The Rhyme of the Factory Acts" nd.

Caroline A. Foley, "Royal Commission on Labour:  The Employment of Women" in Economic Journal, 1893.

I.O. Ford, "Women's Wages and the Conditions Under Which they are Earned" (1893).

S.N. Fox and C. Black, "The Truck Acts:  What they do and what they ought to do" (1894).

E.B. Giles, "History of the Art of Cutting in England" (1887).

Ada Heather-Bigg, "The Wife's Contribution to Family Income" in Economic Journal Vol.IV (1894).

J.A. Hobson, "Problems of Poverty" (1895).

W.H. Hulme, "The English Tailor, A Short History of the Tailoring Trade" (nd 1920s?).  Typescript - Leeds Reference Library.

B.L. Hutchins, "Home Work and Sweating" Fabian Tracts No.130 (1907).

B.L. Hutchins, "Working Women and the Poor Law" (1909).

B.L. Hutchins, "Statistics of Women's Life and Employment" in Journal of the Royal Statistical Society, June 1909 Vol.LXXII.

B.L. Hutchins, "Women in Modern Industry" (1915).

B.L. Hutchins and A. Harrison, "A History of Factory Legislation" (1907 ed.).

W.S. Jevons, "Theory of Political Economy"

W.S. Jevons, "The State in Relation to Labour" (1894).

J.R. MacDonald, "Women in the Printing Trades" (1904).

A. MacKirdy, "Baby Toilers" (1907).

A. Marshall, "Principles of Economics" (1907 edn.).

Anna Martin, "The Married Working Woman" (1911).

Anna Martin, "The Mother and Social Reform" (1913).

C. Meyer and C. Black, "Makers of Our Clothes:  a Case for Trade Boards" (1909).

Alfred Morris, "Civilization's Missing Link - The Case for a National Minimum Wage" (1894).

Richard Mudie-Smith (ed.), "Sweated Industries:  being a Handbook of the Daily News Exhibition" (1906).

Rosalind Nash, "Sweated Industries" (1906).

National Anti-Sweating League, "Sweating and Wages Boards" (nd).

G. Newman, "Infant Mortality - A Social Problem" (1906).

Clementina Black (ed.), "Married Women's Work: being the report of an enquiry undertaken by the Women's Industrial Council" (1915).

Charles Booth, "Life and Labour of the People of London" (1902), seventeen volumes.

Charles Booth, "The Inhabitants of Tower Hamlets (Schools Board Division) their condition and occupations", in Journal of the Royal Statistical Society L. 1887.

Charles Booth, "Conditions and Occupations of the People of East London and Hackney", in Journal of the Royal Statistical Society LI 1888.

Jessie Boucherett, Helen Blackburn and others, "The Condition of Working Women and the Factory Acts" (1896).

A. Bowley, "Earners and Dependents in English Towns in 1911", in Economica, 1921, No.2.

British Association for the Advancement of Science: Committee on the Economic Effect of Legislation Regulating Women's Labour (1903).

Jane E. Brownlow, "Women and Factory Legislation", (1896).

Edward Cadbury, "Experiments in Industrial Organisation" (1912).

E. Cadbury and G. Shann, "Sweating" (1908).

E. Cadbury and others, "Women's Work and Wages: a phase of life in an industrial city", (1906).

Ada Nield Chew, "Victims of our Industrial System in Young Oxford Vol.II Nos. 16, 19 and 20.

W.L.S. Churchill, "Liberalism, and the Social Problem", (1909).

W.L.S. Churchill, "The People's Rights ... selected from his Lancashire and other recent speeches." (1909).

Clara Collet, "Women's Work in Leeds" in Economic Journal Vol.I, 1891.

C.E. Collet, "The collection and utilisation of official statistics bearing on the extent and effects of the industrial employment of women" in Journal of the Royal Statistical Society (1898) LXI.

C.E. Collet, "Women in Industry" (1911).

M.I. Crofts, "Women Under the English Law" (1925).

E. Dilke, "Trade Unions for Women" (1892).

B. Drake, "The West End Tailoring Trade" in "Seasonal Trades" - S. Webb and A. Freeman (eds.) (1912).

B. Drake, "Women in the Engineering Trades" (1917).

Fabian Tract No.50, "Sweating: Its Cause and Remedy" (1895).

Fabian Tract No. 83, "State Arbitration and the Living Wage" (1903 - 2nd ed.).

Fabian Tract No.128, "The Case for a Legal Minimum Wage".

L. Papworth and E. Zimmern, "The Occupations of Women" (1914).

M.S. Pember Reeves, "Round About a Pound a Week" (1914).

Gertrude Tuckwell, "The State and its Children" (1894).

G. Tuckwell, "Women's Work and Factory Legislation: the Amending Act of 1895" (1895).

Gertrude Tuckwell, "The Anomalies of our Factory Laws" in Labour Leader, April 1902.

Gertrude Tuckwell, "The Story of the Trade Boards Act" in Contemporary Review Nov. 1921 Vol.120.

B. Webb and others, "Socialism and the National Minimum" (1909).

B. Webb, "The Wages of Men and Women: should they be equal?" (1919).

S.J. Webb, "The Alleged Differences in the Wages Paid to Men and to Women for Similar Work" in Economic Journal I (1891).

Arnold White, "Problems of a Great City" (1886).

W.H. Wilkins, "The Bitter Cry of the Voteless Toilers (with special reference to the seamstresses of East London)" (1893).

Women's Industrial Council, "Home Industries of Women in London" 1st Report, 1897. Interim Report 1900; Third Report 1908.

Women's Industrial Council, "Women's Wages in England in the Nineteenth Century" (1906).

Women's Industrial Council, "How to Deal with Homework" (1906).

Women's Industrial Council, "The Case for and Against a Legal Minimum Wage for Sweated Workers" (1909).

Women's Labour League, Central London Branch - Questionnaire on seasonal trades (1907).

Women's Trade Union League, "Factory and Workshop Legislation: opinions of HM Inspectors 1895-1900" (1901).

George H. Wood, "Real Wages and the Standard of Conform Since 1850" in Journal of the Royal Statistical Society 1909 No.72.

## Journals and Newspapers

Amalgamated Union of Clothing Workers: Monthly Gazette.

Daily News

Economic Journal

The Friend

Journal of Amalgamated Society of Tailors

Journal of the Royal Statistical Society

Labour Leader.

The Lancet

Leeds Mercury

Morning Post

The Times

Women's Industrial News.  Organ of Women's Industrial Council 1895-1919.

Woman Worker.  Official organ of the National Federation of Women Workers.

Yorkshire Post.


## Secondary Sources

S. Alexander, "Women's Work in Nineteenth Century London:  A Study of
        the Years 1820-1850" in J. Mitchell and A. Oakley (eds.) "The
        Rights and Wrongs of Women" (1976).

Stephen Aris, "The Jews in Business" (1970).

M. Barrett, "Women's Oppression Today:  Problems in Marxist Feminist
        Analysis" (1980).

R.D. Baron and G.M. Norris, "Sexual Divisions and the Dual Labour Market"
        in D.C. Barker and S. Allen (eds.), "Dependence and Exploitation
        in Work and Marriage" (1976).

R. Beer, "Matchgirls Strike, 1888" (Nat. Museum of Labour History,
        Pamphlet No.2 nd).

B. Birnbaum, "Women, Skill and Automation:  A Study of Women's Employment
        in the Clothing Industry, 1946-1972" (unpublished manuscript,
        nd 1976?).

Gladys Boone, "The Women's Trade Union Leagues in Great Britain and the
        USA" (1942 - Columbia Univ. Press).

Borough of Lewisham:  Corporate Planning Unit, Homeworking in London.

S. Boston, "Women and the Trade Unions" (1980).

R.L. Bowlby,  "The Statutory Regulation of Minimum Wages in Great Britain"
        PhD.  University of Texas, 1958.

A. Bowley, "Earners and Dependants in English Towns in 1911" in _Economica_
        1921 No.2.

H. Braverman, "Labour and Monopoly Capital" (1974).

Asa Briggs, "Seebohm Rowntree" (1961).

British Sociological Association, Working Paper to 1974 Conference,
        "Homeworkers in North London".

J. Brown, "Social Control and the Modernisation of Social Policy, 1890-
        1929" in P. Thane (ed.) "The Origins of British Social Policy"
        (1978).

K. Burgess, "The Challenge of Labour" (1980).

D. Blythell, "The Sweated Trades" (1978).

J.A.M. Caldwell, "Social Policy and Public Administration 1909-11"
(PhD Thesis 1956, Nottingham).

H.A. Clegg et al., "A History of British Trade Unions Since 1889", Vol.I
1889-1910 (Oxford, 1964).

S. Crine, "The Hidden Army" (1979).

Roger Davidson, "Llewellyn Smith, the Labour Department and Government
Growth 1886-1909" in G. Sutherland (ed.) "Studies in the Growth
of Nineteenth Century Government" (1972).
Roger Davidson, "Sir Hubert Llewellyn Smith and Labour Policy 1886-1916"
(PhD Thesis 1971, Cambridge).

A. Davin, "Imperialism and Motherhood" in History Workshop Journal, No.5.
Spring 1978.

S.P. Dobbs, "The Clothing Workers of Great Britain" (1926).

B. Drake, "Women in Trade Unions" (1920).

Paul H. Emden, "Quakers in Commerce" (1939).

H.V. Emy, "The Liberal Party and the Social Problem 1892-1913" (PhD
Thesis, London 1969).

F. Field, "Seventy Years On: A New Report on Homeworking" (1978).

A. Fox, "A History of the National Union of Boot and Shoe Operatives
1874-1957" (Oxford, 1958).

F. Galton, "The Tailoring Trade" (1973).

A.G. Gardiner, "The Life of George Cadbury" (1949).

K.R. Gilbert, "Sewing Machines" (1970).

Harold Goldman, "Emma Paterson" (1974).

S. Gwynn and G. Tuckwell, 'The Life of the Rt. Hon. Sir Charles Dilke". (1917)

E. Halevy, "History of the English People in the Nineteenth Century,
Vol.6 The Rule of Democracy (1905-1914) (1961 edn.).

Mary Agnes Hamilton, "Mary MacArthur" (1925).

J. Harris, "Unemployment and Politics" (Oxford, 1972).

J. Harris, "William Beveridge" (Oxford, 1977).

J.R. Hay, "The Origins of the Liberal Reforms" (1975).

J.R. Hay, "Employers' Attitudes to Social Policy" in P. Thane (ed.)
"The Origins of British Social Policy" (1978).

J. Hinton, "The First Shop Stewards' Movement" (1973).

E. Hobsbawn, "Labouring Men" (1964).

Helen F. Hohman, "The Development of Social Insurance and Minimum Wage
Legislation in Great Britain" (1933).

S.J. Hurwitz, "State Intervention in Great Britain, A Study of Economic Control and Social Response, 1914-1919" (New York, 1949).

T.W. Hutchison, "The 'Marginal Revolution' and the Decline and Fall of English Classical Economy" in History of Political Economy, Vol.4 No.2, Autumn 1972.

Islington Borough Community Plan 1975: Topic Paper No.6, Employment.

Roy Jenkins, "Sir Charles Dilke" (1958).

S. Lewenak, "Women and Trade Unions" (1977).

J. Lewis, "The Politics of Motherhood" (1980).

London Trades Council, A History.

J. Morris, "The Gertrude Tuckwell Collection" in History Workshop Journal, No.5, Spring 1978.

J. Morris, "State Reform and the Local Economy" in Economic History Review (forthcoming).

National Union of Tailors and Garment Workers, "Employment in Clothing - a Struggle for Survival" (nd, 1977?).

H. Pelling, "A History of British Trade Unionism" (1963).

E.H. Phelps-Brown, "The Growth of British Industrial Relations" (1959).

A. Phillips and B. Taylor, "Sex and Skill" in Feminist Review, Issue 6, 1980.

Ivy Pinchbeck, "Women Workers and the Industrial Revolution 1750-1850" (reprint 1969).

Austin Reed Ltd., "Fine and Fifty [A History of the Firm published on their golden jubilee]" (1950).

E. Richards, "Women in the British Economy Since 1700: an interpretation" in History Vol.59, No.197. Oct. 1974.

E. Roberts, "Working Class Standards of Living in Barrow and Lancaster, 1900-1914" in Economic History Review Vol.XXX No.2, May 1977.

S. Rowbotham, "Hidden from History" (1973).

S. Rowbotham and J. Weekes, "Socialism and the New Life" (1977).

Peter Rowland, "The Last Liberal Government Vol.I: The Promised Land 1905-1910" (1968).

A.K. Russell, "Liberal Landslide" (1973).

D. Russell and M. Tichelar, "Class Struggle in South London, 1850-1900" (1981).

James A. Schmeichen, "State Reform and the Local Economy: an Aspect of Industrialisation in Late-Victorian and Edwardian London" in Economic History Review 2nd Series XXVIII, No.3, Aug. 1975.

G. Searle, "The Quest for National Efficiency" (1971).

D. Sells, "The British Trade Boards System" (1923).

S. Shah, "Immigrants and Employment in the Clothing Industry: The Rag Trade in London's East End" (1975).

I.G. Sharp, "Industrial Conciliation and Arbitration in Great Britain" (1949).

G. Stedman-Jones, "Outcast London" (1971).

M. Steward and L. Hunter, "The Needle is Threaded" (1964).

P. Thane, "Non-Contributory Versus Insurance Pensions 1878-1908" in P. Thane (ed.) "The Origins of British Social Policy" (1978).

Joan Thomas, "A History of the Leeds Clothing Industry". (1955)

P. Thompson, "Radicals, Liberals and Labour in London, 1880-1900" in Past and Present, 27, 1964.

P. Townsend, "Poverty in the UK" (1979).

TUC, Conference on Wages Councils (1969).

TUC, "Homeworking" (nd).

W.S. Tute, "The Grey Top Hat: the Story of Moss Bros. of Covent Garden" (1961).

Iolo A. Williams, "The Firm of Cadbury 1831-1931".

E. Wilson, "Women and the Welfare State" (1977).

D. Winch, "Economics and Policy" (1969).

## Manuscript Collections

Henry Broadhurst Papers

Clara Collet Papers

Labour Representation Committee: Manuscript Collection.

Margaret MacDonald: Women's Employment Collection.

Reconstruction Committee - Women's Employment Sub-Committee Collection.

Gertrude Tuckwell Collection.

Webb Trade Union Collection. Section A. Vol.47 Women Workers.

Women's Industrial Council Collection.

## Official Papers

(a) Parliamentary Papers

House of Commons Debates

House of Lords Debates

Reports of the Chief Inspector of Factories and Workshops.

    PP1901 X (Cd.668)
    PP1902 XII (Cd.1112 and Cd.1300).
    PP1902 XII (Cd.841)
    PP1903 XII (Cd.1610)
    PP1904 X (Cd.1816)
    PP1904 X (Cd.1979)
    PP1904 X (Cd.2139).
    PP1905 X (Cd.2324)
    PP1905 X (Cd.2569)
    PP1906 XV (Cd.2848)
    PP1906 XV (Cd.3036)
    PP1907 X (Cd.3586)
    PP1907 X (Cd.3323)
    PP1908 XII (Cd.4166)
    PP1908 XII (Cd.3986)
    PP1909 XXI (Cd.4664)
    PP1910 XXVIII (Cd.5191)
    PP1911 XXII (Cd.5693).

Report to the Board of Trade on the Sweating System in the East End of
    London PP1887 LXXXIX (Cd.331)

Report to the Board of Trade on the Sweating System in Leeds. PP1888
    LXXXVI (Cd.5513)

House of Lords Select Committee on the Sweating System.
    First Report; with the Proceedings of the Committee, Minutes
        of Evidence and Appendix ... PP1888 XX (Cd.361)
    Second Report ... PP1888 XXI (Cd.448)
    Third Report  ... PP1889 XIII (Cd.165)
    Fourth Report ... PP1889 XIV Pt.I (Cd.331)
    Fifth Report  ... PP1890 XVII (Cd.169)

Royal Commission on Labour.  Reports of the Lady Assistant Commissioners
    on the Employment of Women PP1893-4 XXXVII (Cd.6894).

Royal Commission on Labour:  Fifth and Final Report.  PP1894 XXXV (Cd.7421).

Interdepartmental Committee on Physical Deterioration Vol.I  Report and
    Appendix.  PP1904 XXXII (Cd.2175).

Return as to the Administration in each County and County Borough during
    1904, by the Local Authorities of the Homework provisions of
    the Factory and Workshop Act, 1901, as shown by the reports of
    the Medical Officers of Health sent to the Home Office under
    Section 132 of the Act ...  BPP1906 CX (Cd.211)

Report of an Enquiry into Earnings and Hours of Labour of the Workpeople
    of the UK.
    Part I   Textile Trades in 1906  BPP1909 LXXX (Cd.4545)
    Part II  Clothing Trades in 1906 BPP1909 LXXX (Cd.4844)
    Part III Building and Woodwork 1910 (Cd.5086) LXXXIV
    Part IV  Public Utility Services 1910 (Cd.5196) LXXXIV
    Part V   Agriculture  1910 (Cd.5460) LXXXIV
    Part IV  Metal, Engineering and Shipbuilding Trades 1911 (Cd.5814)
                LXXXVIII
    Part VII Railway Service in 1907, 1912-13 (Cd.6053) CXIII
    Part VIII Paper, Printing, Pottery, Brick, Glass and Chemicals,
                Food, Drink and Tobacco and Miscellaneous Trades.
                1912-13 (Cd.6556) CVIII.

Report of the Government Factories and Workshops Committee  PP1907 X
     (Cd.3626).

House of Commons Select Committee on Homework:
          1st Report and Minutes of Evidence  PP1907 VI (Cd.290)
          2nd Report and Minutes of Evidence  PP1908 VIII (Cd.246)

Report on Wages Boards and Industrial Conciliation and Arbitration Acts
     of Australia and New Zealand  PP1908 (Cd.4167).

Royal Commission on the Poor Laws and Relief of Distress:  Appendix
          Vol.XVII - C. Williams and T. Jones:  Report on the Effect of
          Outdoor Relief on Wages and the Conditions of Employment.
          PP1909 XLII (Cd.4690)

Royal Commission on the Poor Laws and Relief of Distress:  Appendix
          Vol.XVI:  A.D. Steel-Maitland and R.E. Squire:  Report on the
          Relation of Industrial and Sanitary Conditions to Pauperism in
          London  PP1909 Vol. XLIII (Cd.4683).

UK Home Office:  Summary of Reports on the Administration of the
          Factory and Workshop Act 1901, by local authorities in respect
          of Workshops, Outwork, etc. in the year 1908.  PP1910, XXIX
          (Cd.511)

Committee on Relations Between Employers and Employed, 2nd Report
          PP1917-18, XVIII (Cd.8606).

Reconstruction Committee, Sub-Committee on Women's Employment PP1919,
          XXXI (Cd.9239).

UK Board of Trade:  Handbooks on London Trades - Clothing.  Clothing
          Trades Part 2 - Boys (1915).

UK Board of Trade:  Memorandum on the Working of the Trade Boards Act
          (1913).

UK Home Office:  A Study of the Factors which have operated in the past
          and those which are operating now to determine the distribution
          of women in industry.  PP1929 XVII (Cd.3508).


(b)  Public Records Office

Board of Trade Papers 1907-1909

Cabinet Minutes 1907-1909

Minutes of the Tailoring Trade Board


(c)  Other

Reports of the Chief Medical Officer of Health.
          (i)   London boroughs
          (ii)  Leeds.

earlier proposals for WTC 170-1
fam wage resol<sup>n</sup> 172
factory acts 177-8
WTC bill based on MA 205